$45.⁰⁰

*The World
of the Country House in Seventeenth-Century England*

The World of
the Country House in
Seventeenth-Century England

J. T. Cliffe

YALE UNIVERSITY PRESS ∼ NEW HAVEN AND LONDON

Designed by Kate Gallimore
Typeset in Caslon by Best-set Typesetter Ltd., Hong Kong
Printed in Hong Kong

Library of Congress Cataloging in Publication Data
Cliffe, J. T. (John Trevor), 1931–
    The world of the country house in seventeenth-century England /
J. T. Cliffe.
      p. cm.
    Includes bibliographical references and index.
    ISBN 0-300-07643-6 (cloth)
    1. England—Social life and customs—17th century. 2. Country homes—England—
History—17th century. 3. Country life—England—History—17th century. 4. Land tenure—
England—History—17th century. 5. Landowners—England—History—17th century. 6.
Gentry—England—History—17th century.
    I. Title.
DA380.C57   1999
942.06—dc21   98-49211
                                                                                                          CIP

CONTENTS

ACKNOWLEDGEMENTS

I should like to record my grateful thanks to the following for allowing me to use material in the manuscript collections which they own: the Earl of Verulam, Lord Cobbold, Lord Daventry, Lady Herries, Sir Richard Carew Pole, Sir Ralph Verney and the Claydon House Trust, Major J. R. More-Molyneux, the College of Arms, the Lamport Hall Trust, the Northwick Estates, Olive Countess Fitzwilliam's Wentworth Settlement Trustees, the Trustees of Dr Williams's Library and the owners of the Newburgh Priory manuscripts and the Cunliffe-Lister (Swinton) manuscripts which have been deposited in the North Yorkshire County Record Office.

I also take this opportunity to express my appreciation for the help which I have received from the staffs of the British Library, the Public Record Office, the London Metropolitan Archives, the Lambeth Palace Library and Dr Williams's Library, London; the record offices of Bedfordshire, Buckinghamshire, Cheshire, Cornwall, Derbyshire, East Devon, East Sussex, Essex, Hampshire, Hertfordshire, Norfolk, Northamptonshire, North Yorkshire, Somerset, Staffordshire, Surrey, Warwickshire, West Devon and West Sussex; the Sheffield Archives and the West Yorkshire Archive Service, Leeds; the Borthwick Institute of Historical Research, York, the Hull University Archives and the Yorkshire Archaeological Society Library.

I am grateful to the rector of St Mary's, Beddington, Surrey and the vicars of St Mary's, Harefield, Middlesex and St Mary's, Watford for permitting photographs to be taken of memorials in their churches.

I owe a particular debt to Meg Lewis who has met all my typing needs with great skill and patience and Harland Walshaw who has undertaken a number of special photographic assignments for me, some of which have called for a considerable measure of ingenuity and determination.

INTRODUCTION

This is a study of the country houses of the gentry, their inhabitants, including servants and other employees, and the activities which went on inside and around such houses. It specifically excludes the houses and domestic lives of the nobility which have already received a great deal of attention.[1]

Unlike the nobility, with their precise legal status, the gentry present a major problem of definition. Historians have debated this issue for many years but no general consensus has yet emerged. This is hardly surprising given the heterogeneous character of the gentry in socio-economic terms and the fact that seventeenth-century commentators were unable to produce a satisfactory definition. John Selden the celebrated lawyer and scholar once observed that 'What a Gentleman is, 'tis hard with us to define': in other countries he was known by his privileges; in the courts of law at Westminster he was 'one that is reputed one'; and in the Court of Chivalry he was one who had a coat of arms.[2] For the purposes of this study the following definition has been adopted: 'families owning landed property which were headed by baronets or knights or men described as 'esquire' or 'gentleman' in such official documents as heraldic visitation records, subsidy rolls and hearth tax returns.'

On the basis of this definition the total number of gentry families in the middle decades of the century was probably around 15,000.[3]

Among the gentry there were extremely wide variations in landed income. In 1670 the top end of the income structure appears as follows:[4]

landed income (£ per annum)	number of families
8000	6
7000	4
6000	6
5000	15
4000	39

3000	78
2000	249
1000	920
TOTAL	1317

The wealthiest of these families had larger estates than many of the nobility; and indeed some families such as the Thynnes of Wiltshire and the Shirleys of Leicestershire would shortly be admitted to the peerage. At the other end of the income scale there were large numbers of gentlemen with no more than £50 or £100 a year who were barely distinguishable from their yeomen neighbours.

Some country houses which figure in this study underwent a change of name in the eighteenth century or later, in particular through the substitution of 'Park' or 'Castle' for 'Hall' or 'House'. In such cases the general approach has been to follow seventeenth-century practice. Similarly, no account has been taken of subsequent changes in the names of counties or their boundaries.

In direct quotations the original spelling has been retained with the exception that the pound sign has been modernised. Occasionally the punctuation has been slightly modified in the interests of clarity.

CHAPTER ONE

Houses Fit for Gentlemen

W hen the Cadhay estate in Devon was put up for sale in 1694 the Tudor mansion of the Haydon family (Pl. 1) was described in glowing terms:

> The Mansion Seat being a large uniform stone built House, with all Houses of Office Necessary as Dairy, Bake House, Brewhouse, Barns, Stables, Cowhous, and Hovells, all which are not now to be New built for £8000 . . . The House now being in Repair, not Decay'd or any thing like itt butt on the Contrary very fitt to Receive any Gentleman whatsoever.

As a minimum it was considered necessary that a house fit for a gentleman should be more stylish and commodious than an ordinary farmhouse (though there would usually be farm buildings at the rear); and that it should be situated in its own grounds which ideally should include parkland. The Cadhay estate did not contain a park but it had other attractive features, in particular three acres of garden enclosed with high walls and 'stored with all sorts of fruit', eight acres of orchard with cider-making facilities, a hopyard, a dovehouse and four ponds for the keeping of fish.[1]

The country house was not only a dominant presence in a physical sense: it also represented the kind of economic power which went with the ownership of a landed estate. In normal circumstances the gentry leased out the bulk of their property to tenants whose farming activities were subject to regulation by the manorial courts. At the same time the squire's mansion was often the main source of employment in the parish in view of the requirement for indoor and outdoor servants and for seasonal labour in the gardens and the fields belonging to the home farm. In 1631, for example, it was reported that the township of Burton in Lincolnshire had eighty-eight inhabitants of whom no fewer than fifty lived at Burton Hall, the seat of Sir John Monson.[2] Other forms of power derived from such public offices as deputy lieutenant and justice of the peace. For a range of minor offences a justice of the peace was able to act without reference to his fellow magistrates and dispense summary justice in his own house.

1. Cadhay, Devon.

Sir Henry Wotton was referring to one of the most traditional functions of the country house when he described it as the theatre of a man's hospitality.[3] In the seventeenth century 'hospitality' meant far more than the entertainment of relatives and friends. As Bulstrode Whitelocke put it in a lecture delivered to his family, 'true hospitality . . . is to entertain strangers, and our poor neighbors, and those who are in want of bread'.[4]

Some country houses had an important religious role. In the late seventeenth century Hoghton Tower, the Lancashire mansion of the Hoghton family, was extolled as 'a seat of religion, sobriety, and good order'[5] and other houses belonging to ultra-Protestant families were described in similar terms. In contrast there were parishes where the survival of Catholicism owed much to the fact that it commanded the wholehearted support of the gentry who lived there to the extent that they were prepared to keep chaplains in their houses.

At the beginning of the seventeenth century the gentry owned a wide variety of country houses. At one extreme there were medieval castles and converted monastic buildings; at the other, a multitude of fine new Elizabethan houses, more regular in their design than the older houses and often conforming to an E-shaped plan. Although many of these Elizabethan houses were not particularly large there were a number which testified to the great wealth and pride of their builders such as Howley Hall and Wighill Hall in Yorkshire, Wollaton Hall in Nottinghamshire, Salden House in Buckinghamshire, Longleat House in Wiltshire, Montacute House in Somerset (Pl. 2) and Wembury House in Devon. Howley Hall had cost £30,000, Salden House £33,000, and Montacute House and Wembury House (which was the largest

2. *(right)* Montacute House, Somerset, the seat of the Phelips family.

mansion in Devon) at least £20,000 each.[6] Perhaps inevitably, the families which built on such a lavish scale were not without their critics. In a sermon preached at St Paul's Cross in London in March 1613 Thomas Adams expressed his feelings on the subject in no uncertain terms:

> Our vain-glorious building, to emulate the skies . . . Howses built like pallaces . . . structures to whom is promised eternity . . . Whole townes depopulate to reare up one man's walles . . . brave gates, but never open: sumptuous parlours, for Owles and Bats to flie in; pride begun them, riches finished them, beggery keeps them: for most of them moulder away . . . our Fathers lived wel under lower roofes: this is waste, and waste indeed.[7]

Some gentlemen feared that expenditure on house building could too easily break free from all constraints. In 1604 Sir William Wentworth of Wentworth Woodhouse in Yorkshire warned his son Thomas (the future Earl of Strafford) to avoid superfluity in building, 'for that is a monument of a gentlman that wanted discrecion and iudgment. Let your house be too litle for a daie or twoe, rather then too greate for a yeare'. In the event Thomas Wentworth undertook major building operations and was clearly drawing on his own experience when in 1634 he told his cousin Michael Wentworth, who was on the point of rebuilding Woolley Hall, that 'If you builde a new howse . . . itt is a matter whearin you may shew a greate deale, and a great wante of discretion, itt being nothing so easye a thing to builde well as men take itt to be that knowe it not, and therfore att your perill looke well aboute you'.[8] Sir John Weld, who had bought the Willey estate in Shropshire in 1616, took an even more austere view. In a memorandum which he prepared for the guidance of his son he advised him 'not to be busy in Building . . . nor in too much hospitality' for these could be a means of wasting his estate.[9]

Despite such expressions of concern the gentry continued to build country houses on an extensive scale throughout the seventeenth century except for a brief lull during the Civil War period. The general trend is illustrated in the following table which covers both new houses and houses which were substantially improved or enlarged:[10]

House Building in the Seventeenth Century

	number of houses
(1) building operations concentrated in one of the following periods	
1600–39	681
1640–59	114
1660–99	510
(2) building operations in the periods	
1600–39 and 1640–59	9
1600–39 and 1660–99	61
1640–59 and 1660–99	11
1600–39, 1640–59 and 1660–99	3
grand total	1389

Within these figures there are wide regional variations which may largely be attributed to major differences in the number of wealthy gentry in individual counties. At one extreme, a substantial amount of house building went on in Yorkshire, Cheshire, Northamptonshire, Buckinghamshire, Essex, Gloucestershire and Devon; at the other, it appears to have proceeded at a much more restricted tempo in such counties as Durham, Nottinghamshire, Bedfordshire and Cornwall. At the beginning of the century Richard Carew could write that Cornish gentlemen 'keep liberal, but not costly builded or furnished houses'.[11] In contrast, Fynes Moryson commented in a work published in 1617 that Cheshire 'is a great County of Gentlemen, no other County having so many Knights' houses'.[12]

One of the significant factors responsible for the general building boom was the impact of new wealth as personified by merchants, businessmen, lawyers and Crown officials with social aspirations. Often the purchase of an estate was followed more or less immediately by the construction of a mansion house which proclaimed the arrival of a new county family. Among the houses dating from the early seventeenth century which still survive Temple Newsam in Yorkshire was built by Sir Arthur Ingram, one of the most rapacious and successful businessmen of his generation; Blickling Hall in Norfolk by Sir Henry Hobart (Pls 3 and 4) who was Lord Chief Justice of the Common Pleas;[13] and Caverswall Castle in Staffordshire by Matthew Cradock whose family had made a fortune in the wool trade. Although the *arriviste* usually had a preference for the more traditional kind of design there were exceptions as in the case of Crewe Hall, the Cheshire mansion erected by another Lord Chief Justice, Sir Randle Crewe, between 1615 and 1639. A contemporary, Daniel King, noted approvingly that he 'hath brought into these remote parts a model of that excellent form of building which is now grown to a degree beyond the building of old times for loftiness, sightliness, and pleasant habitation, as in and near unto London we see many in this age of ours'.[14]

Among the commercial and professional families of London and Westminster there was a considerable demand for country seats in the neighbouring counties of Middlesex, Hertfordshire, Essex, Kent and Surrey. According to John Norden the merchants of London were acquiring the best seats in Middlesex for recreation in the summer and as 'withdrawing places' when there was an epidemic raging in the capital.[15] To judge from a first-hand description of the mansion built by Sir Nicholas Crispe, a merchant and customs farmer, near the village of Hammersmith it was one of the most impressive houses in rural Middlesex before the time of the Civil War:

> The Building is very lofty, Regular, and Magnificent, after the Modern Manner; Built of Brick, Corner'd with Stone, and has a handsom Cupola at the Top. It contains several very handsome Rooms, very spacious and finely Finish'd ... The whole House in Building, and the Gardens, Canalls &c in Making, is said to Cost near Three and Twenty Thousand Pounds.[16]

If the *nouveaux riches* were heavily engaged in house building the same is no less true of many of the established gentry. Some country squires were anxious to provide themselves with houses which were more elegant or more

3. Blickling Hall,
Norfolk.

conveniently planned or significantly larger than those which they had inherited. Others were faced with the problem that their houses were decaying with the passage of time and it was necessary for them either to be renovated or even rebuilt. In a commonplace book which they kept the Shann family of Methley in Yorkshire recorded the building operations which were undertaken both in their own parish and in the general neighbourhood. At the beginning of the century two of the minor gentry who lived at Methley, John Flower of Hessle House and Charles Yonge of West House, pulled down their ancient dwellings which were timber structures with thatched roofs and replaced them with stone-built houses. Sir John Savile, a lawyer who had purchased the manor in 1590, repaired Methley Hall, which had been allowed to fall into ruin, and 'brought yt to A fayre house Againe'. His son, Sir Henry, who succeeded him in 1607, had more ambitious ideas. He 'pulled downe the roofe of the house, and builded up the Stone woorke therof higher then ever it was before, and mayd it A flatt roofe and covered it over with Leade' (Pl. 5). In the course of this building programme he had some timber brought from Sandal Castle 'towards the makinge of the Screene' which was set up between the great hall and the kitchen.[17] In 1638 the condition of Carlton House in Yorkshire, the Elizabethan mansion of the Stapleton family, was debated in the Court of Wards. On behalf of the ward, Richard Stapleton, it was claimed that the house had not been properly maintained: rainwater had entered into many of the rooms and damaged the woodwork and other materials. In response to this allegation a servant, Robert Johnson, testified that about four or five years previously he had arranged for the house to be well covered with lead and that he had heard Elizabeth Stapleton, the ward's grandmother, say that during her widowhood she had spent £500 in 'repairing and amending' it.[18] Apart from the injurious effects of age and weather there was the ever-present danger of an accidental fire. In 1636 Sir Peter Wentworth, who was seated at Lillingstone Lovell in Oxfordshire, wrote in a

4. Sir Henry Hobart. Portrait by Daniel Mytens, *c.* 1624. (Blickling Hall).

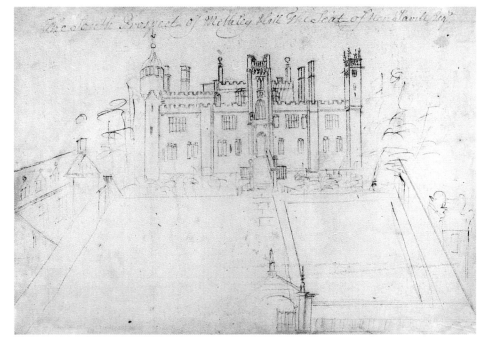

5. Methley Hall, Yorkshire. An early eighteenth-century drawing by Samuel Buck (British Library, Lansdowne MSS 914, fol. 145).

letter to the Privy Council that he had suffered 'very great losse by fire both this yeare and the last' and 'a greate part of his howse' had already fallen or was on the point of falling down.[19] Other country houses which were either destroyed or badly damaged by fire during the early seventeenth century included Sir Richard Hopton's mansion at Canon Frome in Herefordshire; Taplow Court in Buckinghamshire which was said to have been 'burnt down to the ground though yt were of bricke'; Hamells in the Hertfordshire parish of Braughing; Eastoft Hall in Yorkshire where John Eastoft put his total losses at £2000; and Wollaton Hall in Nottinghamshire. The fire at Wollaton Hall, which occurred in 1642, caused serious damage to the interior. The owner, Sir Percival Willoughby, only managed to carry out a few essential repairs before his death the following year and for several decades the house remained 'in the same pityfull condition which the fire had left it in'. During that time the Willoughby family resided at their other seat, Middleton Hall in Warwickshire, and it was not until 1687 that they settled once more at Wollaton Hall.[20]

Improvements to existing houses could take various forms. Timber structures were encased in brick or stone, new wings or ancillary buildings were added and interiors were modernised. During the period 1607 to 1628 Sir Ralph Delaval, one of the wealthiest landowners in Northumberland, made extensive alterations to Seaton Delaval Hall. His son Thomas writes that

> He built the long new house . . . to the garden wall of the grounds, the brewing house . . . He new builded the baking house and part of the kitchen. He sett on the battlements on the fore front of the house. He built the dove-coate . . . He new tabled and set finialls and new topped all the chymneys of the house and buildings.

In addition, he wainscoted a number of rooms, including his own bedchamber and study.[21] In 1625 Barrington Court in Somerset, which had been built in the early sixteenth century, was acquired by William Strode who, as noted by a contemporary, 'bestowed money and labour to restore it to its pristine beautie'. During the course of litigation in 1677 Strode's son and namesake made the point that he and his father had spent £3000 in carrying out improvements and alterations. A Yorkshire squire, Sir Henry Slingsby, referred in his diary to the alterations which he was making at his principal residence, Red House in the parish of Moor Monkton. 'That which I have done in matter of building', he wrote, 'is not much, but here and there a peice which one summer hath begun and finish'd'. During the years 1635 to 1641 his total expenditure on building work at Red House and his other house, Scriven Hall, amounted to £1346 8s 5d.[22]

While the building activities of the country gentry often took the form of beautifying and modernising their ancestral homes they were also responsible for many of the new houses which were going up, though in their case financial considerations could sometimes dictate a protracted timescale. Among the houses which they commissioned in the early seventeenth century were Chipchase Castle in Northumberland (Pl. 6); Burton Agnes Hall in Yorkshire (Pl. 7) for which the original plan was prepared by Robert Smythson[23] and Byram Hall in the same county; Raynham Hall in Norfolk which was designed by William Edge; Aston Hall in Warwickshire; Quenby Hall in Leicestershire; Aldermaston House in Berkshire which John Evelyn noted was 'built *a la moderne*';[24] Broome House in Kent; Charborough House in Dorset; and Dunster Castle in Somerset where George Luttrell employed William Arnold as his architect. Sir William Dugdale the Warwickshire antiquary offered the opinion that 'for beauty and state' Aston Hall 'much exceedeth any in these parts' (Pl. 8). According to his account of the house it

6. Chipchase Castle, Northumberland. Built by Cuthbert Heron in 1621.

7. Burton Agnes Hall, Yorkshire. Built by Sir Henry Griffith, 1601–10.

was begun in 1618 and completed in 1635.[25] In contrast, the building of Broome House proceeded much more quickly, partly no doubt because Sir Basil Dixwell had a more substantial estate revenue than Sir Thomas Holte, the builder of Aston Hall. Sir Basil laid the foundation of his new house in April 1635 and by the autumn of 1638 the project was finished. As early as June 1638 we find him inviting a neighbouring family to Broome House 'wher yow shall meete myselfe and the Gentlemen and Gentlewomen which are of my house, that are very desirous to see yow all there and to eate a cake and drinke a bottle of wine together'.[26] George Ashby, who built Quenby Hall (Pl. 9), had married the daughter of a wealthy London merchant but it was probably no coincidence that about the time the work was completed he was obliged to sell one of his manors. Another major landowner whose building operations appear to have owed much to an advantageous marriage was Sir

8. Aston Hall, Warwickshire. A seventeenth-century print (Sir William Dugdale, *The Antiquities of Warwickshire*, second edition, 1730).

9. Quenby Hall, Leicestershire (John Nichols, *The History and Antiquities of the County of Leicester*, 1795–1811).

John Ramsden of Longley in Yorkshire. In 1633 he successfully negotiated a match with the widow of a London alderman who brought him a portion of over £12,000 and valuable property in Essex, some of which was sold. During the course of Charles I's reign he built Byram Hall, a large three-storeyed mansion with shaped gables, which would become the family's principal seat.[27]

The building of a large country house involved heavy expenditure even when it lacked the grandeur of such palatial mansions as Longleat and Temple Newsam. Quenby Hall cost £12,000 and Broome House, with the stables and other outhouses, £8000 while Sir John Evelyn spent £9000 in rebuilding Leigh Place at Godstone in Surrey.[28] In the early seventeenth century a smaller type of country house could be built at a cost of between £1000 and £3000 as the following examples illustrate:[29]

house	*cost*
Brookmans, North Mimms, Hertfordshire	£1500
Eastwood Hall, Ashover, Derbyshire	£2000
Nelmes, Hornchurch, Essex	£2000
Dorton House, Buckinghamshire	above £2000
Fountains Hall, Yorkshire	£3000
Rowdell House, Washington, Sussex	£3000
Flambards, Harrow on the Hill, Middlesex	£3000

Sir Gilbert Gerard, who rebuilt Flambards, was both a major landowner and a senior official of the Duchy of Lancaster and as such could have afforded the cost of a much larger house but the nature of the site may have proved restrictive. Edmund Byne, the builder of Rowdell House, had an estate revenue of no more than £600 a year and he therefore resorted to the expedient of funding the project through the sale of timber and some part of his personal estate.[30]

Often the timber required for building purposes was provided from the estate. According to an affidavit submitted to the Court of Wards in 1626 Dame Anne Savile, the widow of Sir George Savile of Thornhill in Yorkshire, had ordered the felling of 200 trees for 'the newe buildinge and necessary repaireinge of the Mannorhouse called Thornehill Hall and the outhouses and pales and fences thereto belongeinge and adioyninge'.[31] Some gentry also had stone quarries, though in many areas brick was the preferred material. On the other hand, the expenditure on a building project was not wholly limited to the fabric and foundations: there was also the cost of the plasterwork and the internal fittings. When Sir John Wolstenholme was carrying out improvements to his Yorkshire mansion, Nostell Priory, shortly before the Civil War he drew on the services of Nicholas Stone, the king's master mason, who recorded in his account book that the sum of £32 2s 0d had been received for a chimney-piece supplied in 1640 and set up in 1642. In May 1642 Stone also presented him with an estimate of the cost of ten more chimney-pieces. On the basis that Sir John would himself provide the marble this amounted to £129.[32]

Among the potential hazards of house building were an unbudgeted increase in expenditure and shortcomings on the part of the contractor. In a Chancery suit of 1626 Brian Stapleton of Myton in Yorkshire described the problems which had arisen over his plan 'to builde a new house of Bricke together with a Courte to be walled about'. In October 1623 he had ordered 100,000 bricks but as yet the suppliers had delivered fewer than 50,000. He also alleged that Robert Stanning who had been responsible for superintending the work had been guilty of negligence. On taking stock of progress he had discovered that 'many doores, Chimneyes, windowes and ovens' in the new house had been 'misplaced, false wrought and wrong sett upp'.[33] In his will, which was drawn up in 1632, Thomas Hillersden of Elstow in Bedfordshire left his wife the sum of £500 'to finish the newe buildinge of the howse now in hand upon the scyte of the late dissolved Monastery of Elvestowe'. Following his death, however, the Court of Wards was informed that it would in fact be necessary to spend at least £1000.[34]

When the Civil War broke out in 1642 all building activities were naturally suspended. A few years earlier John Layer the Cambridgeshire historian had noted that Thomas Chicheley of Wimpole was 'now erecting an extraordinary curious neat house near the ancient site'. In the event Sir Thomas (as he became) did not finish building the new Wimpole Hall until after the Restoration.[35] When Sir Richard Wilbraham of Woodhey Hall in Cheshire drew up his will in February 1643 he bequeathed to his son Thomas all the brick and stone at Woodhey and Shotwick 'which I intended to build withall, and all the Tooles which were used and which were myne at my Smithy at Woodhey'. Sir Richard, who was then a prisoner of the royalists, died shortly afterwards and before long the family settled at Weston Park in Staffordshire. For many years Woodhey Hall suffered from neglect and it was not until the 1690s that the Wilbrahams put work in hand.[36]

During the Civil War period at least eighty country houses belonging to gentry families were either completely destroyed or severely damaged while many

10. Mapledurham
House,
Oxfordshire.

more were plundered. Some regions such as East Anglia escaped comparatively lightly but it was a different story in Yorkshire, Buckinghamshire, Devon
and a number of other counties which experienced intensive fighting. Not surprisingly, it was often the royalist gentry whose houses were besieged and
assaulted. Sir John Pakington had the misfortune to lose both his principal
houses, one at Aylesbury in Buckinghamshire and the other at Hampton
Lovett in Worcestershire.[37] During his travels in 1644 Richard Symonds rode
past Sir Charles Blount's mansion at Mapledurham in Oxfordshire (Pl. 10) and
inserted in his diary the comment that 'This faire and large howse is much
spoyled by the rebellious when the Earl of Essex lay at Reading 1643'.[38] In
1645, while he was imprisoned in the Tower, Sir John Glanville's house at
Broad Hinton in Wiltshire was burnt down by royalist troops, apparently with
the aim of preventing the parliamentarians from putting in a garrison. When
John Evelyn visited Broad Hinton in 1654 he found that Sir John was living in
the gatehouse.[39] In a petition which he submitted at the time of the
Restoration a Northumberland landowner, Sir Edward Widdrington, related
that he had lost £1900 by spoil and plunder and that his main residence,
Cartington Castle, which he valued at £8000, had been pulled down.[40]

On the other hand, a number of parliamentarian gentry fared no better. In
1644 a Yorkshire squire, Sir William Lister, informed Parliament that his

11. The ruined castle of the Harleys at Brampton Bryan, Herefordshire.

house, Thornton Hall in Craven, and the barns and stables had been burnt to the ground by Prince Rupert. Some years later his son-in-law John Lambert the parliamentary general wrote that his own house, Calton Hall, was uninhabitable, 'beinge quit puld downe and ruinated' in the recent wars.[41] Others whose houses sustained heavy damage included Sir Robert Cooke of Highnam Court in Gloucestershire, Sir Robert Harley of Brampton Bryan in Herefordshire and Henry Darley of Buttercrambe Hall in Yorkshire. When Harley viewed the ruins of Brampton Castle (Pl. 11) his Puritan temperament led him to declare that 'God Hath brought great desolation upon this place since I saw it. I desire to say the Lord hath given and the Lord hath taken away and blessed be the name of the Lord. I trust in his good time He will rays it up agayn'. As Sir Robert was well aware, it was in such terms that Job had responded to the catastrophe which had befallen him.[42]

Some of the country houses which were destroyed were never rebuilt. The Pakingtons settled at Westwood in Worcestershire and substantially enlarged their house there which had originally been built as a lodge.[43] The impressive ruins at Moreton Corbet in Shropshire (Pl. 12) bear witness to the fact that Sir Vincent Corbet abandoned any idea of restoring his magnificent Elizabethan mansion. Instead he took up residence at Acton Reynald, a few miles away, where the family had a secondary house.[44] In 1648 Thornhill Hall in Yorkshire was burnt down following an accidental explosion which occurred while it was besieged by parliamentarian forces. As a result the owner, Sir George Savile, decided to move to Rufford Abbey in Nottinghamshire where he 'much enlarged and adorned' the house.[45] Generally, however, a house which had suffered damage was rebuilt or renovated, in some cases during the Commonwealth period and in others after the Restoration. In the 1650s Sir Walter Erle, who had been one of the leading parliamentarians in Dorset,

built Charborough House for a second time on the same site as his ill-fated
Jacobean mansion. Some twenty years after its completion Celia Fiennes paid
her relative Thomas Erle a visit and wrote that it was 'a new built house on
the brow of the hill . . . there is a very good hall at the entrance leads you to a
large parlour and drawing room . . . the chambers are good and lofty'.[46]

Contrary to the conventional wisdom there was a substantial amount of
house building in the Commonwealth period which is only partly attribut-
able to war damage. Some new country houses such as Thorpe Hall in
Northamptonshire, Chesterton House in Warwickshire and Gunnersbury
House in Middlesex were built by parliamentarian gentry, including wealthy
Cromwellian officials; others such as Coleshill House in Berkshire and Lees
Court in Kent by royalists or men whose political outlook was distinctly
pragmatic. Often these houses represented a marked departure from the E-
and H-shaped designs of the early seventeenth century. Classical influences
had been slowly percolating before 1640 but they were now having a much
greater impact. In south-east England particularly there was a growing fashion for more compact houses which had neither gables nor projecting wings,
though traditional forms of building were less readily abandoned in the
more remote counties.[47] The front of Chesterton House (Pl. 13) bore a close
resemblance to the Banqueting House in Whitehall which Inigo Jones had
designed when he was still heavily under the influence of Italian classicism.
The building of the new house was set in hand by Edward Peyto in 1655 but
it was unfinished at his death three years later. In his will he indicated that
it was his wish that 'the building I have begun at Chesterton may be finished out of the Rents of the lands in Chesterton which belong after my
decease to my . . . son Edward Peyto . . . Towards which I do give and
appoint that all the Bricks, Stones, Timber and other materialls provided for

13. Chesterton House, Warwickshire. An eighteenth-century drawing (British Library, Additional MSS 29,264, fol. 189).

that building shalbe therein employed'. The Peyto estates were then worth £1200 a year but most of the revenue was earmarked for jointures. Since Peyto's son was a mere child his widow took on responsibility for the work and in 1659 was employing John Stone as the architect. In 1662 Elizabeth Peyto presented the Court of Chancery with a report on the project, explaining that the house which her husband had inherited had been 'ruinous and not fitt for his habitation'. By the time of his death, she went on, the walls of the new house were some four feet high and he had spent £1000 and taken delivery of materials of a great value for the next stage of the building programme. By 1 November 1661 she had herself disbursed £1226 18s 7d and, the Court was assured, she was willing to continue provided she was reimbursed from her son's estate. Some accounts which have survived reveal that in the period 1662 to 1664 (when the house was finally completed) she incurred expenditure of some £1100 on the payment of wages and the purchase of freestone, timber, lead and tiles.[48]

A number of families whose houses had been damaged were unable to make a start on rebuilding or repairing them until after the Restoration, either because of serious financial difficulties or because they had been living in exile on the Continent. At Brampton Bryan in Herefordshire the building of a new house adjoining the ruined castle proceeded slowly at first, mainly on account of the fact that Sir Edward Harley was often absent on parliamentary duty. In August 1660 his steward, Samuel Shilton, informed him that 'for the building at Brompton it is Now att a stand Till your Mind be knowne'. By November 1661 he was able to report that 'The New building is now brought up to the first floor, all except the kitchen chimney'; nevertheless several years were to elapse before the house was finally ready for occupation. In 1687 Sir Edward was amused to hear that someone in Ludlow who had been asking whether he lived in a strong castle had been told that 'the Castle is down, His dwelling neer is a slight thin hous'.[49] In his account of the Devonshire gentry John Prince writes that Ashe House, the seat of Sir John

Drake, was 'burnt and demolished in the times of our late Civil Wars' and 'lay long in ruins'. It was eventually rebuilt by his son, another Sir John, who succeeded him in 1669. In Prince's words he 'enlarged and beautified it to a greater Perfection that it was of before', though on the evidence of an inventory of 1684 the new house was not particularly large.[50] In February 1663 a major building programme was begun at Coughton Court in Warwickshire, the seat of Sir Francis Throckmorton, which had suffered extensive damage at the hands of the parliamentarians. According to the accounts of his steward, Francis Reeve, who exercised a general oversight of the project, it took three years and cost £2355 in all. Among the items of expenditure were the wages of the work force which numbered sixty-two at its peak and the purchase of large quantities of bricks, tiles and Derbyshire lead. In March 1664 there is an entry recording the provision of ale for the labourers 'when the new building was reared' while in May John Dewes swept twenty-six chimneys and was paid at the rate of twopence a chimney.[51]

Aside from war damage, the factors responsible for the high intensity of house building in the later Stuart period were basically the same as those which had been in evidence in the early seventeenth century. At the same time the building activities of many of the country gentry in Charles II's reign may well have received an additional stimulus from their sense of relief at the demise of the republican regime. Sir Daniel Fleming's description of Cumberland and Westmorland, which was written in 1671, contains numerous references to work which had recently been undertaken or was currently in progress within this region. Sir Philip Musgrave had been adding substantially to his principal residence, Hartley Castle, and had also made his house at Edenhall much more 'convenient'. Ferdinando Huddleston was rebuilding Millom Castle which had been ruined in the Civil Wars; William Fletcher of Moresby Hall had 'lately made the house much more beautifull and convenient'; and Sir Francis Salkeld of Whitehall (near Wigton) had 'much beautifyed this seat'. At Hutton in the Forest Sir Henry Fletcher had been obliged to suspend his building work on the outbreak of hostilities but his son Sir George had subsequently fulfilled his intentions, 'he haveing builded very much and made this a stately and convenient Habitation'.[52]

To judge from these and other examples which appear in Fleming's account the Cumberland and Westmorland gentry were mainly engaged in remodelling existing houses, perhaps because their financial circumstances were such that they were unable to embark on anything more ambitious. This also appears to have been the situation in another remote county, Cornwall, but elsewhere many new houses were erected during the latter part of the century, in some cases by the *nouveaux riches* but often by landed gentry who had long been settled on their estates. The more notable houses which have survived from this period include Halswell House in Somerset, Kingston Lacy in Dorset (Pl. 14), Ramsbury Manor in Wiltshire, Sarsden House in Oxfordshire, Melton Hall at Melton Constable in Norfolk, Weston Park in Staffordshire, Sudbury Hall in Derbyshire, Belton House in Lincolnshire and Capheaton Hall in Northumberland. Some of the new country houses reflected metropolitan tastes, others were more provincial in their appearance. Kingston Lacy, which was completed in 1665, was designed by Sir Roger Pratt who was

14. Kingston Lacy, Dorset.

one of the most fashionable architects of the day. In the process his client, Sir Ralph Bankes, may have overstretched his resources: in 1684 the Court of Chancery was informed that he had died heavily indebted and that the estate which he had left had been clogged with interest payments, rent-charges and other encumbrances.[53] In Devon Sir Walter Yonge grew discontented with his modest ancestral home at Colyton and had a new mansion, Escot House (Pl. 15), built in open country. In May 1687 he told his friend John Locke that 'there is no end of charge in building . . . yet I love the building so well that I should be glad to find a meet help to finish it'.[54] Sarsden House was rebuilt

15. Escot House, Devon (*Vitruvius Britannicus*, 1967 edition).

by Sir William Walter in 1693 after a fire in which he was said to have incurred losses amounting to £20,000.[55] Not long after this Sir Walter Wrottesley, the head of one of the most ancient families in Staffordshire, decided that the time had come to replace Wrottesley Hall with a more modern structure. Someone who viewed the work in progress wrote that Sir Walter had 'pulled down the old hall and built a more noble and sumptuous one, now almost finished, 1696. I have heard it would cost near £4000 to finish it'.[56]

During these post-Restoration years there are more frequent references to the employment of architects, men such as Pratt, William Samwell, Robert Hooke, Hugh May and Robert Trollope of Newcastle. At the same time there were a number of gentry who considered themselves to be proficient enough to undertake their own design work or at least to exercise close supervision. According to a contemporary account Sir John Brograve of Hamells in the Hertfordshire parish of Braughing had 'great Skill and Knowledge in Building, and Materials necessary for the same: this inclin'd him to beautify this Seat, and to make his House graceful and pleasant to his Eye'.[57] Similar praise was bestowed on Richard Legh of Lyme Hall in Cheshire (Pl. 16) by the minister who conducted his funeral service in 1687. The deceased, he observed, had rebuilt and 'ennobled' his mansion, 'partly in Effect and partly in Design, and preparations for its finishing . . . In the projecting whereof . . . as himself was the chief Designer, so in Architecture in general he was a great Master'.[58]

The evidence which has survived about building costs in these years presents a varied picture. When Sir Jacob Astley of Melton Constable in Norfolk sought parliamentary cover for a settlement of his estates he considered it necessary to outline his building plans. In a private bill of 1664 the point was made that Melton Hall was 'now wholly decayed and fallen down' and it was his intention therefore to rebuild it 'which will cost him above ffower thousande pounds'. In the event this must have proved to be a highly optimistic forecast (see Pl. 17 for the new house).[59] Following the death of his mother Sir Seymour Pile of Baverstock in Wiltshire inherited an estate at Axford near Ramsbury and decided to make it his seat. During the course of Charles II's reign he built a substantial mansion, Axford House, which cost him £9000.[60] In 1681 the Ramsbury estate was purchased by Sir William Jones, a former Attorney General. He immediately made arrangements for the building of a new house but died the following year. In a codicil to his will he indicated that it was his wish that 'the building of my house at Ramsbury . . . shall proceed and the workmen thereof shalbee paid out of my personal estate According to the agreement I have made with them'. The executors duly carried out his directions and spent a total of £17,257 5s 5d, including the sum of £2445 which was paid to the workmen.[61] On one of her journeys Celia Fiennes noted that at East Tytherley in Hampshire Sir Francis Rolle had 'a fine House and Garden and Groves'. Sir Francis died in 1686 and his widow, Dame Priscilla (who had brought him a large portion), subsequently disclosed that he had laid out some £15,000 in building the house and improving the grounds.[62] Belton House in Lincolnshire (Pl. 18) was begun in 1685 and completed in 1688. The building accounts record the expenditure of £10,000 but the total cost, including the decorative work, may have been around £15,000.

16. Richard Legh.
Portrait by Sir
Peter Lely (Lyme
Park, Cheshire).

The owner, Sir John Brownlow (Pl. 19), could well afford this kind of expenditure since he was one of the richest gentlemen in England with an estate revenue of over £9000 a year.[63]

Whatever the age of a country house there was a need for regular maintenance. Sir Roger Twysden of Roydon Hall in Kent told his son that 'I have ever left my coppis woods full of good store of Standard, for it must bee so that you may take downe 15 or 20 good okes every year or such an howse as this will fall for want of repayr'.[64] Among the papers of the Cary family of Clovelly in Devon there is a composite bill for repairs carried out in 1685.

17. Melton Hall, Melton Constable, Norfolk.

This amounts to £119 2s 5d (as against an estimate of £50) and covers glazing, carpentry, painting and other work. In March 1699 a seven-year window contract was negotiated. A glazier, Charles Cory, undertook to carry out necessary repairs to the windows of Clovelly Court, the stables, the brewhouse and other buildings except those in the gardens. William Cary, for his part, agreed

18. Belton House, Lincolnshire.

19. Sir John
Brownlow. Portrait
by John Riley
(Belton House).

that he would pay him a retainer of £2 a year.[65] As contemporary evidence frequently illustrates, country houses could soon begin to deteriorate through lack of proper maintenance. Sir John Knightley, a Warwickshire baronet who died in 1688, left his estate to a relative, John Wightwick, on condition that he assumed the name of Knightley. Wightwick was then only a child and for some years the mansion house at Offchurch stood empty and neglected. In 1696 the Court of Chancery received a gloomy report on the condition of the house. The roof was 'in great decay' and would need to be replaced, as would the supporting walls. In addition, the floors, wainscot, chimneys and lead gutters were all in a poor state. In the considered opinion of the authors of the report it would be necessary to spend no less than £1250 on refurbishing the mansion and the outhouses.[66]

CHAPTER TWO

The Country House Anatomised

In the seventeenth century a country house would often be approached through a gatehouse where a porter was responsible for controlling entry. Gatehouses were mainly the work of medieval and Tudor builders but they were still being erected in the early Stuart period, though more for show than for reasons of security. Houses where seventeenth-century gate-houses still survive include Burton Agnes Hall in Yorkshire (Pl. 20), Shenton Hall in Leicestershire and Stanway House in Gloucestershire. The first room which a visitor entered on reaching the house was the great hall (Pls 21 and 22) which was usually two storeys high. In many houses this was used as a din-ing-room for the servants and for visitors who were of too lowly a status to be granted the privilege of taking their meals with the family. Most seventeenth-century inventories which have survived offer evidence that the furniture in the hall was very much in keeping with this function: as a rule there were one or two plain tables, together with forms, stools or chairs of no particular quality. According to an inventory of 1668 the hall in Sir Matthew Herbert's Shropshire mansion, Oakley Park, contained a long table, two side tables, a bench, a form, a chair, a picture and a candlestick, all of which were described as 'old and overworne'.[1]

In some country houses which were built in the second half of the century the shape and character of the hall underwent a radical transformation: its height was often reduced to one storey, an elegant staircase was inserted and it became primarily an entrance hall which was meant to impress. The hall at Coleshill House in Berkshire, which was completed in 1662, was an early example of this new approach with the exception only of its height (Pl. 23). When Celia Fiennes visited the house some years later she wrote that the entrance was

> an ascent of severall steps into a hall so lofty the rooff is three storyes, reach-es to the floore of the gallery, all the walls are cutt in hollows where statues and heads carved finely are sett . . . the great Staires goes out of the hall on each side, spacious and handsom . . . the hall was paved with black and whyte marble and had seates round the roome cut in arches in the walls.[2]

At the beginning of the century many country mansions had a large state room, the great chamber, on the first floor. Here the family and their special

guests dined in considerable style and engaged in various recreational activities in surroundings which often bore witness to the owner's wealth and taste. One of the best surviving examples of this type of room is at Gilling Castle in

20. The gatehouse at Burton Agnes Hall, Yorkshire.

21. The great hall at Burton Agnes Hall, Yorkshire.

22. The great hall at Parham House, Sussex which was the seat of the Bishop family.

Yorkshire where it was the principal feature of a building programme carried out by Sir William Fairfax in the middle years of Elizabeth's reign (Pl. 24). This has a handsome ceiling hung with a multitude of pendants, walls with richly carved wainscoting surmounted by a frieze depicting some 370 coats of arms and windows with heraldic stained glass. Although some of the houses built in the reign of James I, among them Hawksworth Hall in Yorkshire and Wistow Hall in Leicestershire, were provided with a great chamber,[3] all the evidence suggests that this practice had been almost completely abandoned before the time of the Civil War. References to a great chamber still appear in

23. The entrance hall at Coleshill House, Berkshire which belonged to the Pratt family.

the inventories of older houses but even in such cases it was not always being used for its original purpose: in 1637, for example, the main items in the great chamber at Everingham Hall in Yorkshire consisted of four pieces of tapestry, a feather bed with curtains, a chair, two low stools and a cupboard.[4]

The eclipse of the great chamber as the main state room in the mansions of the nobility was occasioned by their loss of enthusiasm for the ceremony

24. The great chamber at Gilling Castle, Yorkshire.

25. The Stag Parlour at Lyme Hall (Park), Cheshire.

which they had once considered to be an essential accompaniment to eating at table.[5] Since for the most part the gentry had never been obsessed with ceremony to anything like the same extent their change of attitude may have been principally a matter of following the lead of their social superiors; and indeed it is possible that in some cases the great chamber simply acquired a new name. What is certainly clear is that in the seventeenth century most gentry families took their meals either in a parlour (on the ground floor) or a dining-room (on the first floor). Parlours served both as dining- and sitting-rooms (for examples see Pls 25 and 26). Many country houses had two parlours which were often styled 'great' and 'little' and occasionally 'winter' and 'summer'. In 1618 the dining parlour at Ripley Hall in Yorkshire contained, among other things, a 'long drawe table', a side table, eleven joined stools (which were made of parts fitted together), twelve 'sett woorke

26. The great parlour at Quenby Hall, Leicestershire.

stoules' and two other stools, five chairs, two maps, a chessboard and eleven pictures.[6] An inventory of the contents of Etchilhampton House in Wiltshire which was drawn up in 1682 reveals that Sir Walter Ernle and his family normally dined in the little parlour. Among the items in this room were a plate warmer, a 'heater', two pewter stands 'to set dishes on the table', and a small toasting fork.[7] The term 'dining-room' began to come into general use in the middle years of the century (Pl. 27). In the reign of Charles II the rooms at

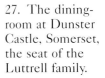

27. The dining-room at Dunster Castle, Somerset, the seat of the Luttrell family.

Arbury Hall in Warwickshire, the Elizabethan mansion of the Newdegate family, included both a great chamber and a dining-room. The great chamber was apparently used as a bedroom while the contents of the dining-room were listed as five pieces of tapestry hangings, three Persian carpets, a couch, eighteen Turkey-work chairs and four Spanish tables.[8] Often the dining-room figured in the improvements which the gentry were making to the interiors of their houses. Towards the end of the century a Devonshire squire, Francis Fulford, embarked on an extensive remodelling of his Tudor mansion at Great Fulford. A visitor who was highly impressed by the results of this work wrote admiringly that the great hall had been richly paved with black and white marble (Pl. 28); that the staircase was 'a piece of great Cost as well as Cunning, being diversyfied with sundry pieces of party-coloured Timber'; and that this led up to a noble dining-room which was 'very sumptuously furnished'.[9]

In the latter part of the century it became the practice, at least in the larger houses, to retire after meals to a drawing- or withdrawing-room (Pl. 29) which was situated next to the dining-room or parlour. There are also occasional references to a smoking or tobacco room which would have been the exclusive preserve of the men. This was at a time when tobacco was considered by many to have health-giving properties.

The long gallery (Pl. 30), which was a feature of many country houses, provided the gentry with a convenient means of taking physical exercise, particularly when the weather was inclement. Some galleries were convert-

28. The great hall at Great Fulford, Devon.

29. The drawing-
room at Lyme Hall
(Park), Cheshire.

ed into bedchambers or used for storage purposes. After the Restoration,
however, there was a growing fashion for turning them into picture gal-
leries. Among the houses where this transformation occurred were Roydon
Hall in Kent, Bessels Leigh House in Berkshire, Shardeloes in
Buckinghamshire, Yarnton Manor in Oxfordshire and Madresfield Court in
Worcestershire.[10]

The amount of sleeping accommodation required in a major country house
was often substantial, not only because of the size of the household but
because of the need to make provision for visitors and their servants. Sir
Hugh Cholmley observes that in the summer of 1638 Sir Christopher
Yelverton and his wife (who was Cholmley's sister) 'with some other friends,
did me the favour to come to Whitby, where they stayed ten weeks; all which
time I was between fifty and sixty in household'.[11] An inventory drawn up
after the death of Sir Robert Phelips in 1638 registers the point that in his
Somerset mansion, Montacute House, there were twenty-eight beds in all,
some of which would have been shared, while in 1661 The Vyne in
Hampshire contained twenty beds 'of all sorts' which were valued at £80.[12]

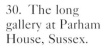

30. The long gallery at Parham House, Sussex.

Bedrooms varied widely both in size and character. At one extreme there was the large and well appointed chamber of the head of the household while at the other there were small dormitories where the ordinary sort of servants slept in conditions which were far from luxurious. In 1699 the best chamber at Sydmonton Court, the Hampshire seat of the Kingsmill family, contained a bed with a valance, silk damask curtains and silk quilts, a japanned looking-glass, a japanned table and stands with leather covers, six silk damask armchairs, an elbow chair, two stools with tapestry cushions, a fire screen, a close stool, four striped muslin window curtains, two iron dogs, a fire shovel and tongs, two earthenware flower pots, a small picture and three pieces of tapestry hangings (for another example see Pl. 31).[13] During the late seventeenth century it was not unusual for the squire to have a dressing-room next to his bedchamber. At Hayne in the Devonshire parish of Newton St Cyres the contents of Sir Arthur Northcote's dressing-room, as listed in 1688, consisted of his clothes, which were valued at £20, a looking-glass, an assortment of books and a sword with a silver hilt.[14] When the nursery was inventoried it appears to have been the practice to ignore the children's toys. Had they been recorded they would have included such items as dolls, drums, whipping-tops, kites and battledores and shuttlecocks.

In some country houses there was a well-stocked armoury which often testified to the fact that the squire was a deputy lieutenant or a colonel in the militia. In 1687 Colonel Richard Fowler of Harnage Grange in Shropshire had an impressive collection of weapons and other military equipment: 17 carbines, 28 muskets, 18 suits of armour, 20 swords, 19 girdles for swords, 36 pike heads, 6 fowling guns, a park gun, another 7 swords and 6 pairs of pistols.[15] In the absence of an armoury a gentleman might choose to display his weapons in the great hall (Pl. 32).

31. The south-
west bedroom at
Quenby Hall,
Leicestershire.

Many country mansions had domestic chapels, though not all of them were still in use. These ranged in origin from the Middle Ages to the seventeenth century and included both free-standing buildings (Pl. 33) and rooms fitted up within the houses which they served. In 1669 Sir Peter Leycester calculated that there were seventeen domestic chapels in his native county of Cheshire which belonged to such families as the Booths of Dunham Massey,

32. Display of
arms in the great
hall at Littlecote
House, Wiltshire
which belonged to
the Popham
family.

33. The early seventeenth-century chapel at Childerley Hall, Cambridgeshire which was the seat of the Cutts family.

the Leghs of Lyme Hall, the Grosvenors of Eaton and the Catholic Stanleys of Hooton. Some of the chapels which he listed were described as ancient but there were others which were of much more recent provenance. The chapel at Crewe Hall was the work of Sir Randle Crewe who had completed the building of his 'sumptuous' new house shortly before the Civil War while at Dunham Massey Hall Sir George Booth (who was a Presbyterian in religion) had converted two ground floor rooms in 1655. In contrast, the chapel at Toft Hall, the seat of another branch of the Leycester family, was by now used for secular purposes.[16] New domestic chapels were making their appearance throughout the seventeenth century. During the years 1675 to 1678 Sir Peter Leycester was engaged in building a chapel for his family in the garden at Tabley Hall where he had been undertaking a major improvement programme. His total expenditure on the chapel, including the communion plate, amounted to £795.[17] Occasionally an inventory records the contents of a private chapel in some detail. At Easton Mauduit Hall, the Northamptonshire seat of the Yelverton family, the upper chapel, as it was termed in an inventory of 1671, appears to have been a gallery reserved for the use of the head of the household and his immediate family since it contained a couch, a number of chairs, some hangings and a fireplace. In the body of the chapel there were eight Common Prayer books, a quarto edition of the Bible, a cushion of old crimson velvet for the reading desk, hassocks and stands, a great Bible in two volumes in the chancel and, on the communion table, a carpet (that is, a covering) and an altar cloth.[18]

Under the procedures of the Church of England it was necessary for a new chapel to be licensed and consecrated by the bishop of the diocese. This presented difficulties during the reign of Charles I when Archbishop Laud and some of his fellow bishops were inclined to regard private chapels with some suspicion because of the fear that they might be used for conventicles. Sir Henry Slingsby the Yorkshire diarist writes that it was for this reason that Archbishop Neile of York refused to consecrate the chapel which his father had built at Red House in Moor Monkton.[19] After the Restoration the ecclesiastical authorities tended to be more indulgent in such matters, though they might lay down some restrictions when granting permission. In 1668 Sir William More of Loseley House in Surrey obtained a licence from the Bishop of Winchester for the celebration of divine service and the administration of the sacraments in his private chapel on the basis that he and his household could worship there on Sundays and feast days whenever it was inconvenient for them to join the congregation at their parish church, St Nicholas in Guildford.[20]

The houses of office, as they were called, consisted in particular of the kitchen, the buttery, the pantry or larder, the still-room, the boulting house where corn was winnowed, the bakehouse, the dairy, the brewhouse, the slaughterhouse and the laundry or wash-house. The kitchen, buttery and pantry were usually on the ground floor, though at Coleshill House in Berkshire they were relegated to a basement.[21] Generally, the other domestic offices were situated in a service wing (which might be at the opposite end of an inner courtyard) or in a separate range of ancillary buildings. In 1639 Archbishop Laud was informed that at Childerley Hall, the Cambridgeshire seat of Sir John Cutts, 'meane houses of Office' had been erected on the ruins of the parish church.[22]

Horses represented one of the gentry's more important assets. Some of the wealthier squires owned as many as 30, 40 or 50 saddle horses, coach horses, cart horses and foals. In 1692 the personal effects of Francis Forrester of Watling Street Hall in Shropshire included a white stallion, nine geldings and twenty-three mares which were valued at £156 5s 0d and a coach and harness which were considered to be worth £10.[23] All country houses had their stables, many of which were rebuilt in the course of the seventeenth century. Sir Roger Burgoyne, who had mansion-houses at both Sutton in Bedfordshire and Wroxall in Warwickshire, frequently complained in correspondence with his friend Sir Ralph Verney about his financial problems and the severe limitations which they imposed on his building plans. In June 1663 we find him writing that when the new stables had been completed at Wroxall they were likely to be 'as empty as my purse'. A decade later he heard that his stables at Sutton had been burnt to the ground but took no immediate steps to rebuild them. Writing from Sutton in February 1675 he declared that 'something must be done before this ruined place be fitt for any gentleman's constant residence, though for the present I think to

34. The late
seventeenth-
century stables at
Melbury House,
Melbury
Sampford, Dorset.

make shift for stables with the outhouses over the way'.[24] Where money was
in plentiful supply the stables often had a certain grandeur. At Chiswick in
Middlesex Sir Stephen Fox, who made a fortune as paymaster to the Army,
built a magnificent house 'after the Modern Manner' together with stables
and other outbuildings which were said to 'look like so many Gentlemen's
seats'.[25] Capacious stable blocks dating from the late seventeenth century
have survived at a number of country seats, including Melbury House at
Melbury Sampford in Dorset (Pl. 34), Arbury Hall in Warwickshire and
Weston Park in Staffordshire. Not altogether surprisingly, the families which
erected these particular edifices – Strangways, Newdegate and Wilbraham –
were among the wealthiest gentry in their respective counties.

Despite the abundance of wood a country mansion usually had a stock of
coal as well as logs and faggots in its back yard. Heating was necessary not
only for general domestic purposes but as a means of forestalling the effects
of damp on the wainscot, tapestries, curtains and plasterwork. During the
course of Exchequer proceedings in 1699 the point was made that James
Dibble, who had been employed as steward by Sir Roger Strickland of
Thornton Bridge in Yorkshire, had been obliged to purchase substantial
amounts of coal in his master's absence since the house was very large and
fires were often made 'to preserve the Rooms'.[26] In the northern counties and
the counties bordering Wales there were many country gentlemen who mined
coal, either on a commercial scale or simply for their own use. In 1624 Sir

Ralph Delaval of Seaton Delaval in Northumberland gave direction in his will that his mansion house should be supplied with 300 wain loads of coal each year out of the colliery which he owned,[27] and other major families such as the Ingrams of Temple Newsam in Yorkshire, the Corbets of Adderley in Shropshire and the Halls of High Meadow in Gloucestershire would also have been self-sufficient in this respect.

As Sir Henry Wotton noted in his treatise on architecture it was important that a country seat should be well-watered.[28] This was a feature which Sir Henry Chauncy the Hertfordshire historian particularly singled out in his description of Watton Woodhall, the seat of the Boteler family. The house, he wrote, was situated in a pleasant park where 'divers christal Springs issue out of the Ground, at some distance before the House . . . They do greatly adorn the Seat, and the Park, and the Hills, the Timber Trees, and these Waters render this Place so very pleasant and delicious to the Eye, that it is account-ed one of the best Seats in this County.'[29] Aside from aesthetic considerations the ready availability of water was a matter of practical necessity. In 1671 John Ashburnham, a courtier who was seated in Sussex, added a codicil to his will for the purpose of authorising his executors to spend as much as they thought fit 'for and towards the finishing of my house att Ashburnham and the Outhouses, Gardens and Courts belonging to the same and bringing the water to the same'.[30] Water was drawn from either a pump or a well in an adjoining yard. An inventory which was prepared in 1679 following the death of anoth-er Sussex landowner, William Morley of Glynde Place, refers to a well house in which there were 'two well bucketts with Chaines and ropes thereto' and 'two Leaden Cesternes'.[31] Many country houses received their water through lead pipes connected with a spring which might be some considerable dis-tance away. In a Star Chamber case heard in 1606 it was deposed that Sir John Chamberlayne's manor-house at Prestbury in Gloucestershire was dependent on a pipeline system introduced about thirty years previously which brought water from a conduit head in grounds known as North Mead. In his bill Sir John alleged that Reginald Nicholas, a former employee of the family who now owned the manor, had instructed his servants to dismantle the pipes as part of a campaign of harassment which he had been waging against him.[32] In a journal which he kept Sir John Lowther of Lowther Hall in Westmorland observed that 'It is not knowne who brought the water to the house which had beene worthie of memorie, a thinge soe convenient and usefull'. In 1659 he wrote that it had been necessary to renew 70 yards of the pipeline and repair the rest, adding that if a grate was placed 'upon the pipe at the well heade, there will not be anie defect for longe tyme'. Five years later, howev-er, he was forced to undertake further renovation work.[33]

In the latter part of the century there is some evidence of more elaborate arrangements for the supply of water. William Thursby, who purchased the Abington estate in Northamptonshire in 1669, not only rebuilt the house but constructed a water-tower and a reservoir which were linked to a stream flowing from a spring called Broadley Head. The tower still survives (Pl. 35): inscribed with his initials and the date 1678, it stands over a well equipped with a water-wheel.[34] According to Robert Plot, the seventeenth-century anti-quary, a similar kind of system was in operation at Hamstead Hall, the

35. The water tower in the grounds of Abington Hall (Abbey), Northamptonshire.

Staffordshire seat of Sir John Wyrley. Here, he writes, 'there is a Corn-mill that pumps water up into a lofty house near it, whence all the Offices of the Hall are served'.[35]

Although Sir John Harington had invented the water-closet in the reign of Elizabeth his pioneering work had been largely in vain. When John Aubrey visited the mansion of the Carew family at Beddington in Surrey during the latter part of the seventeenth century he was intrigued by

> a pretty Machine to cleanse an House of Office, viz. by a small Stream, no bigger than one's Finger, which run into an Engine, made like a Bit of a Fire-Shovel, which hung upon its Center of Gravity; so that when it was full, a considerable Quantity of Water fell down with some Force, and washed away the Filth.

This appears to have been some kind of water-closet but as Aubrey's reaction clearly testifies such a facility was extremely rare.[36] As a general rule the sanitary arrangements in the houses of the gentry consisted of close stools and chamber pots. In 1665 a total of six close stool pans and fourteen chamber pots figured in a schedule of the personal estate which had belonged to Clement Paston of Town Barningham Hall in Norfolk.[37] The provision of close stools was generally confined to the main bedchambers where they were sometimes housed in special closets. For their personal ablutions the gentry relied heavily on the basin and ewer. When Celia Fiennes visited her relative Sir John St Barbe at Broadlands in Hampshire she noted that in a back yard there was 'a Bathing house and other necessarys'.[38] This, however, was highly unusual: seventeenth-century inventories of gentry houses contain no references to bathrooms or bathing houses. On the other hand, it is possible that in some instances the wash-house had a dual function as laundry and bathroom. Alternatively, tubs of hot water might be carried upstairs to the bedchambers of the squire and his family.

Inventories of country mansions often record large quantities of linen and brass and pewter utensils. At the same time it was almost an article of faith that a gentleman should be able to display a collection of gold or silver plate. In many cases this was a relatively modest collection but some of the wealthier squires owned plate worth £500 or more. Following the death in 1636 of Sir Roger Townshend of Raynham Hall in Norfolk his plate was valued at £801 13s 0d and sold to goldsmiths and others for £803 8s 5d.[39] The inclusion of jewellery in probate inventories appears to have been a rather haphazard affair. When Sir Humphrey Forster of Aldermaston in Berkshire drew up his will in 1663 he was anxious to put it on record that his estranged wife, who was living in London, had in her possession various items of great value which rightfully belonged to him. These included three pearl necklaces which had cost him £1460 and two pairs of pearl earrings worth £100.[40] While Sir Henry Wood's personal estate at Loudham Park in Suffolk was being inventoried in 1671 the assessors came across a strong box and the decision was taken to send it unopened to his lodgings in Whitehall where he had held a senior appointment in the court of Charles II. When the box was finally unlocked in the presence of two noblemen and a bishop it was found to contain, among other things, some miniatures by Samuel Cooper, a gold watch and a pearl necklace which was considered to be worth between £1500 and £2000.[41]

In an account of Suffolk written in the reign of James I Robert Reyce commented that there were 'many curious costly builded houses wherein though the meanest gentleman provideth to be well furnished, yett the better sort doe most excell', adorning their buildings 'with costly furniture which every owner seeketh to have'.[42] In a large mansion such as Bramshill House in Hampshire (Pl. 36) (which Celia Fiennes likened to a little town) the value of the furniture in the principal rooms could amount to a substantial sum. James Zouch, who sold the house and estate in 1637, commissioned a detailed valuation of the furniture and was advised that it was worth £2762 5s 3d.[43] On the other hand, probate inventories often record much lower figures in the case of smaller country houses. According to an inventory drawn up in September 1668 Sir Francis Godolphin of Godolphin House in Cornwall (Pl. 37) left a personal estate worth £21,135. Among the range of items listed the money, plate and jewels were valued at £800, household stuff of all sorts at £675, chattel leases at £11,250 and tin together with associated implements at £4000.[44]

In the early seventeenth century few gentlemen appear to have had particularly large collections of paintings; indeed there were some well-to-do

36. Bramshill
House, Hampshire.

squires whose houses were apparently devoid of pictures, though they
would often decorate their walls with tapestries or maps. There were nevertheless a considerable number of families which commissioned portraits,
usually from foreign artists living in England. Sir Anthony van Dyck mainly undertook work for Charles I and members of the nobility but Cornelius
Johnson, who was born in London of Dutch parents, had many clients
among the gentry. Johnson settled in Kent where he enjoyed the patronage
of such families as the Campions of Combwell (Pls 38 and 39), the Filmers
of East Sutton and the Oxindens of Deane (Pl. 40). Beyond the borders of
Kent his clientele included the Pelhams of Halland House in Sussex, the
Kingsmills of Sydmonton and the Coopers of Rockbourne in Hampshire,

37. Godolphin
House, Cornwall
(William Borlase,
*The Natural History
of Cornwall*, 1758).

38. (above, left)
Sir William
Campion. Portrait
by Cornelius
Johnson, 1633.

39. (above, right)
Margaret Campion.
Portrait by
Cornelius Johnson,
1637.

40. (left) Sir
Henry Oxinden.
Portrait by
Cornelius Johnson,
c. 1637.

41. Sir Thomas Lucy, his wife and some of their children. After Cornelius Johnson (Charlecote Park, Warwickshire).

the Temples of Stowe and the Verneys of Middle Claydon in Buckinghamshire, the Lees of Ditchley in Oxfordshire and the Monsons of Burton in Lincolnshire.[45] In his accounts for the year 1638 Sir Thomas Pelham recorded the payment of £4 to Johnson for his portrait and 5s to the boy who brought it.[46] During this period there was a growing taste for group portraits which served as a testimony to family values. Among the gentry who were depicted with their families were Sir Thomas Lucy of Charlecote in Warwickshire (Pl. 41), Sir Thomas Burdett of Foremark in Derbyshire and Sir Matthew Boynton of Barmston in Yorkshire. Boynton was a zealous Puritan who planned to emigrate to New England but eventually went into temporary exile in Holland and it is conceivable that the picture (which has a pastoral setting) was painted while the family was living there.[47] Sir Richard Saltonstall of South Ockendon in Essex and Sir Thomas Aston of Aston in Cheshire commissioned group portraits in which, unusually, their wives are shown in bed: Lady Saltonstall has just been delivered of a child while Lady Aston is pictured both on her deathbed and as she was in life (Pl. 42).

After the Restoration there are more frequent references in inventories to sizeable collections of pictures, at least in the case of the wealthier gentry. Some examples are given in the following table:[48]

family	*date*	*number of pictures*
Bennet of Babraham, Cambridgeshire	1668	67
Blois of Grundisburgh, Suffolk	1681	69
Brownlow of Belton, Lincolnshire	1686	153
Chute of The Vyne, Hampshire	1661	30
Cutts of Childerley, Cambridgeshire	1670	74
Delaune of Sharsted Court, Kent	1678	56
D'Ewes of Stowlangtoft, Suffolk	1685	46
Lenthall of Bessels Leigh, Berkshire	1682	145
Neville of Billingbear, Berkshire	1676	51
Purefoy of Wadley House, Berkshire	1686	45

Pictures were hung in the great hall, the parlours, the great chamber, the dining-room, the withdrawing-room, the long gallery, the staircases and the principal bedchambers. The grand staircase at such mansions as Belton House and Babraham Hall not only provided an attractive setting for a major display of pictures but may in some cases have acted as a stimulus to their acquisition. At Babraham Hall the 'great staircase', as it was called, contained twenty-three small pictures and twenty large ones. In 1668 the 'painted long Gallery' at Osterley Park in Middlesex, which was then the seat of Sir William Waller, had twenty-four pictures on its walls. In the mansion of the

42. Sir Thomas Aston at the deathbed of his wife. By John Souch, 1635 (Manchester City Art Galleries).

Fane family at Burston in Kent there was a room which actually went by the name of the picture gallery: an inventory drawn up in 1692 records its contents as 'three great pictures and nine other old pictures'.[49]

Family portraits continued to be an important element in collections of pictures. When Celia Fiennes visited her relative Hugh Boscawen of Tregothnan House in Cornwall during the summer of 1698 she wrote in her journal that the drawing-room contained pictures of the family. An inventory which was drawn up in 1701 following his death reveals that there were six pictures in this room and that they portrayed his brother Edward, a rich London merchant; his son Theophilus who had died of smallpox at Strasbourg; the Countess of Lincoln who may be identified as the mother of his first wife; his widow Lady Mary; his daughter Mrs Bridget Fortescue; and a kinswoman, Mrs Trefusis.[50] From the reign of Charles II onwards Sir Peter Lely, Sir Godfrey Kneller, Michael Wright and other fashionable portrait painters were receiving commissions from such major landed families as the Brownlows of Belton in Lincolnshire, the Mordants of Little Massingham and the Windhams of Felbrigg in Norfolk, the Shirleys of Staunton Harold in Leicestershire, the Grimstons of Gorhambury in Hertfordshire, the Thynnes of Longleat in Wiltshire and the Onslows of West Clandon in Surrey. If family portraits were valued as a means of keeping alive the memory of loved ones they also had dynastic functions: as one generation succeeded another they became a kind of family history capable of instilling pride of lineage. At Adlington Hall in Cheshire the descent of the estate in the seventeenth century can be traced through the portraits of Sir Urian Legh who was responsible for converting the mansion into 'a stately and commodious house', his son Thomas who died in 1644 while in arms for the king and his grandson Thomas the younger, another royalist officer, who rebuilt the north front at the beginning of Charles II's reign.[51]

A gentleman's portrait collection was not necessarily limited in its coverage to members of the family and their kin; it could also include pictures of kings and queens, statesmen and other persons of note or figures from the classical world. The Alstons of Odell in Bedfordshire had a series of pictures of all the kings of England from William the Conqueror onwards; and the Fortescues of Salden House in Buckinghamshire had a similar set painted on board.[52] Since Sir Gilbert Pickering had been a leading republican it is hardly surprising that there were no royal portraits in his collection at Titchmarsh Hall in Northamptonshire unless a picture of the Duchess of Richmond can be regarded as such. On the other hand, he owned a series of portraits known as the Twelve Caesars. This was a popular set of pictures which figured in the collections of a number of gentlemen: in 1673, for example, Sir Thomas Wendy of Haslingfield in Cambridgeshire bequeathed to a relative his pictures of the Twelve Caesars together with pictures of Alexander the Great, the Emperor Constantine, Scipio, Cicero and Seneca.[53]

Some Puritan gentry considered that representations of Christ and his family smacked of idolatry. In 1671 a nonconformist divine wrote that Richard Hampden of Great Hampden in Buckinghamshire, 'finding a picture of the Trinity amongst his Grand-mother's goods, which fell to him and his sisters, for which he was bid £500, rather threw it into the fire and burnt it'.[54] Given the fact that Sir Gilbert Pickering and his wife were Puritans of the most extreme kind it is intriguing, to say the least, that his son John had a picture of the Virgin Mary in his bedchamber.[55]

The 'landskips' which were sometimes mentioned in seventeenth-century inventories were often tapestry hangings but some men such as Walter Kirkham of Fineshade Abbey in Northamptonshire owned landscape pictures.[56] In the latter part of the century a new subject began to emerge: the country seat. During the reign of Charles II a Dutch artist, Jan Siberechts, produced three paintings of Thomas Thynne's Wiltshire palace, Longleat House. Subsequently he came under the patronage of Sir Thomas Willoughby and painted several pictures of his Nottinghamshire mansion, Wollaton Hall, with its new formal gardens (Pl. 43). An English artist, Peter Hartover, undertook this type of work in north-east England. Among the houses which he depicted were Capheaton Hall in Northumberland which had been built for Sir John Swinburne in 1668 and Harraton Hall in County Durham which belonged to the Hedworth family.[57]

In its general scope the collection of Sir Thomas Spencer at Yarnton Manor in Oxfordshire was perhaps not untypical of its kind. According to an inventory drawn up in 1685 it contained over fifty pictures. The two parlours and the withdrawing-room next to them were hung with portraits of the family and their relations. On the walls of the great staircase there were fifteen pictures whose subject matter, as succinctly described by the assessors, included Covent Garden, a parrot, a Dutchman, a Dutchwoman, two magpies, an ass, 'a Woman milkeing a Goate', a landscape, 'the present King' (presumably James II who had just succeeded to the throne), a horse and a mare. The long gallery was used for the display of portraits which were mainly of royal personages. These were listed as Henry VII and his queen, Henry VIII, King James 'at length', Richard III, Sir Thomas Lovell, Henry V, Cardinal Wolsey and Lord Pembroke. In the new gallery there were a further nineteen pictures but these were not separately recorded.[58]

The major art collectors in the seventeenth century were generally royal or aristocratic. An exception was Sir James Oxinden of Deane in Kent whose father had been a client of Cornelius Johnson. In 1684 he was reported to have paid £310 for a picture of a battle scene, £250 for a picture of Christ confounding the lawyers and about £400 for three other pictures. The following year he and his wife were granted a licence to travel into France where he probably acquired further paintings. Sir James died in 1708 and the Court of Chancery was subsequently informed that he had left 'a very curious Collection of pictures and paintings of the best masters' worth £2000 or more, many of which he had purchased during his travels in Italy and other countries.[59]

In some country houses there was a cabinet or closet of curiosities which often testified to the owner's scholarly disposition. Anthony Wood refers in his diaries to two Warwickshire squires who had cabinets of this sort, Henry Parker of Honington and Ralph Sheldon of Weston. During a visit to Honington Hall in 1678 he was shown 'a cabinet of rarities collected most at Constantinople and other Easterne parts of the world'. Among other things this contained a variety of shells and 'naturall stones', gold and silver medals and coins, 'Turkish pictures and others of England, in miniture', all kinds of looking glasses and 'a piece of Didoes tombe'. Altogether the collection was considered to be worth £500.[60]

Many country gentlemen invested surplus cash in trading concerns such as the East India Company or put it out at interest. In the reign of Charles II John Coke of Holkham in Norfolk, who owned estates in various counties, had what he called a 'greate banck of money in London' which consisted of loans to Sir Robert Viner and other businessmen.[61] Even so, it was far from unusual for a wealthy landowner to keep considerable sums of money in his house, either because he considered this to be the safest option or because he was influenced by Puritan objections to usury. In 1690 we find Richard Bradshaw, who was steward to Sir Cecil Bishop of Parham in Sussex, and Mrs Ann Avelin the housekeeper counting and bagging up money, sealing the bags with their master's personal seal and depositing them in his private closet.[62] In some cases the amount of money hoarded was very substantial. Before departing for London in April 1628 Sir Thomas Pelham of Halland House in Sussex thought it prudent to record in his account book that he had left £1200 in gold in one of his new drawers, £200 in silver in the next drawer and another £200 in silver in the old desk.[63] In the sermon preached at the funeral of Sir Thomas Thynne of Longleat in 1639 the minister stressed that 'although God blessed him with great wealth, and store of coyne, yet hee never put it to Usurie or Interest thereby to increase it, for he held the tolleration of the Law in this Kingdome to bee no sufficient warrant for any violation of the divine Law'. The personal estate which he left was valued at some £19,000. This included £9000 in gold, £5000 in silver, plate worth £500 and household goods worth £2000.[64] Henry Rogers of Cannington Priory in Somerset may perhaps have regarded usury in the same light: following his death in 1672 it was calculated that the ready money stored in his house amounted to £7500.[65] When John Cartwright of Aynho in Northamptonshire died in 1676 Anthony Wood wrote in his diary that he was 'A person charitable, and ready to bestow money where there was need; but otherwise a most covetuous and sordid person'. At the time of his death he had 'as is reported 40 thousand pound laying by him'.[66]

The gentry may well have thought that they were in little danger of being robbed in their own homes, particularly if they had significant numbers of menservants, but occasionally their complacency was rudely shattered. According to a neighbouring landowner Sir William Uvedale of Horton in Dorset was an extremely covetous man who 'got together and hid in his house many thousands of pounds, which were afterwards stolen from him by some that got intelligence of it'.[67] In 1659 a party of six or seven men dressed like soldiers and brandishing swords and pistols managed to gain entry to Lowther Hall in Westmorland by pretending that they had authority to search for arms. From Sir John Lowther's graphic account of the incident we learn that although there were over thirty persons in the house at the time they were no match for the intruders who proceeded to lock up all the servants. After threatening to kill him, he writes, they made 'my wife and daughter open all the lockes, Trunckes and Chests, and took our plate, Money and sume Jewells which they found'.[68]

43. *(left)* Wollaton Hall, Nottinghamshire. Painting by Jan Siberechts, 1697. (Yale Center for British Art).

CHAPTER THREE

Parks and Gardens

In a work published in 1617 Fynes Moryson drew attention to the fact that England had an abundance of deer parks:

The English are so naturally inclined to pleasure as there is no Countrie wherein the Gentlemen and Lords have so many and large Parkes onely reserved for the pleasure of hunting . . . all parts have such plenty of Fallow Deare as every Gentleman of five hundredth or a thousand pounds rent by the yeere hath a Parke for them inclosed with pales of wood for two or three miles compasse.[1]

Although Moryson was deliberately exaggerating his basic proposition was valid. During the seventeenth century the gentry owned some 850 parks.[2] The greatest concentrations were in Yorkshire (which had by far the largest number of parks), Staffordshire, Suffolk, Essex, Surrey, Sussex and Gloucestershire (for an example see Pl. 44). Parks could be as small as 20 acres in size and as extensive as 1000 acres or more. According to a survey carried out in 1636 on behalf of Henry Hildyard his manor of Winestead in Yorkshire contained 2219 acres which included two parks, one of 154 acres and the other (described as the old park) of 42 acres.[3] In contrast, there were many parks consisting of 300, 400 or 500 acres. In 1639, for example, a Northamptonshire squire, Sir Christopher Yelverton, was granted authority by the Crown to impark 500 acres out of an estimated total of 1830 acres within his manor of Easton Mauduit.[4]

The deer park had two main functions. It was a place of recreation where the gentry hunted on horseback and with packs of hounds; and it was also a useful source of food, in particular venison and rabbits. Parks provided their owners with the means to gratify their friends either by inviting them to hunt their deer or by supplying them with gifts of venison. In a Star Chamber bill of 1611 Sir Richard Norton indicated that he favoured the latter practice. According to his explanation of the background Rotherfield Park, which adjoined his Hampshire mansion, was 'furnished with a great nomber of fallow deere and Conyes Aswell for his owne Provision in houeskeeping as to bestowe uppon divers of his good freinds at seasonable tymes of the yeere when he thought good'.[5] At the same time some men viewed their parks as a

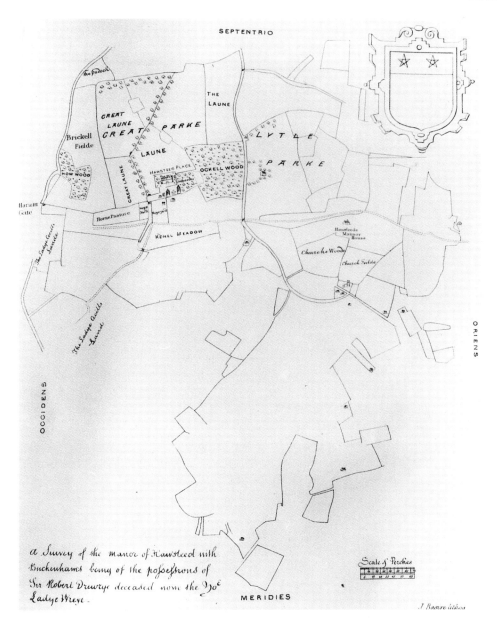

44. A map dated 1616 of the Hawstead estate, Suffolk which until recently belonged to the Drury family. Two parks are depicted. (John Gage, *The History and Antiquities of Suffolk. Thingoe Hundred*, 1838).

means of cultivating persons of power and influence. In another Star Chamber bill Sir Francis Leake of Sutton Scarsdale in Derbyshire stressed that he had been careful to preserve the deer in his park there not only for his own delight and profit but also for the pleasure and recreation of members of the nobility and peers of the realm 'whensoever they do resorte to him'.[6]

Deer were basically of two kinds, the red deer (Pl. 45) and the smaller fallow deer of which there were several varieties. Many squires in the northern counties, the Midlands and the West Country had red deer in their parks while fallow deer, which were far more numerous, were to be found all over England. Some gentlemen who owned herds of both types considered it prudent to keep them apart because of the aggression displayed by the male red deer in the rutting season[7] but it does not appear that this practice was invariably followed.

Just as parks varied widely in their acreage so there were very substantial differences in the size of herds. In 1608 Wedgnock Park in Warwickshire, which belonged to Sir Fulke Greville of Beauchamp Court, contained 108 red deer and about 1500 fallow deer.[8] This, however, was exceptional. More typical were the herds kept by another Warwickshire landowner, Sir Clement Fisher of Packington Hall, and a Norfolk squire, William Windham of Felbrigg Hall. In July 1673 Sir Clement's steward, Thomas Harding, noted that there were 252 deer in his park, together with seventy-nine fawns, while in the winter of 1683 Windham's herd numbered 206 deer and thirty fawns.[9] On the other hand, much smaller herds were by no means uncommon. In a Star Chamber bill of 1613 a Leicestershire squire, Sir Philip Sherard, told the Court that for the last twelve years he had been keeping some thirty deer in Stapleford Park 'for his pleasure and service of his house'. Since the park only consisted of 20 acres the amount of land available was clearly a major constraint on the size of the herd.[10] Similar considerations may well have entered the thoughts of Sir John Gage of West Firle in Sussex when he was drawing up his will in 1633: Plashett Park, he declared, should be kept stocked with 100 or 120 deer and no more.[11]

When a herd was relatively small the emphasis was probably more on the supply of venison than on hunting for pleasure; indeed there are instances where the deer shared the park with considerable numbers of cattle or sheep. In any event there was little sport to be had if the deer became too tame. In 1613 Lawrence Wright of Snelston in Derbyshire informed the Court of Star Chamber that some of his deer in Snelston Park 'were reduced to that

45. Red deer in Lyme Park, Cheshire.

46. A keeper selecting a fat buck (Richard Blome, *The Gentleman's Recreations*, second edition, 1710 (reference L.1.d.16)).

tamenes that they would take bread at the hand' while later in the century Celia Fiennes observed in her journal that in the park of Sir Charles Shuckburgh of Over Shuckburgh in Warwickshire the deer were 'so tame as to come up near the gate which ascends steps to a Court of broad stone'.[12] In contrast, the stags in the park belonging to the Legh family of Lyme Hall in Cheshire were described as 'wonderfull fierce and dangerous'.[13]

Parks were enclosed with fences, hedges or walls which not only shut in the deer but were also a visible assertion of ownership rights. Within the park there was usually a lodge where the keeper lived and kept watch for trespassers (Pl. 46 depicts a keeper at work). In 1694 the contents of the keeper's lodge in the park adjoining Brocket Hall, the Hertfordshire seat of Sir John Reade, included a bed, two pairs of harness, bridles, saddles, two fowling guns, two carbines, four pistols, some nets (which would have been used for catching rabbits) and three steel traps.[14] If the keeper was married the lodge would usually serve as his family home. In 1614 Sir Robert Strode of Parnham House in Dorset alleged in a Star Chamber suit that a band of men who had entered Horn Park with the intention of stealing some young sparrow-hawks had broken into the 'parke lodge or parke howse' and so alarmed the keeper and his wife and children that they had feared for their lives.[15]

From the reign of Elizabeth onwards some gentlemen were seeking to increase their estate revenue by disposing of the deer in their parks and making use of the land for agricultural purposes. In his account of Devon, which was written in the early seventeenth century, Tristram Risdon commented that 'many parks are disparked, and converted from pleasure to profit; from pasturing wild beasts to breeding and feeding of cattle, sheep and tillage'. Similarly, his contemporary Robert Reyce observed that Suffolk now had fewer deer parks than 'it was wont to have . . . In this latter age . . . many of our greatest parkes are layd open, where now many families with husbandry and tillage are maintained'. In some counties parks were also being put to industrial use: in Sussex many parks contained iron forges which fed on the surrounding woodland.[16] On the other hand, new deer parks were being created and existing ones enlarged. In 1623 Sir Robert Napier, a London merchant who had bought the Luton Hoo estate in Bedfordshire, obtained a licence from the Crown to enclose 300 acres for a park. This, however, required the acquisition of some parcels of land and it was not apparently until 1633 that the enclosure of Luton Hoo Park was finally completed.[17] In 1627 Sir Henry Savile of Methley in Yorkshire 'began to take in his newe parke, and by reason that he would not have A common road way through it to the markett or anie place else with Carte and Carrage, he caused the way to be put downe'. In this process he incorporated 'a prettie peece of common . . . and in the next yeare after he had finnished the paile and put deare into his parke, and men began to go the newe way in Anno dom 1628'.[18] During the reign of Charles I the Crown granted licences to impark to a number of major landowners, among them Sir Thomas Metham of North Cave and Sir William Robinson of Newby, both in Yorkshire, Sir Francis Drake of Buckland Abbey in Devon and Sir Edward Stanley of Bickerstaffe Hall in Lancashire.[19]

On occasion such enclosing activities had more serious consequences than the diversion of a road. During the 1630s Sir John Cutts, who was one of the wealthiest squires in Cambridgeshire, depopulated the parish of Childerley in order to enlarge his deer park while Sir Erasmus de la Fontaine of Kirby Bellars in Leicestershire demolished a number of cottages for the same purpose. Both men fell foul of the commissioners for depopulations and in 1640 the latter was fined the substantial sum of £500. Ironically, the hall at Kirby Bellars was badly damaged by fire when it came under royalist attack in 1645 and Sir Erasmus was put to considerable expense in carrying out the necessary repairs.[20]

During the Civil War period many deer parks were despoiled. Fences and hedges were pulled down and the deer were killed or sold or allowed to escape. Although the royalist gentry suffered most in this respect the parliamentarian gentry were certainly not immune. In 1646 Sir Robert Harley the Herefordshire parliamentarian testified that, among other things, his parks at Brampton Bryan and Wigmore had been wholly laid open and destroyed and as a result he had lost at least 500 deer, though he declined to put a cash value on them.[21] In the aftermath of such events some landlords ceased to use their parks for the rearing and preservation of deer. During a tour of Surrey in the reign of Charles II John Aubrey wrote in his journal that James Zouch of Woking House had a park which was three miles in compass but added 'no Deer since the late Wars'.[22] There were others, however, who were determined to re-stock their deer parks. In a petition which he submitted to the king in 1660 Sir Henry Wood of Loudham Park in Suffolk sought authority to take fifty deer from Heveningham Park which was part of the estate of William Heveningham, a parliamentarian who had narrowly escaped execution. His own deer, he explained, had been sold during the late usurpation.[23] During the latter part of the century there are frequent references to the presence of deer in the parks of the country gentry and indeed some men such as Sir William Ducie of Tortworth in Gloucestershire, Sir Edmund Fettiplace of Swinbrook in Oxfordshire and Paul Foley of Stoke Edith in Herefordshire secured royal licences which enabled them to establish new deer parks. Foley obtained his licence in 1688 and not long afterwards he received a visit from Celia Fiennes who wrote that there was 'a delicate Parke above the house, pailed in, that is stored with deare both red and fallow and affords 12 brace in a season'.[24] Occasionally a park which had undergone a change of use reverted to its original role. When the manor of Everingham in Yorkshire was surveyed in 1635 it was noted that within the demesnes there was a park of 378 acres 'adioyning to the house which hath sometimes been in many devisions but nowe lieth all togither'. In 1687 Sir Philip Constable was granted a licence authorising him to 'keep up' the park (which had existed for time out of mind) and to stock it with deer.[25]

   Wherever he was seated the owner of a deer park was only too well aware of the potential threat from intruders who had designs on his deer.[26] During the early seventeenth century some forty gentry brought suits in the Court of Star Chamber against men who were alleged to have hunted and killed deer in their parks. Among these complainants were such major landowners as Sir Peter Legh of Lyme Hall in Cheshire, Sir Thomas Lucy of Charlecote in Warwickshire (whose grandfather appears in the apocryphal story of Shakespeare's deer poaching activities), Sir Roger Bodenham of Rotherwas Court in Herefordshire (who was described by the defendants as 'a greate mann in his Cuntry' with a 'great store of welth'), Sir Thomas Thynne of Longleat in Wiltshire and Sir Reginald Mohun of Boconnoc House in Cornwall.[27] Often an attempt was made to play up the riotous nature of the incursions by laying stress on the number of persons involved and the range of weapons which could include guns, pistols, swords, daggers, pike staves and cross-bows. Many of the accused used the style 'gentleman' and in some cases the Star Chamber proceedings were clearly a product of local feuds or property disputes. Occasionally a keeper or a man formerly employed in that capacity was named as an accomplice or even as a ringleader. In 1614 Sir Henry Baynton of Bromham in Wiltshire claimed that his principal keeper, Thomas Lansier, and his son Edward, along with others, had been unlawfully hunting and killing deer in Spye Park over a period of three years.[28] The following year Richard Shireburn of Stonyhurst in Lancashire alleged that John Holden had been seeking to gain his revenge after he had dismissed him as keeper of his park there 'for sundrie foule faults and misdemeanors'. Holden and his associates, he told the Court, had shot ten red and fallow deer and threatened to kill his keepers.[29]

   Some landowners who sought redress from the Court of Star Chamber described how a series of raids had left their parks seriously depleted. In 1620 William Tirwhitt of Kettelby House in Lincolnshire complained that Roger Leeming and others had not only killed at least forty deer in the park adjoining his mansion but demolished gates and fences so that many of the remaining deer had escaped and were 'utterlie lost and destroyed'. In response to these accusations Leeming and a fellow defendant argued that it was Tirwhitt's cattle which had caused the damage.[30]

At about one o'clock on the morning of 18 December 1608 Richard Carr of Hexham in Northumberland entered the park of Francis Radcliffe at Dilston and shot two does. Unfortunately for him three of Radcliffe's servants were lying in wait and, alerted to his presence by the sound of gunfire, found him carrying one of the does on his back. Carr immediately took flight but his pursuers were able to apprehend him.[31] It was, however, rare for any poachers to be caught red-handed, not least since they frequently operated in large and well armed bands. In such circumstances some keepers hastily retreated while others were physically assaulted. In a Star Chamber case of 1610 Thomas Middleton of Leighton in Lancashire related that a band of men who had been poaching deer in the New Park within his manor of Yealand Redmayne had attacked Christopher Bisbrowne his keeper and Edmund Haggaite, another of his servants. Both had been severely wounded and, he added, 'have ever sithence languished and still doe languishe of their said wounds in greate perill of their lives'.[32]

In Sussex Sir Thomas Pelham of Halland House was involved in an increasingly bitter dispute with a neighbouring family, the Lunsfords, which nearly cost him his life. For killing deer in Halland Park, assaulting one of his keepers and other offences Thomas Lunsford the younger was heavily fined by the Court of Star Chamber and as a result decided to take his revenge. In August 1633 Sir Thomas was returning from church in his coach when Lunsford and his servant Morris Lewis suddenly emerged from a copse at the side of the road and mounted an attack with swords and pistols. The assailants, however, failed in their purpose and were soon arrested. Eventually Lunsford managed to escape from Newgate prison and fled abroad. In 1637 he was tried *in absentia* in the Court of Star Chamber when it was decided that he should be fined £5000 and required to pay £3000 in damages to Sir Thomas and that he should be imprisoned during the king's pleasure. Following his return to England two years later he obtained a royal pardon, took part in the military expeditions against the Scots and earned even greater notoriety when in December 1641 the king appointed him lieutenant of the Tower.[33]

In the unsettled times following the first Civil War there was an upsurge in the amount of deer poaching which led the republican government to resort to legislation. In 1651 it was enacted that anyone found guilty of stealing or killing deer in a forest, chase, park or other enclosed ground would be liable to a fine of £15.[34] On 11 June 1660, shortly after the restoration of the monarchy, three deer poachers entered Sir Metcalfe Robinson's park at Newby Hall in the North Riding of Yorkshire where they were challenged by Richard Batty the keeper. Batty was severely wounded and subsequently died and as a result Sir Metcalfe offered a reward of £10 a head for the capture of his assailants. In the event they managed to escape abroad but two of them were later executed.[35] Although new legislation on deer poaching was approved in 1661[36] its impact appears to have been negligible. During the reign of Charles II Lyme Park in Cheshire, with its large herds of red and fallow deer, continued to be raided by poachers and the owner, Richard Legh, suspected that a neighbouring family, the Leghs of Adlington Hall, might be heavily involved. Although the latter denied any responsibility relations between the two families became distinctly cool.[37]

In the opinion of Fynes Moryson there was no other country in the world 'where all sorts of men alot so much ground about their houses for pleasure of Gardens and Orchards'.[38] As contemporary evidence abundantly testifies, the country gentry often took a close personal interest in horticultural matters, not least because of the way in which gardens could provide a handsome setting for their houses. Thomas Stanley, a Cheshire squire who was later created a baronet, wrote in a memorandum book that in 1625, shortly after he and his wife had taken up residence at Alderley Hall, 'I made 2 gardens, the one at the house wherein I sett younge Apricock trees, Cherries and Plumms . . . the other garden being low in the walks. The same tyme I began to plant my orchard'.[39] According to his son, Sir John Reresby of Thrybergh in Yorkshire, who entered into his inheritance in 1629, 'was exactly curious in his garden, and was one of the first that acquented that part of England (soe far north) with the exactness and nicety of thos things, not only as to the form or contriveance of the ground, but as to excellency and variety of fruits, flowers, greens, in which he was rather extravagant then curious'.[40] Although Sir Thomas Pelham was one of the leading parliamentarians in Sussex during the first Civil War he did not consider it necessary to neglect his gardens. In 1643, while the whole future of England was in the balance, he was buying garden trees, plants and seeds for his grounds at Halland House.[41] In Bedfordshire the Osbornes of Chicksands Priory, who had supported the royalist cause, and the Lukes of Wood End, who had been actively engaged on behalf of Parliament, managed to establish some kind of rapport through a common interest in gardening. In 1653 we find Dorothy Osborne writing in a letter to William Temple that Sir Samuel Luke 'has growne soe kinde as to send to mee for some things hee desyr'd out of this Garden, and withall made the offer of what was in his, which I had reason to take for a high favor, for hee is a nice florist'.[42] A decade later, when Philip Lord Wharton was seeking a husband for one of his daughters, he received a report on the character of Hungerford Dunch of Little Wittenham in Berkshire who was the heir to an estate worth £5000 a year. The young man, he was told, had a great affection 'to the best, both men and things; much of his time and delight taken up in his Gardens and Orchards'.[43]

Many gentry collected books on horticulture and in some cases sought advice from men with specialist knowledge and expertise. In 1667 Sir Edward Harley of Brampton Bryan in Herefordshire suggested to a friend that he should contact Mr Thomas Floyd of Whitminster in Gloucestershire who was 'very happily versed in vegetable experiments'.[44] Sir Dudley Cullum, who took great pride in his garden at Hawstead Place in Suffolk, benefited from the guidance of John Evelyn whose reputation as an expert on horticultural matters owed much to his published works which included *Sylva*, a discourse on tree husbandry. Writing to Evelyn in 1694 he expressed his delight at the effectiveness of the stove which, acting on his directions, he had installed in his capacious greenhouse.[45]

47. Gardening activities at Aspenden Hall, Hertfordshire, the seat of the Freeman family. Engraving by Jan Drapentier, *c.* 1700 (Sir Henry Chauncy, *The Historical Antiquities of Hertfordshire*, 1826).

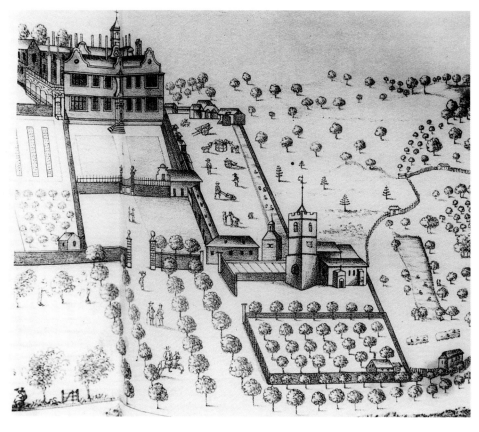

As a general rule a country squire employed one full-time gardener and brought in casual labour to assist him as occasion required (some gardening activities are depicted in Pl. 47). The gardener was usually the most highly paid of the outdoor servants[46] but his work could be extremely arduous. In his diary Sir Henry Slingsby of Red House in Yorkshire recorded the death in 1640 of his gardener Peter Clark who had served the family for over a decade and added that 'he was for no curiosity in Gardening, but exceeding laborious in grafting, setting and sowing; which extream labour shortn'd his days'.[47] Some gardeners displayed a certain independence of spirit which may not have been unconnected with the particular nature of their occupation. Two letters received by Sir John Reresby of Thrybergh, the second baronet, while he was in London graphically illustrate this point. In the first letter, which was written some time in the reign of Charles II, he was informed that his wife 'cannot gett the Gardener to worck as yu ordered' and that as a consequence she had been obliged to seek the assistance of a kinsman who had sent his own gardener to prune the trees and vines. No doubt this episode resulted in the dismissal of Sir John's recalcitrant employee. Subsequently, in 1686, Thomas Robotham, his steward, reported that, as directed, he had obtained a new spade for the gardener 'but he is not pleased with it; he desiars youar honor to get him one bought at London and to send it and rather then be without it he wil pai himself for it'.[48]

On the other hand, the enthusiasm for gardening which was so much in evidence among the gentry could mean that the activities of the gardener were subject to very close supervision. During the latter part of the century Sir

Walter St John and his family lived for most of the year in his mansion at
Battersea in Surrey and only visited his seat at Lydiard Tregoze in Wiltshire
during the summer months. Even so, his wife, Dame Johanna, felt compelled
to issue detailed instructions to Richard Rudler, the gardener at Lydiard
Tregoze. On one occasion she wrote in a letter to Thomas Hardyman, who
was the steward there, that

> I have sent Rudler some seed of Portingal Melons, also som roots of
> Shallotts. Let him carfully plant them in the Kitchen Garden so that no
> Hog may come at them. I bid Richard send down an orang colered
> cowslip root. He must git Joan and old goodwife Woolford to git violet
> roots out of the woods and Plant them in the orchard . . . Also I have
> sent som seed of Larkspur 2 sorts, the one is the ordinary sort, the other
> double. Let him plant flowers of the sun and Hollyhocks on the bank
> under the rails and balesters of the garden, which bank is in the
> orchard, and plant stocks or some thing against the dead wal in the gar-
> den next the bowling green and let him compas the lawrel round the
> cort with pols as he did the woodbine by the Hal dore to fence it from
> the children.[49]

The range of equipment used in gardens and orchards was not inconsider-
able. An inventory drawn up in 1632 at Hatfield Priory, the Essex seat of Sir
Thomas Barrington, lists a variety of items, including a grafting saw, three little hoes and a large one, an axe, a bill or billhook, two spades, four watering
pots, three scythes, standing ladders and four other ladders, a grindstone,
three stone rollers and a wooden roller, two turf spades, two baskets, two
wheelbarrows, two pairs of garden shears and two rakes.[50] The most
significant item missing from this schedule is the lawn mower which only
made its appearance in the nineteenth century. For lawns and bowling greens
it was necessary to rely on scythes, shears and rollers. In 1664 no fewer than
eleven rollers were recorded in an inventory of Sir Humphrey Forster's personal estate at Aldermaston House in Berkshire.[51]

A striking feature of many country estates was the abundance of trees. In
1692 it was calculated that within the Norfolk manor of Oxnead where the
Paston family was seated there were 8917 trees of various kinds: oak, ash,
aspen, walnut, poplar, elm, fir, sycamore and cherry.[52] Trees provided shade
and shelter, fuel for domestic and other purposes and material for the construction and repair of buildings and fences. There was also a fashion for
planting avenues of trees in order to beautify and add a touch of grandeur to
the approaches to the house (Pl. 48). In 1690 Sir Clement Fisher's mansion at
Great Packington in Warwickshire was described as 'a sweet seat, near the
road, with a park on the other side, with a fair lodge and an avenue of fir-trees
to the hall'. The same traveller, however, had some reservations about Sir
Charles Wolseley's seat at Wolseley in Staffordshire which drew from him the
verdict that it was a 'fair house with fine gardens, but a very ill avenue to it'.[53]
From an economic standpoint the gentry were fully conscious of the fact that
their trees were a valuable asset. Some men sold wood on a regular basis to
augment their income while a financial crisis often led to the wholesale deple-
tion of timber trees.

48. The Lucy mansion of Charlecote, Warwickshire with its long avenues of trees. Painting by an unknown artist, *c.* 1700 (Charlecote Park).

As contemporary diaries and journals indicate, many country squires had a particular liking for fruit trees and bushes. During the 1630s Sir John Oglander of Nunwell House in the Isle of Wight wrote in his commonplace book that he had planted two young orchards with his own hands: one contained several varieties of apple and pear trees while in the other there were cherries, damsons and plums. In addition, he was responsible for introducing quinces, apricots, figs and melons at Nunwell.[54] In a work published in 1686 Robert Plot wrote that in the gardens of Rowland Okeover at Okeover Hall in Staffordshire (Pl. 49) there were 60 different sorts of apples, 20 sorts of pears, 16 sorts of cherries, 35 sorts of apricots and other plums, and 7 sorts of nectarines and peaches.[55]

Orange trees were first introduced into England by Sir Francis Carew of Beddington in Surrey during the reign of Elizabeth. When John Evelyn visited Beddington House in 1658 he wrote that it was 'famous for the first Orange garden of England, being now over-growne trees, and planted in the ground, and securd in winter with a wooden tabernacle and stoves'. In 1690 the Court of Chancery ruled that the trustees of Francis Carew, who was then a minor, should appoint agents and receivers of the revenue from the estate and instruct them 'to repair the Mansion house and Edifices thereunto belonging and keepe up the Gardens and take care of the Orange trees, repair the Orange house and other the ffarme houses'.[56] In the late seventeenth century a number of other gentry families were cultivating orange trees, among them the Bonds of Peckham and the Claytons of Marden in Surrey, the Botelers of Watton Woodhall in Hertfordshire and the Cullums of Hawstead in Suffolk.[57]

Walnut trees were valued both for their fruit and the timber which was used for making furniture and gunstocks. They were particularly abundant in Surrey which in Thomas Fuller's view produced some of the best walnuts.[58] In August 1655 John Evelyn wrote in his diary that the seat of Sir Francis Stydolfe, Norbury House in the Surrey parish of Mickleham, was environed with innumerable elm and walnut trees and that he had been told that the latter provided their owner with a considerable revenue. In his will, which was drawn up in 1676, Sir Richard Stydolfe the son bequeathed to his heirs all the walnut trees on his estate with the proviso that his wife should be allowed four bushels of walnuts every year.[59]

Although limited in scope by modern standards the range of flowers available was by no means lacking in variety. It included roses, daffodils, tulips, violets, lilies, sunflowers, hollyhocks, lupins, pinks, marigolds, peonies, poppies, anemones, hyacinths, carnations and primroses. The main sources of supply were London and provincial nurserymen but some gentlemen also looked to the Continent. When Sir Ralph Verney was re-stocking his gardens at Claydon House in Buckinghamshire during the 1650s he imported roots,

49. Okeover Hall, Staffordshire (Robert Plot, *The Natural History of Stafford-shire*, 1686, British Library reference Eve.c.2).

seeds and flowers, together with ornamental trees, from Holland and France.[60]

Few descriptions of country house gardens as they existed in the early seventeenth century have come down to us and it was not until the latter part of the century that gentlemen's seats came to be regarded as an appropriate subject matter for paintings and engravings.[61] Probably Elizabethan influences remained strong and the garden at Breckenbrough Hall in Yorkshire may well have reflected the prevailing fashion at this time. In 1618, when the Lascelles family was planning to sell the estate, it was reported, among other things, that there was 'a very fayre square garden, adjoyning on the south side of the house, with delicate walks, having on both sides thorne hedges finely cutt, arbours, and good store of excellent fruite trees'.[62] In a work first published in 1624 Sir Henry Wotton argued that gardens should be irregular or at least should be 'cast into a very wilde Regularity'. One of his favourite gardens was that which had been created by his friend Sir Henry Fanshawe at Ware Park in Hertfordshire. In his estimation there was nothing comparable to this 'delicate and diligent curiosity' on the Continent. Sir Henry, he explained, 'did so precisely examine the tinctures and seasons of his flowers that in their settings the inwardest of which that were to come up at the same time should be always a little darker then the outmost, and so serve them for a kind of gentle shadow'.[63] John Chamberlain the celebrated letter writer visited Ware Park in 1606 when the project was already well advanced and wrote that Sir Henry was employing a work force of over forty men, 'for the new garden is wholy translated, new levelled, and in a manner transplanted, because most of the first trees were dead with being set too deepe'. What he found particularly striking was that instead of placing a knot garden in the middle (in accordance with Elizabethan practice) Sir Henry was making a fort with ramparts, bulwarks and other authentic features. In this respect Sir Walter Erle of Charborough House in Dorset had similar ideas. Having fought in the Netherlands, he 'valued himself upon the sieges and service he had been in; his garden was cut into redoubts and works representing these places'.[64]

Some years after completion of the new garden at Ware Park another large-scale project was put in hand at Somerleyton Hall in Suffolk. According to a contemporary Sir John Wentworth, having no children, 'bestowed a great deale of cost in waterworkes, walkes, woods, and other delights' and 'left one of the most delightfull dwellings in England'. A system of waterworks involving the use of hydraulic engines had already been installed in the gardens at Hatfield House[65] but it was still a comparatively new development. Sir John died in 1651 and not long afterwards Thomas Fuller visited Somerleyton Hall, which was then occupied by his widow, and was equally impressed by its surroundings. Here, he wrote , 'summer is to be seen in the depth of winter in the pleasant walks, beset on both sides with fir-trees, green all the year long, besides other curiosities'.[66]

During the late seventeenth century many country squires embarked on major garden schemes, in some cases following the building of new houses. In 1679 the Court of Chancery was informed that Sir Thomas Rous of Rous Lench in Worcestershire had spent thousands of pounds on improving his

50. Sudbury Hall, Derbyshire with its new gardens. Painting by Jan Griffier, *c.* 1700 (Sudbury Hall).

gardens and building walls.[67] In Hertfordshire Sir Humphrey Gore of New Place in Gilston 'did much adorn the House with Walks and Gardens' and 'made a pretty Park to the same'.[68] In Derbyshire George Vernon, who commanded an income of some £3000 a year, not only rebuilt Sudbury Hall but laid out the formal gardens depicted in a view of the seat which he commissioned from Jan Griffier (Pl. 50).[69] In Lancashire Sir Nicholas Shireburn, a wealthy Catholic, took up residence at Stonyhurst in 1695 and over the next five years spent some £1600 on the gardens there.[70]

The transformation of country house gardens in this period owed much to French influences, though after the Revolution of 1688 Dutch influences also began to have an impact. In this process the emphasis was on formality, symmetry and elegance and the gentry became accustomed to employing such terms as vista and parterre. Characteristic features of the new style gardens were raised terraces and stairways, avenues, gravel and green walks, boxed hedges and dwarf trees, statuary, canals, pools and fountains. At Great Packington in Warwickshire Sir Clement Fisher, who succeeded his uncle in 1683, not only built a new mansion but 'adorned it with delightful Gardens, Statues, canals, Vistos, and other suitable Ornaments'.[71] In the neighbouring county of Staffordshire the formal gardens at Patshull Hall inspired wonder and admiration. These were the creation of Sir Richard Astley, a man of great wealth who had estates in several counties worth some £1800 a year. When Robert Plot visited Patshull Hall in 1680 he wrote that Sir Richard's seat was 'the most delicious mansion in this county . . . The gardens about it have delicate vistas opening quite through them, with many stately gates of iron work, curiously painted and gilt, leading into them with mounts and places of repose at the ends. In them are most curious water-works, and great variety of

51. One of the garden pavilions at Montacute House, Somerset.

them.' At the front of the house a large fountain threw up a column of water to a great height while to the east there was 'a long fair canal . . . at the South end whereof is a delicate grotto'. Around the house were plantations of trees and avenues with double rows of elms.[72] In the course of her northern journey in 1698 Celia Fiennes took the opportunity to inspect the gardens which she had heard were 'the finest and best kept'. Among the features which engaged her attention were the multitude of statues in grass plots, a grove with all kinds of evergreens which afforded a whole series of prospects or vistas, and a large pond or 'sheete of water' with 348 lead pipes at its edges and a sluice.[73]

During the reign of Elizabeth some gentlemen had erected banqueting houses or pavilions in their gardens. In the course of the seventeenth century there are references to such buildings in various parts of the country, including the seats of major landed families at Montacute in Somerset (Pl. 51), Bessels Leigh in Berkshire, Burston in Kent, Over Shuckburgh in Warwickshire, Pishiobury in Hertfordshire and Wythenshawe in Cheshire.[74] When Bulstrode Whitelocke was living at Fawley Court in Buckinghamshire during the 1630s he made a fish pond and on the arch which he built across it 'sett a neate banquetting house, having the prospect of the Thames under it, and of the woods above it'.[75] In the latter part of the century many gentry had summer or garden houses. In some cases this may possibly have been

52. Arbury Hall, Warwickshire, the Newdegate family seat, with its formal gardens and pavilions. Drawing by Henry Beighton, 1708 (Birmingham City Archives, Aylesford Country Seats, vol. 1/16).

merely a change of nomenclature but as a general rule they appear to have been much simpler structures than the banqueting houses and to have served as places of retirement rather than dining chambers. In 1682 the Lenthall family had both a banqueting house and a garden house at Bessels Leigh. The contents of the banqueting house were described as ten old chairs and five pictures while in the garden house there was an old bedstead.[76]

53. Stanford Hall, Leicestershire.

For the most part the formal gardens of the late seventeenth century (as illustrated in Pl. 52) were swept away when the Georgian fashion for landscape gardening gained the ascendancy. One consequence of this development was a greater sense of isolation, though it did not necessarily represent a radical departure from the past. Even in the seventeenth century there were a number of country houses such as Childerley Hall in Cambridgeshire[77] which were ensconced in parkland. In 1697 Sir Roger Cave of Stanford in Northamptonshire decided to build himself a new mansion on a different site from the ancestral home and this was erected on rising ground in the middle of his park (Pl. 53). Inevitably this resulted in greater seclusion. A further implication was perhaps unforeseen, that Stanford Hall was henceforth situated in Leicestershire.[78]

CHAPTER FOUR

The Squire's Wife

In 1691 a Cornish baronet, Sir John Carew of Antony House, bequeathed to his wife all her wearing apparel and all such jewellery, watches and gold and silver medals as she had in her possession.[1] In the seventeenth century the wife of a country gentleman often owned little or no property of any kind, at least while her husband was alive. The marriage portion which she brought with her was payable either to her father-in-law or her husband if he had already succeeded to the family estate. As a general rule her husband took over any landed property which she might have at the time of their marriage, whether it had been inherited from her family or settled on her as a jointure by a previous husband. This was not an automatic process: it was a matter which had to be addressed in the negotiations over the marriage settlement and on occasion it could involve some hard bargaining. In 1661 Sir Rowland Lytton of Knebworth in Hertfordshire married Dame Rebecca Lucy who had already buried two husbands. Through her first marriage she had valuable jointure lands in Suffolk and as part of the marriage settlement it was agreed that Sir Rowland should receive £500 a year out of them while the remainder of her estate, both real and personal, was conveyed to trustees on the basis that it would be wholly at her disposal.[2] This kind of arrangement, however, was not particularly common. More often the wife's landed possessions were completely assimilated, though she would normally have a substantial jointure settled on her as a *quid pro quo*.

In most gentry families the wife was financially dependent on her husband to a degree which some women must have found irksome and frustrating. In 1628 Sir Thomas Pelham of Halland House in Sussex gave his wife, Dame Mary, £100 to buy new clothes as a preliminary to a journey which she was about to undertake to see her relatives in Cheshire. Subsequently, in 1634, he recorded in his accounts that he had allowed her £25 to cover her expenses at Bath where she hoped (vainly as it turned out) to recover her health.[3] On the other hand, some of the wealthier gentry adopted an arrangement under which the wife received a regular allowance (which came to be known as pin-money) to enable her to meet the cost of clothes and other personal expenses. In June 1640 Sir James Thynne of Longleat in Wiltshire, who had an estate revenue of £6000 a year, married Lady Isabel Rich, a daughter of

Henry Earl of Holland, and shortly before this it was reported that he had offered to provide her with £500 a year for her separate maintenance and to buy a house in London and another one in the country.[4] During the second half of the century a number of major county families followed this practice, among them the Guldefords of Hempstead Place in Kent, the Carylls of West Harting and the Pelhams of Halland House in Sussex, the Stydolfes of Norbury in Surrey, the Clerkes of Watford and the Cravens of Winwick in Northamptonshire, the Offleys of Madeley in Staffordshire and the Gascoignes of Barnbow Hall in Yorkshire. At one extreme Sir Robert Guldeford allowed his wife £100 a year while at the other Sir William Craven allocated £600 a year out of an estate worth £1500 a year for the same purpose. In 1659 Sir John Pelham's wife was receiving an allowance of £320 a year which was intended to cover her own needs and the cost of bringing up the children.[5] Such families were, however, no more than a small minority; in the main the gentry considered it sufficient to settle a jointure commensurate with the marriage portion.

More serious than the general lack of financial independence was the threat to life inherent in frequent pregnancies which were occasioned not only by the inadequacy of the contraceptive methods available but by the husband's concern that the continuance of the male line should be assured. Two entries in the accounts of Sir Daniel Fleming of Rydal Hall in Westmorland help to illustrate this point. In April 1675 he wrote that his wife, Barbara, had died shortly after being delivered of a boy 'to the great loss of mee her afflicted husband and of fourteen children, all liveing, whom God preserve'. In the other entry he noted that Dame Margaret Fenwick (who was the wife of Sir Robert Fenwick) had 'dyed suddenly at Hutton, August 12, 1686, she killing herselfe – as it was reported – and she haveing been very melancholly ever since the birth of her last child'.[6] Not infrequently a squire married two or three times; indeed Sir Gervase Clifton of Clifton in Nottinghamshire had no fewer than seven wives of whom four died without issue (see Pl. 54). On the other hand, a woman who managed to survive the perils of child-bearing often outlived her husband.

Wives who came from distant counties sometimes found the change of locale unsettling, either because of the loss of regular contact with their families and friends or because of the nature of their new environment. During the Civil War period John Gell, the eldest son of Sir John Gell of Hopton Hall in Derbyshire (whose wife left him in 1648), married Katherine Packer, a daughter of John Packer of Shellingford in Berkshire. Some years later she began to correspond with Richard Baxter the Puritan divine who was always ready to dispense spiritual advice. In April 1657 she wrote that 'I have bin put to my choise and yet have willingly chosen rather to live here farre from friends and in noe pleasant country' because of the Presbyterian ministers in the area who fully satisfied her religious needs. She went on to tell him, however, that 'I delight not in any thing, not in the company of friends or in any comforts'. Although 'many a time I goe about my house and amongst my servants . . . I had rather locke my selfe up in a roome alone amongst my bookes for meditation'.[7] In 1652 Sir John Lowther of Lowther Hall in Westmorland took as his second wife Elizabeth Leigh, the daughter of a Norfolk squire and

54. Memorial to
three of Sir
Gervase Clifton's
wives in Clifton
parish church,
Nottinghamshire.

the widow of a Surrey landowner. In his journal he observed that he and his new wife 'were more tymerous then in our former choyses by reason of the remotness of freinds to both, distance of Cuntryes and manor of liveinge betwixt north and south'. In the event, he noted, his wife proved to be a lover of 'a Cuntry course' despite his early forebodings in that respect and they both found great contentment.[8]

For a young woman who had enjoyed the pleasures of the *beau monde* in London a country life did not necessarily have a great deal of attraction. Lady Elizabeth Livingston, who was the daughter of a Scottish nobleman, James Earl of Newburgh, had been brought up at the court of Charles II where she had been serving as a maid of the Privy Chamber to the Queen. In 1670 her father prevailed upon her, much against her will, to marry Robert Delaval, the son and heir of Sir Ralph Delaval of Seaton Delaval in Northumberland, one of the most remote counties in England. Before long her husband fell into bad company but in any event the marriage appears to have been doomed from the start. In a book of meditations she wrote that

> It cannot be denyed but that it was very naturall for a person of my age to have liked better staying in a place where I was every day much court-ed by people of the best quality, and where I was much favour'd by the queen my mistresse, then to retier to a contry house, where notwith-standing the prospect of a hapy, peacefull dwelling for a time which I had figured to myselfe . . . I did not scape haveing many uneasy houers.

During their marriage they often lived apart and for a period of two years she resided in Holland. In 1681, not long before her husband's death, she left Seaton Delaval for Scotland with the parting remark that Sir Ralph 'is foole and knave governed by his sott wife'.[9]

The difficulty involved in adapting to new circumstances seems to have been particularly acute when southern brides were transplanted into north-ern counties where the terrain was wild, the weather often unkind and the inhabitants rough in speech if not in manners. All over England, however, rural seclusion could breed melancholy as well as induce a feeling of tran-quillity. Dame Damaris Masham, the wife of Sir Francis Masham of Otes Hall in Essex, had inherited a love of intellectual pursuits from her father, Ralph Cudworth the Cambridge Platonist. Writing to her friend John Locke the philosopher in 1687 she complained that 'I am Certainlie Plac'd in the Wretchedest Neighborhood in the whole World and never had so Violent a Desire in my life as now to good Companie'.[10] When the husband was serv-ing as an MP his wife was usually left at home and in some decades there were long periods in which she had to endure the lack of companionship. During the years 1660 to 1681 John Swinfen, who was seated at Swinfen Hall in Staffordshire, and Sir Edward Harley of Brampton Bryan in Herefordshire spent much of their time at Westminster with a consequential disruption of their family life. In December 1660 Swinfen informed his wife that he considered it unlikely that Parliament would be dissolved on the appointed day and added that 'There is nothing I long for more than to be att home and to enioy yours and my family's company'. A year later he was lamenting that 'Wee maye now keep our Christmas asunder, which makes it the lesse chearful to us both. I pray God supply our absence by his Gracious presence'.[11] Dame Abigail Harley frequently intimated in correspondence with her husband that she was unhappy about his lengthy absences on par-liamentary duty. It was of no small concern to him, he assured her in July 1664, 'to be from you whom God hath made so dear to mee, for without complement you are more to mee then all the world besides, therefor remember to be kind to mee when we meet'. Lady Harley, however, con-tinued to pine for his company. In December 1670 she expressed the wish that 'som way may not be contrived that every winter I may not be from you as I have bin a great many winters'. Sir Edward, for his part, could offer her no firm assurances. 'I hope', he wrote, 'that in good Time God wil hasten our comfortable meeting'.[12]

As an antidote to melancholy or boredom the wife of a wealthy squire might go and stay with relatives or friends or visit one of the more fashionable spa resorts. In July 1678 Lady Harley was at Bath. Writing from Westminster her husband suggested that if possible she should make the acquaintance of Sir Harbottle Grimston's wife who was also there; Sir Harbottle, he explained, was Master of the Rolls and he was 'much obliged' to him.[13] Some families wintered in provincial towns while others sojourned in London for months at a time.[14] Before the outbreak of the Civil War it was comparatively rare for a gentleman's wife to travel abroad but the situation began to change with the exodus of royalist families seeking temporary exile during the 1640s and 1650s. After the Restoration it was not unusual for a well-to-do squire to take his wife with him when embarking on a journey to the Continent. In the years 1684 and 1685, for example, Sir Thomas Samwell of Upton and Sir William Craven of Winwick in Northamptonshire, Sir William Drake of Shardeloes in Buckinghamshire, Sir James Oxinden of Deane in Kent and Thomas Hatcher of Careby in Lincolnshire secured passes authorising them and their wives to travel to France or other Continental countries.[15] Exceptionally the wife was unaccompanied by her husband. In December 1683 Dame Eleanor Dymoke, the wife of Sir Charles Dymoke of Scrivelsby in Lincolnshire, was given permission to go abroad with her son and daughter, four servants, a coach and four coach horses and a saddle horse.[16]

In his treatise *Of Domesticall Duties* William Gouge the Puritan divine wrote that 'Some wives pretend that they cannot endure the smoake of the citie, other that they cannot endure the aire of the countrie'. A wife, he stressed, must be prepared to live in whatever place her husband preferred. She had specific duties to perform, in particular the ordering of household affairs and the rearing of the children.[17] As a general rule the squire's wife was expected to manage the task of keeping the house stocked with provisions; to oversee the arrangements for meals, particularly when the family was entertaining special guests; to ensure that the principal rooms were furnished and decorated to an appropriate standard; and to exercise control over the female staff. Besides the administrative skills required it was considered important that she should have some degree of proficiency in such arts as cookery, preserving fruit, distilling and needlework.

In the family memoirs which they compiled Sir Christopher Guise of Elmore in Gloucestershire and his grandson Sir John Guise did not hesitate to criticise some of the women in their family for neglecting to fulfil the obligations which went with their position in the household. Dame Elizabeth Guise, the second wife of Sir William Guise (who died in 1642), 'never could be brought to take care of the house or estate'; in fact she was nothing more than 'a goship, a makebate, a wastall'. Similarly, Sir John's mother (who was also called Elizabeth) was 'of an indolent temper and ill versed in the busines of the world'.[18] On the other hand, many of the wives of country squires were warmly praised for their good housekeeping. Lady Margaret Wroth, who was an aristocrat by birth and the wife of Sir Thomas Wroth of Petherton Park in Somerset, was 'very discreet, prudent and active . . . in the conduct of her family, setting forth with her own hands divers works and businesses in her house, always doing some good, protesting that

55. Dame Anne
Twysden.

she could not endure idleness'.[19] According to her eldest son, Dame Anne
Twysden (Pl. 55), the wife of Sir William Twysden of Roydon Hall in Kent,
was a thrifty housekeeper 'yet very noble in her disposition, excelent to con-
trive any building or to adorne an house'.[20] Eleanor Evelyn, the wife of
Richard Evelyn of Wotton in Surrey, was highly regarded for what her diarist
son called 'Oeconomiq prudence' while Dame Anne Corbet, the wife of Sir
John Corbet of Adderley in Shropshire, was described as 'a frugall and provident lady'.[21] Following the death of his mother, Mary Crewe, in 1690 Sir
John Crewe of Utkinton Hall in Cheshire wrote in his journal that she was
'the best parent, the truest friend, the best mistress, the greatest housekeeper of her rank, and the most pious Christian of her time'. No doubt he
was responsible for the inscription on her memorial in the parish church of
Tarporley which proclaims that 'in constant and free housekeeping' she was
'not inferior to any of her quality and time'.[22]

Besides discharging her domestic responsibilities the squire's wife was often
heavily engaged in charitable activities within the general neighbourhood.
Both wives of Sir James Langham of Cottesbrooke in Northamptonshire,
exemplify the kind of Puritan gentlewoman who was noted both for her
intense personal piety and her compassion for the poor and needy. His first
wife, Dame Mary, was always ready 'to do Good to poor distressed Persons,
especially those of the Household of Faith; visiting, edifying and comforting
them . . . and relieving their Necessities'. Lady Elizabeth Langham, for her
part, took care when going on a journey 'to furnish her Poor-man's Purse with

such Monies as were fit to be distributed amongst necessitous People' as she might meet.[23] Charitable work was undertaken by women of all religious persuasions, including Catholics as well as Protestants. One of its most important aspects was the provision of medical care for the many who could not afford professional treatment. Gentlewomen not only prepared medicines and pills in their still rooms but often assumed the role of physician or nurse. In Norfolk Dame Alice L'Estrange, the wife of Sir Hamon L'Estrange of Hunstanton, 'did great service to the poor in the way of surgery'. In 1616 she dressed the wounds of a missionary priest, Thomas Tunstal, who had injured himself when escaping from Wisbech Castle. Dame Alice was not aware that he was a Catholic priest but when she told her husband about her new patient his suspicions were immediately aroused and he had him arrested.[24] Dame Lucy Jervoise, the wife of Sir Thomas Jervoise of Herriard in Hampshire, was described at her funeral in 1641 as a lady of excellent understanding in housewifery, surgery and physic. 'She was helpful', the minister recalled, 'to such as were hurt and maimed, sick and diseased. And as her Skill this way was more than ordinary, so most ready and willing was she to be at much Charge to bestow any Pains to further their Recovery'.[25] Similarly, Anne Ratcliffe, the wife of Edward Ratcliffe of Hitchin Priory in Hertfordshire, was said to have been knowledgeable and skilful in surgery and always ready to help the lame and indigent.[26]

Some women were not content simply to perform the functions which were regarded as falling within the female domain; they wanted additional outlets for the employment of their talents and energy. In 1617 John Chamberlain wrote in a letter to a friend that Dame Elizabeth Winwood, the wife of Sir Ralph Winwood the Secretary of State, had been primarily responsible for an extensive programme of improvements which had been carried out in the grounds of their new mansion at Ditton Park in Buckinghamshire. This work had taken the form of building a dovehouse, paving the courtyard, providing a supply of excellent water, making fish ponds, damming or filling up a moat, planting a great orchard and laying out a spacious garden with delicate arbours and enclosing it with a fine brick wall.[27] At Weston under Lizard in Staffordshire Dame Elizabeth Wilbraham (Pl. 56), the wife of Sir Thomas Wilbraham, supervised the building of the present house, Weston Park (Pl. 57), during the reign of Charles II. To assist her she had a copy of Palladio's *First Book of Architecture* which is still in the library there.[28] Sir John Lowther of Lowther Hall in Westmorland was full of admiration for the book-keeping expertise of his first wife, Dame Mary. In his journal he observed that she was a good accountant who kept his books of accounts over a period of twenty years. During that time, he went on, she recorded receipts and disbursements amounting to some £20,000 and 'I cannot say I ever lost £5 soe careful shee was to give content and keepe all perfect and strayght'.[29] Sir John clearly did not feel that it was strange or unseemly for a gentlewoman to apply herself to this kind of work. Nor did Sir Drayner Massingberd of South Ormsby in Lincolnshire who stipulated in his will that his daughters should be taught 'all sorts of Learning needfull and usefull for them and particularly that they be made perfect in Arithmatick and Casting up Accounts'.[30] Occasionally a squire allowed his wife an opportunity to engage in a business activity. In his

56. Dame
Elizabeth
Wilbraham.
Portrait by Sir
Peter Lely
(Weston Park,
Staffordshire).

will, which was drawn up in 1630, Sir William Stonhouse of Radley in
Berkshire bequeathed to his wife, Dame Elizabeth, 'all that stock of monie
which by her carefull good huswiferie shee hath acquired by my allowance
out of her dayrie at Suggoth and elsewhere'.[31] Lady Margaret Boscawen, the
wife of Hugh Boscawen of Tregothnan in Cornwall, took on responsibility for
marketing the tin extracted from her husband's mines and, notwithstanding
an aristocratic upbringing (as one of the daughters of Theophilus, Earl of
Lincoln), appears to have had the necessary business acumen for such a
demanding task.[32]

What is particularly striking about the business activities of gentlewomen is
the extent to which they became involved in estate management. In some
cases the wife handled such matters while her husband was away from home.

In his autobiography Bulstrode Whitelocke writes that during his absences his first wife (who was the daughter of a London merchant) 'carefully and prudently mannaged my affayres' and adds that 'I found none so good stewards as my wives'.[33] Since Sir Marmaduke Constable of Everingham in Yorkshire was a Catholic it is probable that his periodic absences were mainly the product of fears about the potential consequences of his recusancy. In January 1672 his wife, Dame Anne, submitted to him certain requests in writing to which he signified his agreement. In this somewhat unusual document she proposed that Sir Marmaduke should confirm her right to all the rents, cash and goods which her mother had left her, with the corollary that she had the power to dispose of them as she wished; that he should declare that she had not prejudiced his estate by her management of it during his absence or at any other time; and that if he should absent hmself again he should give full authority to her and his steward, George Constable, to manage his estate or alternatively appoint his own manager, paying her an appropriate maintenance allowance.[34]

In other cases the wife assumed responsibility for estate matters because her husband was incapacitated in some way. Edward Lingen of Stoke Edith in Herefordshire, who was one of the most substantial landowners in the county, was formally declared a lunatic by the Court of Wards and in accordance with its directions was kept under restraint in his own house. In a petition submitted in 1634 his wife, Blanche Lingen, told the Privy Council that

57. Weston Park, Staffordshire.

for about nine years she had been managing his estate and had repaid debts amounting to nearly £3000, discharged mortgages and stocked the demesne lands with cattle.[35] Sir John Hobart of Blickling in Norfolk owned an estate worth over £4000 a year but found it necessary to mortgage some of his property and by May 1640 had incurred debts totalling £11,400. During the illness which eventually led to his death in 1647 it was decided that his wife, Lady Frances, who had already shown herself to be a capable housekeeper, should take charge of all his affairs. Her chaplain, John Collinges, relates that 'Perceiving her dear Husband engaged in a great debt, she undertook the management of his whole estate, and auditing all his accounts, and that to so good a purpose that in a few years she had shortened his debt Six thousand pounds'.[36] As a young man Sir Francis Wolryche of Dudmaston Hall in Shropshire had fathered three daughters by his wife, Dame Elizabeth, but for many years was 'very weak and infirm' in both mind and body and indeed was officially designated as a lunatic. Accordingly the management of his affairs was entrusted to his wife and his daughter Margaret who continued to exercise this responsibility until his death in 1689.[37]

It is an indication of the confidence which she inspired that the squire's wife was often appointed as the executrix of his will, though on the other hand his landed property might be settled on trustees if a minority was in prospect. At his death in 1670 Sir John Russell of Chippenham in Cambridgeshire left his son (who was then a minor) an estate worth £1500 a year but it was encumbered with debts amounting to £6000 or £7000, including the sum of £2000 which had to be raised for the marriage portions of his daughters. In these circumstances his widow, Dame Frances (who was a daughter of Oliver Cromwell), entered into an agreement with the trustees who allowed her to take over management of the estate. She proceeded to improve the revenue arising from the demesne lands of the manor of Chippenham from £300 to £550 a year and in order to speed up the payment of her husband's debts spent no more than £200 a year in maintaining herself and her children.[38]

In many gentry families the relationship between the squire and his wife was one of mutual affection and respect. On 18 February 1690 Elizabeth Pollexfen, the daughter of a judge, Sir Henry Pollexfen, became the third wife of Sir Francis Drake of Buckland Abbey in Devon and wrote in her memorandum book 'then came Sir Francis and myself together; I pray God send us many happy years together, for I really love, honour and esteem him with all sincerity, nor do I question but he has the same regard for me'. Four years later she was exulting in her happiness which was due in no small measure to her husband's 'extraordinary love and affection'.[39] When drawing up their wills some gentlemen took the opportunity to commend the virtues of their wives. Sir Henry Fanshawe of Ware Park in Hertfordshire commented that he had always found his wife, Dame Elizabeth, 'to have been most true and lovinge to me' and that through long experience he was well acquainted with 'her Godlie Disposition, wisdom, Discretion and naturall affection to her Children'.[40] Sir Francis Barrington of Hatfield Broad Oak in Essex, who was a thoroughgoing Puritan, gave direction that his wife, Dame Joan, should be the sole executrix of his will, 'havinge in my lief time found her everie waie moste faithfull and carefull for the good of my selfe and myne. Yea I must acknowledge that I have found her soe good a wief in everie kinde as that I cannott sufficientlie expresse my love and confidence in her'.[41] Sir William Wray of Ashby in Lincolnshire, who married Olympia Tufton in 1652, declared that she had been 'a most deare and loveing wife in the Course of our lives' and exhorted their children to accept her government and tuition.[42] Sir Thomas Hervey of Ickworth in Suffolk was so deeply saddened by the loss of his wife, Dame Isabella, in 1686 that he decided not to marry again and on each succeeding anniversary of her death composed some verse to her memory. In 1690 his anniversary poem included the following lines:

> But here I must unto the world present
> That vast and ne're before enjoy'd extent
> Of happiness by man which I enjoy'd
> With her, was always full and never cloy'd.
> To her my joys and griefs I did impart,
> Into her bosome pour'd out all my heart.
> She tooke upon her all domestick care,
> By love she taught her children how to fear;
> Her bounty did engage her servants so
> As the Centurions could not faster goe.
> Her charity diffusive did extend
> Not to relations only, or a friend,
> But all without exception did pertake
> Of that for her own God and conscience sake.[43]

A cynic might argue that a gentleman would be naturally inclined to look favourably on a wife who fully respected his authority as head of the household. There is a hint of this in an entry which Sir Roger Twysden of Roydon Hall in Kent made in his private diary following the death of his wife, Dame Isabella, in 1657. 'Never man had a better wife', he wrote, and in describing her attributes listed piety, mildness, temperance, sweetness of nature, judgment, patience and humility. On the other hand, his son Sir William testifies that her self-abnegation extended well beyond the relationship between husband and wife. 'I may say', he observed in his notebook, 'that I never knew a better either wife, parent, or friend, in all which relations shee seemed rather to live to others then to her selfe'.[44] Lady Mary Jolliffe (Pl. 58), who was married to William Jolliffe of Caverswall Castle in Staffordshire, was not necessarily submissive but certainly believed that it was a wife's duty to help and support her husband in every possible way. Although she was a daughter of Ferdinando Earl of Huntingdon she was not disposed to pride herself on the fact that she was a person of greater social standing than her husband. At her funeral in 1678 the minister stressed that she was

A Wife precisely observant, from the smallest things to the greatest, provident and careful in all the Concernments of her worthy Husband, studying and contriving his Interests and Satisfaction in every thing. She was

58. Lady Mary Jolliffe. Engraving by an unknown artist.

such a Wife . . . in whom he had all joy and delight. To which he made the most affectionate returne of Kindness, Love, and tenderest Care.

Perhaps the only disappointment of their life together was the failure to produce a male heir.[45]

On the other hand, it is a truism that domestic bliss is not a state of affairs which can ever be guaranteed or taken for granted and, as recent studies have shown, the upper classes undoubtedly had their share of failed marriages. In the course of the seventeenth century at least seventy major gentry families experienced serious marital difficulties which usually resulted in the husband and wife living apart. Divorce was extremely rare at this time but not infrequently an ecclesiastical court would grant a judicial separation and stipulate the amount of alimony to be paid by the husband.[46] In 1617 the High Commission at York decided that a wealthy Yorkshire squire, Sir John Vavasour of Spaldington, should allow his wife £50 a year for maintenance until such time as it should please God to move them to live together again and that he should also be financially responsible for bringing up the children. In 1625 Lady Vavasour (who was characterised by her husband as extravagant) was still refusing to return to him.[47] After the Restoration the Court of Arches was prepared to adopt a more generous attitude when awarding alimony and some gentlemen were ordered to pay £300 a year or more. From the 1650s onwards it was also becoming relatively common for a private separation agreement to be concluded without resort to litigation.

In July 1677 Sir Francis Throckmorton of Coughton in Warwickshire (Pl. 59), a leading Catholic squire, gave a formal undertaking that his wife, Dame Anne (Pl. 60), would receive an annuity of £300 so long as they lived apart and authorised his steward, Robert Grey, to pay it from the rents which came in.[48]

Dorothy Osborne was not apparently indulging in irony when she wrote in 1653 that it was often the wife who was responsible for fomenting domestic quarrels:

> What an Age doe wee live in where 'tis a Miracle if in ten Couple that are married two of them live soe as not to publish it to the world that they cannot agree . . . to my friends I cannot but confesse that I am affrayde much of the fault lyes in us, for I have observed that Generaly in great famely's the Men sildom disagree, but the women are alway's scolding, and tis most certain that, lett the husband bee what hee will, if the wife have but patience (which sure becoms her best) the disorder cannot bee great enough to make a noise, his anger alone when it meet's with nothing that resists it cannot bee loude enough to disturbe the Neighbours.[49]

Shrews and termagants were by no means uncommon in seventeenth-century England. Sir Samuel Grimston of Gorhambury House in Hertfordshire, who is said to have been 'a mild man of kindly disposition', had the misfortune to take as his second wife Lady Anne Tufton, a domineering woman who was not slow to pick a quarrel, usually over matters of religion. Growing tired of her ranting, he had a small room built near his billiard room where he could spend at least part of the day alone with his books. This haven of peace, which was only accessible by a narrow stairway, he jocularly called his 'Mount pleasant'.[50]

Some marriages were probably destined to fail, either because of significant differences in temperament or because the husband and wife were both strong-minded individuals with a propensity for self-assertion. Henry Sacheverell of Morley Hall in Derbyshire, who was one of the wealthiest landowners in the county, appears to have been an introvert who preferred a reclusive life. In 1609, when he was being considered for the office of sheriff, it was reported, among other things, that 'he hath a very great witt, and is a good scoller' but was inclined to be moody and melancholy; that he lived very privately; and that he had separated himself from his wife of whom the county had a high opinion.[51] Sir Thomas Elmes of Green's Norton in Northamptonshire and his wife, Dame Margaret, were a hot-tempered couple who were always quarrelling and eventually decided that they would be happier living apart. When Sir Ralph Verney (who was Dame Margaret's brother) invited them to a family gathering at his Buckinghamshire mansion, Claydon House, in 1653 Sir Thomas replied that 'Your sister and myself do live so unlovingly together that I have no heart to come to her freindes; neither do I like to have my freindes come to mee, least they should take notice of her unkindnesse to mee'. Although Sir Thomas occasionally resorted to physical violence Sir Ralph was not dis-

59. Sir Francis
Throckmorton.
Portrait by Gerard
Zoest (Coughton
Court,
Warwickshire).

Sᴿ FRANCIS THROCKMORTON BARᵀ
DIED *1680*

posed to regard his sister as an entirely innocent party, calling her 'as cap-
tious a sister as she has been a wife'.[52]

In many cases the wife left her husband, either by mutual agreement or
more often without his prior knowledge or consent. Her departure might be
occasioned by physical or mental cruelty though there could also be other
causes. Sir Richard Hawksworth, who was seated at Hawksworth Hall in
Yorkshire, was fined for committing adultery and in 1627 his wife, Dame
Mary, went to live with her parents at Ribston Hall, taking their infant son
with her. During the course of legal proceedings in 1632 it was said that Sir
Richard had initially allowed her to manage his estate and that she had been
affronted when he had subsequently decided to assume this responsibility
himself.[53] In 1632 Katherine Goring, a daughter of George Lord Goring,
became the wife of Edward Scott, the son and heir of Sir Edward Scott of
Scot's Hall in Kent, but within five years they had parted. Writing from

ANN DAUGHTER OF JOHN MOUNSON ESQ^R
OF KINNERSLY COM, SURREY WIFE TO
S^R FRANCIS THROCKMORTON BAR^T DIED 1728

60. Dame Anne Throckmorton. School of Sir Peter Lely (Coughton Court, Warwickshire).

London in June 1637 she told her husband that 'whensoever a happy agreement shall be made for us both' she would be ready to return to him 'on a day's warning'. Some time later she asked her mother-in-law to obtain Sir Edward's permission for her husband to travel abroad. If that could be arranged, she went on, 'I will go with him myself, I will leave all my friends, and when we return again will live where he will have me to live . . . As things now stand we are both most unhappy'. This proposal, however, appears to have come to nothing and when she returned to Scot's Hall in 1646 the servants denied her entry. In a petition which he submitted to Parliament in 1656 Edward Scott related that his wife had deserted him many years before and that at Oxford and elsewhere she had given birth to children by other men. Accordingly he requested Parliament to grant him a divorce and to declare that these children were bastards. The petition was referred to a committee which took evidence from witnesses. Timothy

Rookes, an ancient servant of the family, not only supported his master's allegations but testified that at one point Scott had been kidnapped at his wife's instigation and taken to London where he had been kept under restraint until Cromwell had secured his release. When the couple appeared before the committee it was noted that Katherine Scott had 'a very bold face, but seemeth old' while her husband gave the impression that he was simple-minded. In the event no decision was taken and in 1662 she began proceedings in the Court of Arches for the restitution of conjugal rights. Scott died the following year and in his will bequeathed his estate to Thomas Scott, 'whome notwithstanding the malice and Suggestion of evill affected persons to the contrary I doe hereby owne and acknowledge my legitimate sonne'. This may perhaps have been a case of wishful thinking: the young man had been born at Oxford during the Civil War and it was suspected that Prince Rupert was the father.[54]

During the latter part of the century there are references to matrimonial disputes in a number of cases heard in the Court of Chancery. In 1664 Dame Anne Forster, the widow of Sir Humphrey Forster of Aldermaston in Berkshire, told the Court that about twenty years ago she had been so unhappy that they had separated 'which was not through any cause by her given'. This was after she had borne him no fewer than sixteen children.[55] In Lincolnshire Sir Anthony Thorold of Marston Hall married Anna Maria Harrington in 1683 while he was still a minor. Not long afterwards she decided to leave him, a development which her father attributed to his son-in-law's 'evill Councellors, and evill Company'. In June 1685 Sir Anthony secured a pass to travel into France and in the following November died there, leaving no issue.[56] In a Chancery bill of 1699 Sir Thomas Gascoigne of Barnbow Hall in Yorkshire, who was the head of a prominent Catholic family, described the failure of his marriage to Magdalen Curwen who was the daughter of a Cumberland squire. During the marriage negotiations in 1683 it had been agreed that a jointure of £500 a year should be settled on her and that she should have £100 a year for pin-money 'to bestow, lay out and doe what she would withall for her own private use'. For about two years they had lived very happily together but 'takeing some Causeless displeasure' against him she had secretly left his house and never returned 'which hath been a great Losse and detriment . . . in the Government and Order of his family and household Affaires'.[57]

If the squire's wife survived her husband she was usually able to enjoy the kind of financial independence which as a general rule had been denied her during her married life. Among the wealthier families it was common practice to settle a jointure of £300, £400 or £500 a year, depending on the size of the marriage portion, while in some exceptional cases a widow was assigned property worth £1000, £1500 or even £2000 a year. The living accommodation included in these arrangements might be a town house in London or elsewhere or a secondary house in the country but not infrequently the widow was expected to share the family's principal residence with the heir and his wife. Since this could lead to friction some gentlemen thought it prudent to lay down precise lines of demarcation. In his will, which was drawn up in

1682, a major Cornish squire, John Pendarves of Roskrow, stipulated that his wife Bridget should 'hold and enjoy all the Roomes, both Cellars, ground Roomes and Chambers, from the Parlor door Eastward which extend and lye in the greene Court . . . and Backyard to the same adjoyning with liberty of Ingresse, Egresse and Regresse by all usuall and Convenient ways to the same'.[58]

CHAPTER FIVE

The Wider Family

In 1648 Sir John Kaye of Woodsome Hall in Yorkshire observed in his memorandum book that 'My family consists of 27 persons' (Pl. 61). By 'family' he meant not only his wife, children and stepchildren but all his full-time servants and the resident schoolmaster who was teaching the children.[1] For, in common with his fellow gentry, Sir John took it as self-evident that in his relationship with the servants he had a dual role as employer and *paterfamilias*.

Servants were a major presence in the domestic world of the country gentry. The actual number of servants which a gentleman employed naturally depended to a large extent on his particular financial circumstances but there were also other factors such as the size of the house, the scale of his farming activities, the nature of his housekeeping and the importance he attached to outward manifestations of wealth and rank. At the same time it was not unusual (though practice varied) for agricultural labourers to be engaged on a weekly or daily basis as occasion demanded. A work book belonging to the Newdegates of Arbury in Warwickshire records that in November 1689 there was a casual labour force of thirty-seven but that it had been decided that for the future there should be no more than twenty-six at a time.[2]

From the evidence of family papers, Chancery records, poll tax returns, wills and other sources of information it is possible to build up a comprehensive picture of the size, composition and levels of remuneration of the full-time establishments of servants in the country houses of the gentry.[3] At the bottom end of the economic scale a gentleman with an income of £100 or £200 a year might have no more than four or five servants living under his roof. At the other extreme Sir Thomas Wentworth, the future Earl of Strafford, who had inherited an estate worth £6000 a year, employed no fewer than fifty servants at his principal seat, Wentworth Woodhouse in Yorkshire (Pl. 62).[4] Such a large establishment, however, was comparatively rare outside the ranks of the nobility. Generally speaking, the major county families which commanded an income of £1000 a year or more had between ten and thirty servants who were in receipt of annual wages. After the Restoration even the wealthiest of these families appear to have adopted a more rigorous approach in regulating the size of their domestic establishments, though there was the

61. Woodsome Hall, Yorkshire.

occasional exception: according to John Prince, who published an account of the leading Devonshire families in 1701, Sir Coplestone Bampfield of Poltimore 'did not only live up to' a very plentiful fortune 'but beyond it,

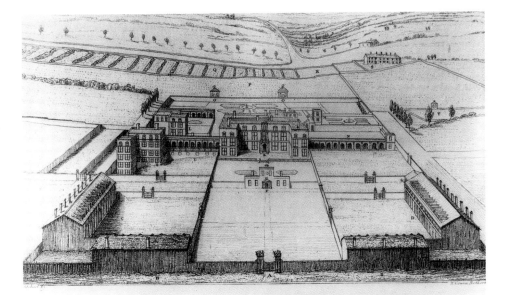

A. The principal entry.
B. Two stables.
C. Brewhouse, bakehouse, &c.
D. A stable.
E. Coach-house and stable.
F. Porter's lodge.
G. A tower.
H. The kitchen.
I. Vaults, over which is the passage from the hall to the kitchen.

K. The house.
L. Another tower, both which have good lodgings.
M. A banquetting-house, and the lead walks.
N. An orangery.
O. Two summer-houses.
P. A grove.
Q. The orchard.
R. The kitchen-garden.
S. The gardener's house.
T. The bowling-green.

62. A drawing of Wentworth Woodhouse, Yorkshire as it was in the seventeenth century (Joseph Hunter, *South Yorkshire*, 1828).

always keeping about him a great Retinue'.[5] A number of factors may have been responsible for the general inclination to exercise tighter control over staffing levels: the financial consequences of the Civil War; the agricultural depression of the later Stuart period in which landlords experienced difficulty in getting in their rents on time and finding new tenants; and the growing tendency for the richest families to sojourn for long periods in London and its more salubrious suburbs. This latter development had a potential impact not only on the number of household servants in the country but on the level of activity of the home farm.

In the larger establishments particularly the servants had a social hierarchy of their own. When a survey was carried out in Gloucestershire in the summer of 1608 it was noted, among other things, that William Dutton of Sherborne had fourteen and Sir Henry Poole of Sapperton fifteen gentlemen and yeomen servants and that they each had nine husbandmen servants.[6] Among the female servants there was often a waiting gentlewoman who was employed as the personal attendant and companion of the squire's wife and would almost inevitably become a close confidante. Besides these social distinctions there were also significant differences in the educational background of servants. Many families had at least a few servants, usually of low status, who were illiterate or at best semi-literate, though this was clearly not regarded as a serious impediment to the performance of their duties. Following the death of Sir William Paston, who was seated at Oxnead in Norfolk, in October 1610 his executor, acting on the directions in his will, gave legacies to eleven of his servants and of these no fewer than eight acknowledged receipt by inscribing a mark in place of a signature (Pl. 63).[7] At the end of the seventeenth century and beyond this practice was still very much in evidence. Among the papers of William Cary of Clovelly Court in Devon there are a number of receipts for wages paid to his servants. At Christmas 1699 John Madge inserted his mark; in April 1701 John Devenshere and John Meeke appended their signatures while Nicholas Balch and John Howard made their marks; and in May 1701 James Davey and Katherine Licence also resorted to the use of a mark.[8]

Male servants had a wide range of responsibilities and were of many different types. Besides the ordinary servingmen and farm labourers they included the estate or land steward, the house steward, the clerk, the bailiff, the butler, the cook, the brewer, the coachman, the groom, the porter, the gardener, the keeper of the park, the warrener, the huntsman and the falconer. Sometimes two of these specialised functions might be merged: in 1625, for example, Sir Francis Stonor of Stonor in Oxfordshire had a servant called John Wallis who was both coachman and brewer, a combination which some of his fellow gentry might have regarded as potentially lethal.[9]

The house steward, who was responsible for the running of the household, was a much less familiar figure than the estate steward. In the latter part of the century he was to be found only in the mansions of the richest families such as the Brownlows of Belton in Lincolnshire, the Cokes of Holkham in Norfolk and the Longs of Whaddon in Wiltshire.[10] The clerk performed the duties of a secretary and might also be required to assist in the management of the estate. In a legal case heard in 1697 Nathaniel

63. List of Sir William Paston's legacies bequeathed to his servants, 1610 (British Library, Additional MSS 27,447, fol. 150).

Corles, gentleman, testified that Sir Edward Mosley of Hulme in Lancashire had employed him as his clerk; that as an addition to the duties associated with this appointment he had acted as receiver of part of his revenue; and that he had produced a first draft of Sir Edward's will which was now the subject of litigation.[11] The butler was another man of considerable standing in the household. He was responsible for the supply and storage of all kinds of drink and had sole charge of the buttery and the wine and beer cellars.

The servingman was satirised in a work written by Sir Thomas Overbury 'and other learned Gentlemen his friends' in the reign of James I:

> He tels without asking who ownes him by the superscription of his livery. His life is for ease and leasure, much about *gentleman-like* . . . He is commonly proud of his master's horses, or his Christmas: hee sleepes when he is sleepy, is of his religion, only the clock of his stomack is set to go an houre after his . . . He never drinks but double, for he must be pledg'd . . . His discretion is to bee carefull for his master's credit, and his sufficiency to marshall dishes at a table, and to carve well.[12]

While the main function of the servingmen was to wait at table they could also be called on to undertake a variety of other tasks, including the delivery of messages, the reception of visitors, the handling of heavy loads and the performance of escort duties when the squire or members of his family went on journeys. A large group of liveried servants travelling with their master could be an impressive sight. When the new lord president of the Council of the North arrived in Yorkshire in 1619 he was met by his kinsman Sir Richard Cholmley of Whitby who was 'attended with twenty of his own servants, all well mounted, and in handsome liveries of grey cloth trimmed with silver lace'.[13] If, however, the employment of servants on escort duties was considered important for reasons of prestige it also reflected a need for physical security in view of the dangers presented by highwaymen and other marauders.[14] In a Star Chamber case of 1610 Sir Richard Tracy related that on a journey from Hampton Court in Herefordshire to his house at Hasfield in Gloucestershire he had been accompanied by nine or ten servants, partly 'for attendance' and partly for the safeguarding of a consignment of money which amounted to some £860.[15] When Mary Bishop, one of the daughters of Sir Cecil Bishop of Parham in Sussex, went up to London in April 1690 there were seven servants 'attending the coach'. For this journey she was given £40 while the servants each received 1s 6d for 'expenses in drink'.[16]

As a general rule the male servants in the larger households heavily outnumbered the female servants whose range of duties was more circumscribed.[17] Even so, there were various categories of maidservants, including personal maids, cook maids, kitchen maids, chambermaids, laundry maids and dairy maids. Although most cooks in country houses were male the employment of cook maids became more common as the century progressed; and it was also not unknown for a woman to be made responsible for the brewing of beer. According to one seventeenth-century writer there were many attributes to be looked for in a good maidservant. She must be 'carefull, faithfull, patient, neat and pleasant . . . cleanly, quicke and handsome, and of few words, honest in her word, deed and attire, diligent in a househould'. At the same time she must be skilled in washing, baking, brewing, sewing and spinning but (he reiterated) 'chiefly in holding her peace'.[18]

After the Restoration there was a significant growth in the number of female housekeepers. The responsibilities of the housekeeper included the control and supervision of the maidservants and the purchase of food and other supplies for the household, a function which could involve the handling of considerable sums of money.[19] Often her employer was a widower and if he had young children she may conceivably have acquired the role of surrogate mother. Sir John Langham of Cottesbrooke in Northamptonshire, who was a widower for many years, clearly had a very high regard for his housekeeper, Mrs Waters. In his will, which was drawn up in 1670, he left her a handsome legacy of £200 with the comment that he had found her 'very faithfull and serviceable to mee. Therefore I would have my Children to love and respect her the more for my sake'.[20] On the other hand, a wealthy landowner might employ a housekeeper for the sole purpose of relieving his wife of the burden of responsibility for the ordering of household affairs which had traditionally been regarded as one of the prime duties of women in her position.

During the late seventeenth century there are occasional references to black servants who appear to have been acquired mainly for their curiosity value. In his memoirs Sir John Reresby of Thrybergh in Yorkshire observes, in an entry for the year 1676, that he had a fine Moor 'about sixteen years of age (given me by a gentleman . . . who had brought him out of the Barbadoes) that had lived with me some years, and dyed about this time of an imposthume in his head'.[21] When Sir John Maynard, who was seated at Gunnersbury in Middlesex, drew up his will in 1690 he listed a number of servants who were to be rewarded with legacies and added 'the black boy I leave and commend to my wife's care of him'.[22]

The recruitment of servants was a matter of great concern to the gentry. Sometimes a close relative or distant cousin might be taken on as the estate steward or house steward or as a personal attendant or general factotum. In the main, however, servingmen and maidservants were drawn from the families of farmers and agricultural labourers within the same county or adjacent counties. Many were raw and untrained in respect of domestic service at the time they were engaged but there were some who had already gained experience in other households. In his diary Sir Henry Slingsby of Red House in Yorkshire writes that while he was in London as a member of the Long Parliament his wife hired a maid, Anne Kirk, who had previously served Thomas Lord Fairfax of Denton until his death in 1640.[23] While it was a sensible precaution to seek some form of character reference before a new servant was engaged there are indications that this practice was not always followed. In a letter which he received from a relative Sir Charles Yate of Buckland in Berkshire was told that a maidservant who had recently been hired by his wife was reported to have commented that her mistress was 'a very good Lady' but her master was 'a fantasticall man'. His informant went on to say that she was reputed to be 'a light housewife', meaning presumably that she was frivolous or idle, and that she had once been 'turned out of service for being druncke'.[24]

When the gentry were faced with the need to recruit servants with special expertise such as cooks, gardeners and coachmen their thoughts often turned to London as potentially the most fruitful source of candidates. In July 1625 Sir Hugh Smyth of Ashton Court in Somerset received a letter from London in which his correspondent wrote that

> I have inquired also after a servant, such a one as you desired. I can yet comend none . . . many young and inexperienced men hath offered

themselves unto me, whose frinds and fortunes I know not, I know you will not like them. When I heare of one for your purpose I will send you word. I will rather wish you none than wish one unfitt your imployments.

In February 1642 his son Thomas, who was now the head of the family, was having problems with his gardener. Writing from London to his steward he told him that 'I have this night had a Gardyner in treaty with mee, but wee can not yet agree; therefore keepe my intentions close, and see what amendment you can make in Swayne'. Before he dispatched his letter, however, there were further developments which enabled him to finish on a more optimistic note: 'Since I wrote this same the Gardyner has better thought of my tearmes and I believe will accept them; therefore lett the other steere his owne wayes'.[25] During the Civil War period Dame Dorothea Drake, the wife of the parliamentarian Sir Francis Drake of Buckland Abbey in Devon, informed her brother Charles Pym, who was then in London, that it was her husband's earnest prayer that he would find them a good cook. Whether Pym was able to satisfy this urgent plea remains unclear.[26]

In 1673 Sir John Reresby was hoping to secure the services of a French cook in an attempt to keep abreast of metropolitan fashion. Probably he was unfamiliar with the satirical comment in Sir Thomas Overbury's book of characters that a French cook 'doth not feed the belly but the palate . . . The servingmen call him the last relique of popery, that makes men fast against their conscience. He can be truly said to be no man's fellow but his master's: for the rest of his servants are starved by him.'[27] In response to Reresby's request for assistance John Sayer, who was acting as his agent in London, reported that he had eventually made contact with Francis the French cook but he would not come to Thrybergh Hall for less than £20 a year; nor, he went on, 'can I hear of any that will if they can doe any thinge that is fitting for a person of quality'. Sayer had also spoken to the clerk of the kitchen to the Duke of Buckingham who knew all the French cooks in London. He had promised him that he would try and find a cook who would be willing to serve Sir John for £10 or £12 a year but he doubted whether this would be easy. Some years later when Sir John was again seeking a cook his requirements were apparently more modest. In August 1686 his friend Sir Henry Goodricke, who was seated at Ribston in Yorkshire, wrote in a letter to him that 'as to the Cook, I had appointed my Steward Prichard to certifye for his honesty, and that he had served me one year, but further neither he nor any other had direction to affirme'.[28]

For thoroughgoing Catholic families and the more zealous kind of Protestant families the field of choice was limited in some degree by religious considerations. In the case of a Catholic family it was clearly important that all the household servants were at least sympathetically disposed towards the faith which their master espoused; otherwise there was a danger that information about the family's clandestine activities, including the harbouring of priests, could find its way to the civil or ecclesiastical authorities. On the other hand, a penal statute of 1606 made it an offence to keep recusant servants and any employer who transgressed could be heavily fined.[29] The impact of this statute is graphically illustrated in a memorandum book which belonged to Richard Cholmley of Brandsby Hall in the North Riding of Yorkshire.

Cholmley was a convicted recusant whose house was on the circuit of the Jesuit mission. On 13 December 1606 he wrote that 'All my Catholicke servants went from me' which may be construed as meaning that he had felt it necessary to dispense with the services of those who had been indicted for recusancy. In August 1607 he appeared before the Northern High Commission and, as we learn from the official record, was informed that he must not retain any recusant servant in his house or service. Two years later there is the cryptic entry in the memorandum book that Cholmley had paid 10s to the clerk of the peace 'not to retourne recusant servants'. From 1611 onwards, however, some of his servants were presented for recusancy, though they were never more than a small proportion of his total establishment. In March 1620 he received the disturbing news that he had been fined £360 for keeping four recusant servants. His response was to resort to litigation and as a result the fine was apparently never paid.[30] In the reign of Charles I the statutory provision relating to servants became a dead letter following the introduction of a new fining system and for the rest of the century it was possible to employ recusant servants without running the risk of incurring financial penalties specifically on this account. In 1651 the Dorset committee informed the republican government that all the servants of Humphrey Weld of Lulworth Castle were papists but this was primarily with the aim of exposing him as a zealous Catholic.[31]

For Protestant squires who paid more than lip-service to the religion which they professed there was no lack of advice available from Puritan authors and ministers on the criteria to be applied when recruiting servants. The head of a household, wrote William Perkins, must 'make a good choice of his servants which is then done when he inquireth after such as feare God and be willing to serve him'. Masters, declared Robert Cleaver, should take care 'to hire religious and godlie Servants to doe their worke and businesses'. In a letter addressed to Dame Joan Barrington in February 1630 Ezekiel Rogers, who held one of the Barrington livings in Yorkshire, stressed that 'the servants who are about you should . . . be of the choicest for godlines'.[32] Such exhortations reflected the Puritan concept of the godly household but as John Dod pointed out the kind of God-fearing servants of whom he approved were likely to be very faithful and diligent in performing the duties for which they were employed.[33]

In practice the recruitment of servants for a godly household could present difficulties. Another Puritan writer, William Gouge, observed with feeling that 'Many servants are of so impious a minde as of all masters they will not serve such as are religious, and make conscience to instruct their servants in the way to salvation'.[34] Some Puritan landed families went to great lengths to ensure that they had servants whose religious sympathies were in harmony with their own or who were willing to accept their spiritual guidance. According to his biographer Sir Nathaniel Barnardiston of Kedington in Suffolk had many excellent servants, 'his Family being a true Nursery for the qualifying and accomplishing such; so that one, who was well acquainted with his Family, affirms that at one time he had ten or more Servants so eminent for Piety and Sincerity that he never saw the like, all at once, in any Family in the Nation.'[35] Sir Robert Harley (Pl. 64) of Brampton Bryan in

64. Sir Robert
Harley. Portrait by
Peter Oliver.

Herefordshire would often remark that 'I care not for a good servant if He do not fear God' and this was an important factor in his choice of servants for which he was able to draw on advice and assistance from his clerical associates. After the Restoration the same kind of approach was adopted by his son Sir Edward (Pl. 65) whose religious beliefs were so austere that he refused to allow his servants to undertake any journeys on the Sabbath. In March 1674 Ralph Strettell, a nonconformist divine resident in London, informed him that he had made enquiries about the man who had been recommended to him for the post of butler; that he had received a highly satisfactory account of his fidelity and diligence; and that since he was currently unemployed he was prepared to come down straightaway. No doubt Harley regarded it as self-evident, given the source of his information, that the candidate would not feel out of place in a godly household.[36]

When a servant was hired on a full-time basis it was usual for the new recruit to enter into an agreement or covenant with the head of the household; hence such servants were often known as 'covenant servants'. A typical agreement of this kind covered the broad span of duties to be performed together with the pay and other conditions of employment which were to apply. In one of his account books Sir Roger Twysden of Roydon Hall in Kent noted that he had taken on John Dudney as his groom on 23 July 1632 and that the bargain he had made with him was that he would give him £4 a year and a cloak once every two years. Subsequently, in October 1632, Dudney received 30s to buy himself a cloak.[37] During the years 1681 to 1686 Sir

65. Sir Edward Harley. Portrait by Samuel Cooper.

Robert Throckmorton of Coughton in Warwickshire kept a careful record of the dates on which he had engaged his servants and the financial terms which had been agreed upon. Among other things, he undertook to pay John Flint the groom £6 a year, Margaret Huggins the cook maid £5 a year, Ralph Wyhon the butler £8 a year, Frances Beddle a kitchen assistant £2 10s 0d a year, John West the head husbandman £6 a year and James Sturdy the gardener £10 a year. Occasionally, however, Sir Robert declined to commit himself over the level of remuneration. In February 1683, he writes, Luke Sturdy came to be 'my boye to wayte on me and has no settled Wages' while in June he hired Ambroise Charles as his postillion on the basis that he was 'to have yearely what I thinck fitt'.[38]

Among the papers of the Buller family of Shillingham in Cornwall there is an agreement between Francis Buller and Nathaniel Arnold which records the latter's appointment in November 1674 as his gardener, under-butler and footman. In this agreement Buller laid down his requirements in some detail. Along with his responsibilities as gardener Arnold was 'to goe with the Coach', 'to helpe to sawe and bring in wood', 'to helpe in the Stables' and 'to helpe to brew with my Coachman if I brew'. Besides undertaking to perform these multifarious duties Arnold promised to be civil and well-mannered and 'to goe hansom and whole'. In return Buller agreed to pay him an annual wage of £5 and to provide him with a new livery every year.[39]

In many households there were at least one or two long-serving retainers whose relationship with the squire and his family was one of profound

66. Memorial to three servants of the Morrison family in St Mary's church, Watford.

HENRY DICKSON ∣ GEORGE MILLER ∣ ANTHONY COOPER
DECEASED THE ∣ DECEASED THE V ∣
XXV OF FEB 1610 ∣ OF APRIL 1613 ∣

HERE LYETH BVRYED THE BODIES OF HENRY DICKSON
GEORGE MILLER AND ANTHONY COOPER WHO WERE LATE
SERVANTS TO Sᴿ CHARLES MORRISON KNIGHT DECEASED &
AFTER CONTYNEWED IN SERVICE Wᵗʰ DOROTHIE LA: MORRISON
HIS WIFE & Sᴿ CHARLES MORRISON KNIGHT AND BARRONETT
THEIR SONNE, BY THE SPACE OF 40 YEARS IN MEMORY
OF THEM THE SAYD DOROTHIE LA: MORRISON HATH
VOVCHSAFED THIS STONE AND INSCRIPTION

mutual respect. During the reigns of Elizabeth and James I the Morrison family of Cassiobury in Hertfordshire had three employees, Henry Dickson, George Miller and Anthony Cooper, who served them for forty years. So highly regarded were they that Dame Dorothy Morrison took the unusual step of erecting a memorial to them, with brass figures, in her parish church at Watford (Pl. 66).[40] The Kentish squire Sir Roger Twysden thought it fitting to record that Thomas Bates,

> a true and faithfull, carefull and Trusty servant of myne that had served my father and me 34 years dyed at my house at Eastpeckham the 27th day of March 1662. He loved me truly and ever took a singular care of me in all journeys whatsoever. I shall never have hys like, nor my sonne after me.[41]

More generally, however, there was often a steady turnover of servants in the houses of the gentry. Servants died, sometimes at a relatively early age, or contracted debilitating illnesses which rendered them unfit to work; left to marry or to take up employment elsewhere; found themselves dismissed or refused a further term of service; or occasionally ran away. Some maidservants married with the blessing of their employers; others resorted to marriage as the only legal means of freeing themselves from their commitment to serve for a minimum period.[42]

In certain circumstances (quite apart from a civil war or the sale of the estate) a domestic establishment could be faced with a major upheaval. If a gentleman was experiencing financial difficulties an obvious form of retrenchment was to economise on the number of servants he employed. In December 1612 Robert Throckmorton of Coughton in Warwickshire received a letter from his grandfather Thomas Wilsford in which he emphasised the need for him to put his affairs in order and added that 'I would alsoe be glad to heare of the Lessening of your howshould, otherwyse yow will growe as fast in debt as your Grandfather', meaning Thomas Throckmorton, 'was wount to doe'. In fact the young man had already taken the necessary action in March when he had reduced his establishment of servants from twenty-six to fourteen. Among those who had been discharged after receiving their Lady Day wages were Throckmorton Whittle, 'Olde Boulton', Parker 'the Spaniell boy' and Susan the malt maid.[43]

In the reign of Charles I James Zouch, whose principal seat was Woking House in Surrey, was in much greater financial straits, partly as a result of the debts he had inherited and partly through his own extravagance. In January 1638 his father-in-law Francis Lord Mountnorris told him that according to the information which Andrew Conradus, who was Zouch's steward, had provided the unpaid debts amounted to some £13,240 while the estate revenue was £1990 a year out of which £600 a year was payable to his mother and a further £400 a year was earmarked for annuities. On completing his analysis of the situation he urged Zouch to 'consider whether you have not sound reason to induce you to live within a narrowe compass unles you will sell more land'. More specifically, he suggested that he should limit himself to an income of £200 a year until all the debts had been paid. 'I am well pleased', he went on, 'to hear you have dismissed some of your superfluous servants and I seriously pray you not to keep a man or maid more then necessity compells'. In this event he was confident that when his mother was made aware of the magnitude of his debts she would be willing to take in Zouch, his wife and four or five servants for £100 a year.[44]

Another development which could have serious implications for the staff of country houses (and indeed for the neighbouring poor) was the growing enthusiasm among the wealthier landed families for the social life of London and some of the provincial cities and towns. In the early seventeenth century the government became increasingly concerned about the number of country gentry who were sojourning in the capital. This, it was feared, could have many adverse consequences, including the neglect of public duties and the decay of hospitality. In a series of proclamations the government commanded such persons to return to their own counties but its efforts proved largely ineffective. In 1635 the Attorney General presented the king with a lengthy list of individuals who had defied the Crown's directions, among them some of the most substantial landowners in England.[45] Sir Thomas Cotton, who was the richest gentleman in Huntingdonshire, had a sizeable mansion at Conington in the northern part of the county but was not often seen there. In 1644 the parliamentary authorities were informed that before the time of the Civil War he and his family had been living at his house in Westminster for 'the most part of every yere' and that his visits to Conington had been infrequent. Since his Conington estate, which was said to be worth £1500 a year, was given over entirely to pasture farming it must be considered doubtful whether the promotion of local employment figured prominently in his thinking.[46]

After the Restoration the growing attractions of London, with its theatres, pleasure grounds and parks, exercised such a powerful influence that more and more county families were drawn to the capital. At the same time there may also have been subsidiary factors at work: for example, Dame Beatrice Smyth, the wife of Sir Thomas Smyth of Hill Hall in Essex, told her sister in December 1664 that if a parliamentary seat could be found for her husband it was his intention to buy a house in Lincoln's Inn Fields.[47] Many of the families which purchased or took leases of town houses owned estates in southeast England but there were some which were seated in more distant counties such as Cornwall, Devon, Norfolk, Lincolnshire and Yorkshire. A number of Lincolnshire gentry had houses in the metropolis during the reign of Charles II, among them Sir Robert Bolles of Scampton, Sir John Brownlow of Belton, Sir Anthony Irby of Boston and Sir William Wray of Ashby.[48]

When a landowner decided to turn his back on country life one of the immediate consequences was the breaking up of his household. In the autumn of 1655 Sir John Hobart of Blickling in Norfolk had a full-time establishment of twenty-seven indoor and outdoor servants. In the latter part of his life, however, he was residing in London and his magnificent country house in its 300 acres of parkland was like an abandoned ship. According to some accounts which were drawn up after his death in 1683 he had by this time no more than seven employees in Norfolk who were in receipt of annual wages. These included an estate steward, a housekeeper, a bailiff, a park keeper and a man who was responsible 'for looking to the Gardens and grounds at Blickling hall'. Other entries record expenditure on airing the rooms and furniture at Blickling Hall and a payment to Thomas Wright, the former cook, for making a swan pie which had been dispatched to Sir John in London.[49]

An event which had potentially serious implications for the whole body of servants was the death of the head of the household. Sweeping changes in the household could follow if the heir was a cousin who had no sense of obligation towards the existing staff; or if the deceased's property was divided up among female heirs; or if the estate descended to a son who was still only a child or adolescent. When the heir was a minor he would often be brought up in his guardian's house, along with any brothers or sisters. Alternatively, arrangements might sometimes be made for him to live in the house he had inherited but with only a handful of servants to meet his needs. When Sir William Kingsmill of Sydmonton in Hampshire died in 1661 he was succeeded by his son William who was a mere infant with a far from robust constitution. For some years Sydmonton Court stood virtually empty but in 1672 it was decided that the young heir and his two sisters should return there since their physicians were of the opinion that they would benefit from the 'naturall Ayre'. Besides the steward and the bailiff who were managing the estate their guardian employed five servants to attend them at a total cost of £60 a year. In addition, they were provided with music masters, dancing masters and French language teachers.[50]

Occasionally a country squire might take the opportunity when preparing his will to name one or two servants whom he was anxious to commend to his successor. More frequently, he might show his concern for the future welfare of the servants by giving direction to his executor that the household should be kept together for a specified period after his decease so that they would have a reasonable breathing-space in which to find new employment. This requirement was usually occasioned by the fact that the testator either had no male issue or thought it likely that his son would succeed him while still a minor. In 1626 Sir Edmund Bowyer of Camberwell in Surrey stipulated in his will that for a period of six months after his death the executors he had nominated should not discharge any of his household servants but should supply them with food and drink and pay them their wages. During that time, he added, 'my servants maie provide them newe services'.[51] In 1633 Sir John Gage of West Firle in Sussex made similar arrangements but on the basis that these should continue for three months. At the end of this period his executors were to put Firle House in the care of a few servants 'whome they shall thincke fitt to keepe up my said house'. If any of his present servants were considered to be capable of undertaking this function they should be chosen in preference to others. The executors, he went on, should 'continewe some fewe servants there untill my eldest sonne shall attaine unto his full age'.[52] Sir John St John owned a large mansion at Battersea on the Surrey side of the Thames. Despite its proximity to London it had all the appearance of a country house with its barns, gardens, orchards, fishponds and a dovehouse. When Sir John drew up his will in 1645 he inserted the provision that all servants living with him at Battersea at the time of his death 'shall if they will accept of itt have entertainmente of meate, drinke and lodgeinge' there for half a year after his decease 'or for soe much of that time as they shalbe out of Service or want other imployment; whereby such of them as are able maie get their livelyhood soe as they doe by all that time demeane themselves religiously, soberly and honestly and carrie themselves respectfully towards my Executors and the rest of my Trustees.'[53]

CHAPTER SIX

Servants and Masters

According to Fynes Moryson, writing in 1617, there was a proverb then in currency that England was the hell of horses, the purgatory of servants and the paradise of women 'because they ride Horses without measure, and use their Servants imperiously, and their Women obsequiously'.[1] When, however, a country gentleman put pen to paper on the general subject of servants it was on the implicit assumption that the employer was more likely to have reasons for complaint than his employees. In a memorandum of advice which he drew up for the benefit of his son Sir John Weld of Willey in Shropshire urged him to keep no idle servants, 'for they are masters'.[2] Sir Miles Sandys argued, in a work which appeared in 1634, that the head of the household must pay particular attention to the moral well-being of the servants:

> There is a care to be had of their Soules . . . I meane not Puritanically to Catechize them . . . but, as neere as you can, to beate down Sinne in them, especially that of Swearing. Suffer them not to enterlard their Discourse with Oathes: for believe it, the hand of God will lighe heavie upon that House where Blasphemers dwell.[3]

William Higford, who was seated at Dixton in Gloucestershire, had some words of advice on the management of servants in a manuscript prepared for his grandson which was published posthumously in 1658. Servants and domestics, he observed, 'are ill companions, lest they prove insolent'. It was important that his grandson should set a good example to his servants so that he would be better able to govern them. At the same time he should ensure that they were all gainfully employed and insist on them rendering accounts, 'lest by remissness they grow idle and unserviceable'. And it was a matter of 'very great necessity, especially for Oeconomy and Government of your House' that he should be well versed in arithmetic so that he could keep a close watch on his expenditure.[4]

More comprehensive guidance on the obligations of both servants and masters was to be found in works by two Puritan authors, Robert Cleaver's *A Godlie Forme of Householde Government* and William Gouge's *Of Domesticall Duties*.[5] Masters, wrote Cleaver, should keep their servants from idleness and bring them up in honesty and comely manners and in all virtue. They should be 'carefull of their servants' good estate . . . not onely in providing for them wholesome meat, drink and lodging, and otherwise to help them, comfort them, and relieve and cherish them as well in sicknesse as in health'. Those who fell sick should be accommodated separately from the rest of the servants and should be given more choice and dainty food. In the matter of discipline the husband should rule and correct the menservants and his wife the maidservants 'for a man's nature scorneth and disdaineth to bee beaten of a woman, and a maides nature is corrupted with the stripes of a man'.[6] For Gouge it was a crucial requirement that servants should be respectful and obedient. In the larger households the servants could be 'so full of curtesie as not a word shall be spoken by their masters to them, or by them to their masters, but the knee shall be bowed withall: they can stand houre after houre before their masters, and not once put on their hat'. On the other hand, there were some servants who were unwilling to accept correction. This was a reprehensible attitude: criticism and blows should be borne with patience. A trembling fear was necessary 'in regard of the small love that servants commonly beare to their masters', though masters should not strike them too frequently. While idleness was the commonest fault of servants there was also the danger that they might contaminate the master's children 'with their filthy and corrupt communication, teaching them to sweare, blaspheme, and use all manner of uncleane speeches'.[7] On this point John Aubrey relates that Sir John Danvers once told him that when he was a young man the main reason why the gentry were anxious that their sons should travel abroad was 'to weane them from their acquaintance and familiarity with the Serving men: for then Parents were so austere and grave that the sonnes must not be company for their Father; and some company man must have'.[8]

Some country squires were considered to be exemplary masters. When Sir Hugh Portman of Orchard Portman in Somerset was laid to rest in 1629 the minister testified in his funeral sermon that he had been a 'munificent and open-handed Master'.[9] At the funeral of Sir Thomas Lucy of Charlecote in Warwickshire, who died in 1640, the minister commented that 'An house-full of Servants have lost, not a Master but a Phisitian; who made (as I am informed) their sicknesse his, and his physick and cost theirs'.[10] In his book on Hertfordshire Sir Henry Chauncy singled out his contemporary Sir Charles Caesar of Bennington, who died in 1694, as a model employer in the way he managed his household. According to his account Sir Charles

> was very regular in his Life, and orderly in his Family, which made the Lives of his Servants very easie, and his House very quiet, never repremanding a Servant oftner than once, and if the Party offended again, he was silently discharged without Noise or Notice of his Displeasure: this created in them an Awe and a great Observance to him; he was very generous to all whom he employed, but seldom pardoned a Slight to his Person or a Contempt of his Business.[11]

Sir Henry Slingsby the Yorkshire diarist appears to have treated the short-comings of his servants with an even greater degree of tolerance. In 1639 he wrote that at his chief mansion, Red House, no fewer than five cooks had come and gone over a relatively short period; that most of them had been excessively fond of drink; and that on occasion they had gone missing for several days at a time. Even so, he went on,

> I never part'd with any of them till I made them as glad to be gone as I would have them. I never grew passhionate with them, nor threaten'd them much if I found them serviceable otherwise, but still sought to win them from the habits of drinking, by fair means, willing to accept their future promise of amendment, which I took so often for satisfaction, and they every time less able to perform, the habit growing yet more upon them, that rather than they should not enjoy the vice of drunkeness with more quietness and freedom, they would at last be glad that I would take occasion to turn them away.[12]

If some gentlemen were good masters, at least by the standards of the time, there were others who governed their servants in a distinctly autocratic manner. Thomas Dutton of Dutton in Cheshire, who died in 1614, was commended by the preacher at his funeral for the tight discipline which he had maintained in his household. His servants, it was stressed, were dutiful and diligent 'both for his credit and his profite; he abhorred idlenesse in his servants . . . he appointed them such offices and imploiments that every one in his house had either a sweating brow or a working braine'. To judge from his account books Sir Cecil Bishop of Parham in Sussex (Pl. 67) was a man of the same kidney. While it was not unusual for the head of a household to pay the poll tax levied on his servants he took a very different view of the matter. In 1690 the housekeeper, the cook, the butler and other servants who had gone with him to London were assessed at 12d per head for poll tax purposes and Sir Cecil decided that it was entirely appropriate that these sums should be deducted from their wages. As revealed in the accounts for 1690 and 1691 he also considered the abatement of wages to be a fitting punishment for various breaches (some of them extremely trivial) of his strict disciplinary code. The cook was fined on several occasions for not stuffing a shoulder of veal, for not roasting the beef and (more mysteriously) 'on account of a pudding'. Other offences which were dealt with in the same way included drunkenness, time wasting on journeys and unauthorised absences. In lists recording the hiring of servants many of the names have the bare annotation 'dismissed'. So rapid was the turnover of staff that in the years 1690 to 1694 Sir Cecil had six cooks, five butlers, six gardeners, three coachmen and five postillions.[13]

In country houses generally servants could be sacked for a variety of reasons, including stealing, persistent drunkenness, disobedience, incompetence and chronic indolence. In an estate book of Sir Clement Fisher of Great Packington in Warwickshire there is an account written by his steward, Thomas Harding, of the dismissal of a cook, Thomas Brickelbanck. On 16 March 1676 Brickelbanck sought permission from his master to go to Coventry but Sir Clement turned down the request, 'knowing his way which was to borrow money or to take things upon trust and promise it should bee paid when hee received his wages and had non to receive'. Brickelbanck went nevertheless and on his return Sir Clement told him that he was dispensing with his services. Among other things, this meant that he automatically forfeited

possession of a house and grounds which he held from his master so long as he was employed at Packington Hall. On Sunday 19 March an announcement was made in the parish church to the effect that no one should lend him money. The following day he departed, leaving behind his wife and four children. On 21 March Sir Clement instructed his steward to take two men with him as witnesses and inform Mrs Brickelbanck that she should immediately give up the grounds which had been assigned to her husband and that she would have to vacate the house on Midsummer Day. The meeting, however, did not go exactly according to plan: in a spirited response the poor woman declared that 'shee would take this for noe warning' unless she had it from the mouth of Sir Clement himself.[14] Exceptionally, the dismissal of a servant could have the most far-reaching consequences for the family. When Sir Thomas Gascoigne of Barnbow Hall in Yorkshire (Pl. 68) found himself on trial in 1680 on a charge of high treason it was a predicament which had largely been brought about by two former servants who had accused him of participating in a Catholic conspiracy. Both men had been sacked for gross misconduct: Robert Bolron, who had been manager of the Gascoigne coalmines, for misappropriating funds for which he had been responsible and Lawrence Mowbray, who had been employed as a footman, for stealing money and jewellery. In the event Sir Thomas was acquitted.[15]

67. Parham House, Sussex.

68. Sir Thomas Gascoigne (on the right) and his brother John, Abbot of Lambspring. Painting by an unknown artist (Lotherton Hall, Yorkshire).

When the Wyrleys of Hamstead Hall in Staffordshire had a minor servant problem they little thought that it would culminate in Star Chamber proceedings. In July 1616 Knightley Wyrley, the wife of Humphrey Wyrley, felt obliged to write to the mother of one of her maidservants, Susan Holland, who had sorely tried her patience. Susan, she told her, was 'verie negligent and slothfull and I have often admonyshed her of it by faire meanes to amend but because I sawe it did her noe good I sought to reforme it with a little wand'. As a result Mrs Bridget Eyre (who was a friend of the Hollands) had been spreading stories about her cruelty, as she represented it, in the town of Birmingham and had also accosted some of her other servants in the streets there. It was not clear to her, she went on, 'what trust is comytted to Mrs Eyre of your daughter but she must not controll nor teache me what I have to doe'. She would have been willing for the sake of her parents to allow Susan to complete a full year's service 'and to take paynes with her to doe her good, but since there is suche adoe thereof I am a wearie of it and would intreate you to send for her home'. According to a Star Chamber bill in the name of Humphrey and Knightley Wyrley the next development was the arrival at Hamstead Hall of a party consisting of Richard Holland, who was Susan's brother, their sister Joyce, who was accompanied by her husband, and the garrulous Bridget Eyre. Humphrey Wyrley, who was a magistrate, was away from home on official duty and in response to their clamours his wife came down from her chamber to meet them. Almost immediately a quarrel broke out and Bridget Eyre 'forgetting her sexe and all womanhood or Civility laid violent hands' on Knightley Wyrley and scratched her cheeks while Richard Holland threatened to stab one of the servants who came to her assistance.

The defendants, for their part, offered a rather different version of the episode. Mrs Wyrley, it was claimed, had assaulted Mrs Eyre 'and pulled her band from her necke and rent her gowne and did otherwise greatlie abuse her'.[16]

The financial obligations of the country gentry in respect of their servants consisted of the payment of wages, the supply of liveries and the provision of food, drink and accommodation. The system of wage regulation (involving maximum rather than minimum rates) which had been introduced under the provisions of the Statute of Artificers of 1563 applied to servants in husbandry but not in the main to household servants or other categories of outdoor staff.[17] In theory therefore a country squire had a free hand in determining the wages of most of his full-time employees though in practice he was forced to take at least some account of market conditions in the neighbourhood and indeed in London if his recruiting activities extended so far. As a rule the estate steward (who is the subject of a later chapter) was the highest paid of all the servants. Before the time of the Civil War the wages of male cooks were usually below £10 a year while those of butlers, gardeners and coachmen tended to be well below. After the Restoration there is evidence of an all-round increase in wages but as the following table illustrates the wages of particular types of servants could vary widely:

Servants' Wages, 1660–1700: The Broad Parameters

male servants	*annual wages(£)*
cook	4 to 25
butler	3 to 10
gardener	4 to 20
coachman	3 to 10
female servants	
housekeeper	6 to 10
cook maid	3 to 9

Exceptionally, Alexander Popham of Littlecote in Wiltshire was prepared to pay £40 a year for the services of a new cook who came down from London in July 1699. Mr Thrift, as he was called, was already sufficiently wealthy to be able to employ his own maidservant.[18]

A clearer picture of the pay relativities between one type of servant and another can be obtained from the accounts of individual families. At the time of his death in 1669 Sir William Drake of Shardeloes in Buckinghamshire had a total of nineteen servants. Among these employees the estate steward was receiving £40 a year, the butler and the coachman £8 a year each and the gardener £12 a year while the wages of the maidservants ranged from £1 10s 0d to £5 a year.[19] Some twenty years later Sir Cecil Bishop of Parham in Sussex was paying £30 a year to his estate steward, £20 a year to the cook, £10 a year to the butler, £12 a year to the gardener, £9 a year to the coachman, £10 a year to the housekeeper and £3 a year each to two housemaids.[20] In the northern counties the wages of household servants were generally lower than those in the counties of south-east England. In the early 1690s the wages bill of Sir Thomas Haggerston of Haggerston in Northumberland included £8 a year for the housekeeper, who was a relative, and £3 a year each for the butler and cook maid. None of the other servants received more than £5 a year.[21]

Wages were sometimes paid on a quarterly but more usually on a half-yearly basis, at Lady Day and Michaelmas. One of the points stressed by Robert Cleaver and William Gouge when discussing the obligations of employers was that servants must be given their wages when they fell due.[22] While many of the gentry were punctilious in this respect there were some squires like William Morley of Glynde in Sussex and William Cary of Clovelly in Devon who thought nothing of delaying payment for two years or more.[23] In a few cases at least this was occasioned by severe financial difficulties. Thomas Danby of Thorpe Perrow in Yorkshire had inherited an estate worth over £2000 a year but it was heavily encumbered and an attempt to put up the rents led to the departure of many of the tenants. Following his murder in London in 1667 his widow wrote that he had not paid any of his servants 'for some three or foure yeares together'.[24]

For a country squire the wages bill for his servants could represent a significant, though by no means a predominant, element of his expenditure. The following table, which relates to the wages of full-time servants, covers a selection of families with incomes of £1000 a year and upwards:

Annual Wages Bills[25]

family	year	total sum per annum (£)
Caryll of West Harting, Sussex	1632	97
Barrington of Hatfield Priory, Essex	1640	113
Smyth of Long Ashton, Somerset	1641	100
Pelham of Halland House, Sussex	1641/2	138
Willoughby of Risley, Derbyshire	1653	200
Hawksworth of Hawksworth, Yorkshire	1658	59
Pelham of Halland House, Sussex	1660/1	224
Gage of West Firle, Sussex	1680	135
Throckmorton of Coughton, Warwickshire	1684	122
Clifton of Clifton, Nottinghamshire	1686	260

The wearing of livery clothes, which was a common practice in the larger households, not only ensured that the servants were well turned out but was also an important factor in the promotion of a corporate spirit. The Stapletons of Carlton in Yorkshire dressed their servants in blue; the Tichbornes of Tichborne in Hampshire favoured dark green as their livery colour; and the Cholmleys of Whitby in Yorkshire and the Bonds of Peckham in Surrey had a preference for grey.[26] In some families, however, the livery colour appears to have varied according to the type of function. The accounts of Sir John Pelham of Halland House in Sussex record the expenditure of £106 12s 0d on liveries in 1660, including £26 6s 0d for livery lace for the blue suits, £12 10s 8d for black and grey material for the suits of the footboys and £1 14s 4d for two yards of grey cloth for the huntsman.[27] This level of expenditure was rather out of the ordinary even for a family as wealthy as the Pelhams. More typical was the spending pattern of another Sussex landowner, Sir John Gage of West Firle, who paid £11 3s 7d for liveries in 1679 and £30 17s 1d in 1680.[28]

On occasion a servant might be given money in lieu of the livery which his master had undertaken to provide. In his accounts John Kendall, who served as steward to Sir Thomas Barrington of Hatfield Priory in Essex, noted that in 1640 he received £2 10s 0d 'for the want of my livery for two yeares'.[29]

Besides the cost of wages and liveries there was the expenditure involved in the provision of food and drink. In the seventeenth century this tended to be a hidden cost which was not readily quantifiable, partly because it was subsumed within the general housekeeping expenses and partly because of the contribution made by the home farm. Nevertheless there is some evidence which reveals contemporary perceptions about the matter. In his will, which was drawn up in 1682, Sir Robert Carr of Aswarby in Lincolnshire expressed the wish that the trustees he had nominated should employ John Burslem to manage the estate and that besides a salary of £50 a year he should be allowed £10 a year for his diet if he had to make his own arrangements. A decade later Francis Basset, a Devonshire squire seated at Heanton Punchardon, gave direction that annuities of £15 each should be paid to two of his servants but with the caveat that they should only receive £10 if they were provided with diet and lodging at Heanton Court.[30] In the light of such evidence it is clear that the expenditure on food and drink for the servants must often have represented a substantial addition to the wages bill.

On a journey which she made into Berkshire that indefatigable traveller Celia Fiennes visited Coleshill House (which had been built for Sir George Pratt in the Commonwealth period) and noted approvingly that on each side of the gallery there were 'severall garret roomes for servants furnished very neate and genteele'.[31] In the country houses of the gentry the accommodation provided for the servants consisted of a number of chambers or garrets, in some cases as many as a dozen or more, which on the evidence of probate and other kinds of inventories were rarely so well-appointed as to justify such unqualified praise. On the other hand, there were various types of servant who enjoyed the privilege of occupying single rooms which were often better furnished than the communal bedrooms. These included in particular the steward, the clerk, the housekeeper, the bailiff who had responsibilities in the immediate neighbourhood, the butler, the cook, the gardener, the coachman, the groom, the huntsman and the falconer. According to an inventory of Hunstanton Hall, the Norfolk seat of the L'Estrange family, which was carried out in 1670 the steward's chamber contained a bedstead with a canopy, a feather bed with a bolster, pillow, blanket and coverlet, a rug, a chair, five stools, two little trunks, two chests, an old pair of virginals, a fire 'sifter' and tongs, a close stool and a lantern.[32]

Male servants of the inferior sort were housed in dormitory accommodation. Where farm labourers were employed on a full-time basis they were often lodged separately from the servingmen. At the same time it was customary for the footboys to be given their own chamber. As a general rule the ordinary kind of menservants were accommodated in unheated and sparsely furnished rooms which were situated in the upper storey of the house or over the stables or other outbuildings. Their beds were of two types: the half-headed bed which had no tester or canopy and the truckle bed which was a low bed equipped with wheels.

A personal maid usually had a room of her own which was adjacent to her mistress's chamber. Katherine Palmer, who served in this capacity in the house of a Surrey landowner, Sir Edmund Bowyer of Camberwell, actually owned the furniture in the room which she occupied. An inventory of her possessions which Sir Edmund, who acted as her executor, submitted for probate purposes in 1663 lists, among other things, a wainscot chest, a chest of drawers, a table and a bedstead; and in her will she bequeathed some of these items to his daughter Margaret.[33] Generally, however, the maidservants were housed in communal quarters which were not markedly superior in any respect to those of the servingmen. The maids' chamber at Bramshill House in Hampshire was probably of a rather higher standard than most. In 1634 the contents of this chamber (which would normally have had four occupants) consisted of two half-headed bedsteads, two feather beds with bolsters and blankets, five damask chests, two trunks, two stills, a pair of iron andirons (indicating that there was a fireplace), three linen wheels, 'one bathing tubbe', a table, a cupboard, a reel for winding thread, three rugs and two standing candlesticks.[34] Not long after this the Zouch family sold the Bramshill estate and made Woking House in Surrey their principal residence. In February 1664 Jane Greethurst, a servant at Woking House, wrote a letter to her friend Mary Stotcher which affords us a tantalising glimpse of conditions in the maids' chamber there. The latter had until recently been a fellow servant and following her departure (she related) ' my Lady doe spake very well of you and doe give you A verry Good report'. After conveying the good wishes of the rest of the servants she went on

> ffor my part I am not sattisfyed in my mind whether I were best to goe or stay. I have been soe much alone since I lost your good company which have troubled me very much; I have never laught when I was in Bed since you went away ffor I have noe body to spake to, neither was I warme in my Bed till I put on my Stockinges. I am not troubled now to provide a Chayre ffor I doe not thinke my Bedfellow which I have now good enough to sit in my Chayre.[35]

Before the time of the Civil War it was unusual for the servants to have their own dining-room: generally they ate either in the great hall or the kitchen. One of the earliest references to a servants' hall occurs in 1654 when an inventory was carried out at Aston Hall, the Warwickshire mansion which Sir Thomas Holte had completed in the reign of Charles I.[36] During the latter part of the century such references become more frequent. There were servants' halls or dining-rooms at Orchard House, Orchard Wyndham in Somerset, Charborough House in Dorset, Broadlands and The Vyne in Hampshire, Aldermaston House and Bessels Leigh House in Berkshire, Shardeloes in Buckinghamshire, Ambrosden House and Yarnton Manor in Oxfordshire, Lilford Hall in Northamptonshire, Welham Hall in Leicestershire, Markeaton Hall in Derbyshire and Belton House in Lincolnshire.[37] Significantly, most of these houses had been built either since the Civil War or shortly before and in some cases at least the introduction of a servants' hall must have been occasioned by the new design concept which transformed the great hall into a stylish entrance lobby. In 1664 the servants' hall at Aldermaston House, the seat of the Forster family, contained a large table, a form, a side cupboard, two 'old turkey chaires', an elbow chair, two Turkey work stools and a candlestick. At Yarnton Manor in 1685 the servants' hall was not so well furnished but the walls were adorned with six old pictures of horses.[38] Exceptionally, the Drake family at Shardeloes also had a special room which was described in 1669 as 'the Sick man's Chamber' and in 1698 as the room 'for the Servants that are Sicke'.[39]

As might be expected, it was regarded as self-evident that the linen provided for the servants would not be of the same fine quality as that which was used by the squire and his family. When the personal effects of Sir Edward Monins of Waldershare in Kent were inventoried in 1666 it was noted that they included fifteen servants' tablecloths and twelve servants' towels.[40] Similarly, an inventory compiled in 1685 following the death of Sir Willoughby D'Ewes of Stowlangtoft in Suffolk lists thirty pairs of servants' sheets which were appraised at £7 10s 0d and five coarse tablecloths for servants which were judged to be worth 7s 6d.[41]

Over and above their wages the servants in a country house could expect to receive gratuities when their master entertained visitors. In 1658 Sir John Pelham the Sussex landowner went on a journey into northern England with the object of seeing his relations there and in the course of his travels meticulously observed the custom of rewarding the servants at the houses where he stayed. As recorded in his accounts he gave £3 12s 6d at Burton Hall in Lincolnshire, £3 10s 0d at Rufford Abbey in Nottinghamshire and £3 8s 6d at the houses of the Wilbraham family in Cheshire and Staffordshire.[42] In September 1697 Paul Foley of Stoke Edith in Herefordshire played host to his friend Sir Edward Harley who was no doubt interested in the state of progress on his new house. At Sir Edward's departure his servant William Thomas made a note of the gratuities which had been handed out: 2s 6d each to the butler, the coachman and a chambermaid, 2s 2d to the cook and 3s 6d to the groom.[43]

While the death of a squire inevitably aroused anxieties about the future of his household there was at least some prospect that he would have made bequests to the servants. In the main the gentry did not forget their servants when they drew up their wills, though there were wide divergences of view about what was fitting. Occasionally all the full-time servants were individually named among the recipients of legacies but usually a more selective approach was adopted. Those who were frequently singled out in this way included the steward, the butler, the cook and the personal attendants; men and women who had faithfully served the family for many years; and the servants who were looking after the testator during his final illness. In such cases a legacy could take various forms: some landed property, a lease on easy terms, a life annuity, a sum of money and even the squire's clothes.

Life annuities, which in effect were a kind of pension, were only rarely granted on a significant scale. In 1675 William Dutton of Sherborne in Gloucestershire, who had an estate worth over £6000 a year, charged it with annuities totalling £91 a year which were to be paid to twelve servants whom he regarded as particularly deserving.[44] Sir John Borlase of Bockmer House in the Buckinghamshire parish of Medmenham made provision in 1684 for the payment of annuities to ten servants. These ranged from £10 to £40 a year and represented a total charge of £190 on an estate revenue of £3500 a year.[45]

For the remainder of the servants (usually the majority) who were not individually named it was common practice to grant them legacies equating to their wages for six months, a year or two years, on the basis that these were over and above the wages which would be due to them as of right. Sometimes, however, this was subject to a caveat laying down a qualifying period of service. In 1613 Sir Thomas Vincent of Stoke D'Abernon in Surrey bequeathed a whole year's wages to those of his male staff who at the time of his death would have served in his household for at least seven years while in 1639 his son Sir Francis employed the same basic formula but with the exception that female servants were not specifically excluded.[46] When drawing up his will in 1624 Sir John Sydenham of Brympton in Somerset considered it appropriate to distinguish between three kinds of servants in determining the arrangements for the payment of legacies. The covenant servants in his household were to be given a year's wages besides their normal wages while the other household servants 'with whome I have made noe contracte for wages certaine' were to receive 20s each. The third category consisted of the outdoor servants 'which shalbe in my Liverye, or Service, at the tyme of my deathe'. Each servant of this type was to have a mourning cloak and a ring of gold costing 20s with the inscription *memento magistri*. The idea of such a ring was highly unusual but there was also a certain irony about it as may be judged from some of the comments which his kinsman Humphrey Sydenham felt at liberty to make in the course of the sermon which he preached at his funeral. 'His outward deportment', he told the congregation, was 'sowre and rough' and his passions 'somewhat windy and tempestuous'.[47]

On occasion the legacies distributed among the general body of servants took the form of straightforward cash payments which were entirely unrelated to their wages. These could be as modest as £1 per head but some testators were much more generous. In 1648 Richard Knightley, a Puritan squire who was seated at Fawsley in Northamptonshire, gave direction that the sum of £20 should be paid to every servant except those for whom separate provision had been made.[48] For his part Richard Winwood of Ditton Park in Buckinghamshire took the view that in such matters it was necessary to draw a distinction between the menservants and the female servants. In 1687 he stipulated in his will that the men should receive £20 per head and the women £10 per head.[49]

Now and again a will contains references to individual servants which hint at domestic problems whose precise nature can only be a matter for conjecture. Sir Nicholas Bacon of Shrubland Hall in Suffolk periodically amended his will in the light of new developments within his household. In the original version, which is dated 13 May 1686, he gave a legacy of £20 to Edward Inolds, the boy who waited on him. Subsequently, however, he cut him out of his will, describing him as 'that ungratefull rogue', and transferred the legacy to one of his women servants, Mary Radnall. In later additions he stressed that John Hanes was to have only his bare wages and not a farthing more if he was still serving him at the time of his death; reduced Mary Radnall's legacy to £5; and increased the legacies payable to two other female servants.[50] In

1697 Sir Richard Earle of Stragglethorpe in Lincolnshire named his servant Thomas Waller as a legatee, 'begging of him to be sober'. Waller was to receive £20 a year but this grant would be void if he married Mrs Moyle, one of the servants of Sir Richard's mother. Despite this proviso Mrs Moyle was given a legacy of £5.[51]

In the later Stuart period especially some of the wealthier gentry were prepared to make testamentary provision for their servants on a scale which obliged their executors to raise very substantial sums to meet this commitment. Apart from annuities Maurice Barrow of Barningham in Suffolk gave £649 in all; Sir Peter Wentworth of Lillingstone Lovell in Oxfordshire £1295; Sir Harbottle Grimston of Gorhambury House in Hertfordshire £460; and Sir William Portman of Orchard Portman in Somerset £760.[52] In a book published in 1644 Grimston had declared that ' if thy children and servants offend grievously, correct and chastise them severely'; on the other hand, he was described by a contemporary as 'an excellent Master to his Servants'.[53] Although Wentworth was descended from one of the Puritan leaders in the Elizabethan House of Commons he had a reputation for sexual promiscuity which had led Cromwell to call him 'a noted whoremaster'; nevertheless he rewarded some of his servants not only with money but with copies of Puritan sermons and other religious works.[54]

CHAPTER SEVEN

Estate Stewards

I n the seventeenth century many of the wealthier gentry in all parts of the country employed stewards to manage their estates.[1] Although a major landowner sometimes thought it prudent to act as his own steward this was no easy task in the case of a large estate which might include property in several counties. The practice of engaging an estate or land steward was already well established before the time of the Civil War but it became even more common after the Restoration. One reason for this development was a significant increase in the number of absentee landlords who resided for much of the year in their London town houses. At the same time it may well have reflected the greater difficulties involved in estate management during the agricultural depression which prevailed in the latter part of the seventeenth century. In this situation the employment of an intermediary to deal with a recalcitrant tenantry had obvious attractions for the kind of landlord whose paramount concern was the preservation or enhancement of his estate revenue.[2]

In some cases the appointment of a steward was the product of special circumstances such as a decision by the head of a family to travel abroad for a time or the succession of a minor who was committed to the care of a guardian. In 1680 Sir Francis Hungate of Huddleston Hall in Yorkshire took himself off to the Continent, apparently as a result of allegations that he had been involved in a Catholic plot, and before his departure brought in John Simpson, who lived in the neighbouring town of Sherburn, to manage the estate during his absence. Sir Francis died in London after returning from the Continent and in a Chancery suit of 1685 his son, Sir Philip, claimed that Simpson had received some £1700 but had declined to render any accounts. In the light of this episode the young squire felt it necessary to seek advice from his cousin Sir John Reresby on such matters as how he could acquire knowledge of his yearly income without being cheated.[3] When a family with substantial landed possessions sustained a minority it was common practice for the guardian to delegate responsibility for them to a steward. One of the consequences of the abolition of the Court of Wards in 1646 was that the Court of Chancery eventually took on some of its functions. In the later Stuart period it was the responsibility of Chancery officials not only to endorse the appointment of a steward to look after a ward's estate but also to monitor his performance. In what was a typical document of its kind the Court decreed in 1668 that Mr Robert Guy should manage the estate which had descended from Sir Oliver St John of Woodford in Northamptonshire to his son and heir; that he should be allowed a salary of £20 a year; and that he should submit annual accounts of the receipts and disbursements.[4]

The estate steward was sometimes called the agent (which foreshadows modern usage), the receiver or even the bailiff (though bailiffs had much more limited functions). His basic duties were to manage the estate as efficiently as possible and, more specifically, to negotiate and draw up leases, to receive the rents, fines and other profits arising and to keep detailed accounts of the estate revenue and the associated expenditure. In addition, he was often responsible for superintending the activities of the home farm, purchasing livestock and selling timber and other commodities. According to a Chancery bill of 1659 Sir Robert Shirley of Staunton Harold in Leicestershire had employed Anthony Atkinson as his 'Chiefe agent' for many years and had entrusted him with receiving the rents and profits of his whole estate, contracting for and making leases to the tenants and 'the whole ordering and manageing of the said estate'. Similarly, the responsibilities of John Treis, who served as steward to the Carew family of Antony House in Cornwall in the latter part of the century, included such tasks as receiving the rents, making contracts for leases and disbursing money for cattle, corn and provisions for the family.[5] In the case of the larger estates the steward might be supported by several bailiffs who were mainly employed on rent collection. In 1688 Sir John Harpur of Calke in Derbyshire, who was then only an infant, owned an estate worth over £3000 a year which included property in Cheshire and Staffordshire. The management of this extensive patrimony required the services of a steward, John Harpur, who collected some of the Derbyshire rents himself; an assistant, Thomas Jackson, who was paid £20 a year for keeping accounts and drawing up rent-rolls; and six bailiffs who were responsible for gathering in the remainder of the rents.[6]

If the steward had no legal background the squire would often arrange for a lawyer to preside over the manorial courts, though this was not strictly necessary. The court steward (as he was sometimes called) received a fee for his services and might also have the opportunity to secure further remuneration as the family solicitor when there was legal business to be transacted. In his will, which was drawn up in 1633, Sir John Gage of West Firle in Sussex made it clear that he was anxious that Robert Pickering should continue both as steward of all the courts of his manors, hundreds and leets and as solicitor for causes relating to his estate.[7] During the reign of Charles II Alan Garway acted as steward of the manorial court at Harrow in Middlesex and was paid a fee of £2 on each occasion together with £1 for auditing the bailiff's accounts. In June 1679 we find him writing to the landlord, Sir James Rushout of Maylards Green in Essex, in an attempt to rectify a misunderstanding which had arisen. After acknowledging in formal language that the court books belonged to Sir James he added that 'as to the stewardshipp if yow shall please to Continue mee I shall Confesse my selfe further obliged'. In a draft reply which was probably identical with the final version Sir James observed

69. Swillington
Hall, Yorkshire.
Engraving by
Johannes Kip
(British Library,
Lansdowne MSS
898, fol. 65).

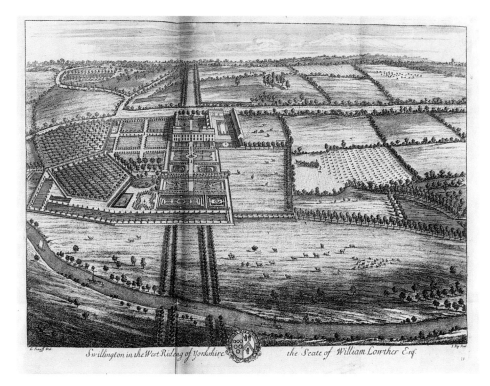

Swillington in the West Riding of Yorkshire   the Seate of William Lowther Esq.

that considering the friendship which had always existed between them he
had been surprised by what Garway had said to him about the court books at
their recent meeting. He went on to assure him, however, that 'as I have been
alwayes satisfyed with your management in the stewardship at Harrow I have
not the least mistrust but that I shall have reason to bee soe still, and therefore am very willing to continue it to you'.[8]

Besides his estate management duties the land steward might be called
upon to undertake a variety of other tasks, including the overall supervision
of the whole body of servants and the payment of their wages, the handling
of bills of all kinds, the maintenance of general expenditure accounts and the
raising of loans or lending of money at interest. John Mattison, who was Sir
Arthur Ingram's steward in Yorkshire, was responsible for overseeing his
building operations at York, Sheriff Hutton and Temple Newsam while
Francis Reeve performed a similar function on behalf of his master, Sir
Francis Throckmorton, during the rebuilding of Coughton Court in
Warwickshire.[9] In 1692 William Lowther entered into possession of the
Swillington estate in Yorkshire but shortly afterwards he and his wife went to
live in Bedfordshire where they remained for several years. During their
absence it was left to the steward, John Cockhill, to superintend a building
programme which involved the refurbishment and beautifying of Swillington
Hall (Pl. 69).[10]

Some stewards were drawn from the ranks of the minor gentry, others from
yeomen families or the urban middle classes. Although there were many who
styled themselves 'gentleman'[11] this was more often a reflection of their professional status, as they perceived it, than of their social origin. Exceptionally,
Nicholas Parker, who was the agent or steward of the Ferrers family of
Tamworth Castle, had his pedigree registered at the heraldic visitation of

Parker, of Tamworth.

K. 3, p. 156.

Hemlingford Hundred.   Warwick 7ᵉ Aug: 1683.

Taken from a Impression of a Seal produced by Mʳ Parker and referred himself to the Books of Kent or Essex. [*No colours given.* ? *Argent, a chevron Gules between three mullets Sable, on a chief Azure as many bucks' heads couped Or.*]

Edmund Parker of═Margaret daũr
Great Bloxwich in │ of . . . . Homer
Com̃ Staff: ob: circ: │ of Worcestersh:
ann: 1630.

2. William and | 1. Nicholas Par-═Joan daughter | 1. Eliz: mar- | 2. Alice mar-
3. John Officers | ker of Great │ of Jnᵒ Shep- | ried to Josias | ried to Cor-
in the Service | Bloxwich afore- │ herd of Wal- | Clarkson of | nelius Belli-
of His late | said obijt circa │ shall in com̃: | Langham Hall | son of Great
Majestie, died | ann: 1668 æt: 60 │ Staff: (and also | near Colches- | Bloxwich
unmarried. | et supra. │ sole heir). | ter in Essex. | aforsaid.

2. Joan and | 3. Eliz: wife of William | 4. Hannah wife of | 5. Margaret
Sarah died | Priest of Footherly in | Charles Baynton of | now living
unmarried. | paroch de Shenston in cõ | Tamworth Attorney | unmarried.
 | Staff: | at Law. |

Nicholas Parker of Tamworth═Sarah daũr: of Edward | 1. Alice wife of Edward
now living ætat: circ: 44 │ Parker sometime of yᵉ | Hincks of Walsall in
annoᵉ 1683. │ Borough of Derby. | com̃ Staff:

1. Edmond | 2. Nicholas | 3. William | 1. Sarah | 2. Dorothy | 3. Mary
æt: 8 ann: | æt: 6 añ: | æt: 2 et | æt: 12. | æt: 9 et | æt: 4 et
 | | ampl: | | ampl: | ampl:

Nich: Parker

70. The pedigree entered by Nicholas Parker at the heraldic visitation of Warwickshire in 1683 (*Harleian Society*, lxii, 1911).

Warwickshire in 1683 (Pls 70 and 71).[12] On the other hand, Richard Smethurst who served Sir John Crewe of Utkinton Hall in Cheshire was content to be described as 'yeoman' in legal documents[13]; and he was by no means unique in this respect.

The Prospect of
TAMWORTH
from the road on the South
East part of the towne.

71. Tamworth Castle, Warwickshire. A seventeenth-century print (Sir William Dugdale, *The Antiquities of Warwickshire*, second edition, 1730).

A number of families employed relatives as their stewards. Following the death of Sir James Altham, an Essex landowner who was seated at Mark Hall in Latton, the estate descended to his brother Leventhorpe. Since Leventhorpe Altham worked at East India House in London he decided in 1680 to appoint a steward and assigned this responsibility to his cousin Michael Altham, a clergyman who had been nominated by Sir James as one of the trustees of the estate. It was agreed that the latter should receive a salary of £50 a year; that he and his family should live at Mark Hall; and that he should take any profits which might arise from the gardens, orchards and pigeon house. In 1681 he was able to acquire the church living of Latton, which was in the gift of the Altham family, without having to forfeit the living of Eastwick in Hertfordshire which he already held.[14]

Relatively few stewards had been to Oxford, Cambridge or the Inns of Court, though it is significant that they were sometimes keen to send their sons there. Some lawyers were prepared to serve as estate stewards as well as court stewards but they were not particularly numerous. Perhaps the most distinguished of them was Samuel Eyre, a barrister of Lincoln's Inn, who was subsequently made a judge and honoured with a knighthood. For some years he acted as estate steward to his kinsman Sir Kingsmill Lucy of Faccombe in Hampshire and his son Sir Berkeley, an infant, who succeeded him in 1679. This, however, was an unusual arrangement: it is clear that his stewardship was very much a part-time activity and that his salary of £20 a year was no more than a modest addition to his income as a barrister.[15] More often the lawyer who was employed as an estate steward was a local attorney with limited financial prospects. In 1686 Sir William Kingsmill of Sydmonton in Hampshire persuaded Thomas Colnett, a Winchester attorney, to come and live with him and manage his estate. When Colnett made his will in December 1695 he was apparently no longer in Sir William's service but was anxious to put it on record that there was £400 owing to him from his former employer.[16] Richard Eare was an attorney who lived at Saltash in Cornwall. In his capacity as a public notary he witnessed the will of Sir John Carew in 1691 and this may possibly have been his first contact with the Carew family of Antony House. In 1698 he accepted an invitation from Sir John's widow to serve as steward of the family estate in succession to John Treis who had recently died. As steward he presided over the manorial courts as well as undertaking all the duties which his predecessor had performed. In 1705 Sir William Carew, who had just succeeded his brother, claimed in a Chancery suit that Eare had failed to account for any of the money he had received but he emphatically denied the allegation. When drawing up his will in 1707 Eare observed in the preamble that he had been moved to take this step by drafting the wills of others.[17]

Occasionally a steward was appointed from within the household. In a Chancery case of 1679 Dame Margaret Pratt, the widow of Sir George Pratt of Coleshill in Berkshire, responded angrily to a bill presented by John Bond who had served both her husband and herself as their estate steward. In his will Sir George had made bequests of £20 each to Bond, his wife Patience and his son John but Dame Margaret sought to demonstrate that his confidence had been misplaced. Bond, she recounted, had originally been 'a low and mean servant' who had attended on Sir George in his chamber and at meal times. As steward he had been systematically enriching himself at the expense of the estate. Although he had only been paid a salary of £12 a year in this capacity she claimed that he was now worth nearly £1000 a year whereas her own estate was daily decreasing.[18] During the reign of Charles II the Barringtons of Hatfield Priory in Essex had two stewards, John Hawkins and Tobias Hewitt, who had risen from the general body of household servants. In his younger days Hewitt had been Thomas Barrington's personal attendant both at the schools which he attended and at Trinity College, Cambridge. He had continued to serve him after his marriage to Lady Anne Rich in 1664 and had eventually been appointed as his steward with responsibility for an estate worth £2000 a year. In view of his long association with the Barrington family it is not surprising that he should have been deeply disturbed over the growing rift between his master and mistress. Writing to an associate of Lady Anne he suggested that if she was willing to live at Hatfield Broad Oak this would be very welcome to his master. 'I know' he went on, that 'my Lady hath a little avertion to the place but I wish with all my soule my Lady would forgett what's past . . . and appley herselfe' to Sir John (her father-in-law) 'with that obleigeing nature which whare her Ladyship pleased to bestowe it allways conquers'. By this time, however, there was no longer any possibility of a reconciliation.[19]

Some stewards were recruited from other households, though this does not appear to have been a common practice. In an Exchequer case of 1674 John Brewster, who was then employed as Sir John Hobart's estate steward at Blickling Hall, testified that he had previously worked for another Norfolk squire, John Coke of Holkham, as his house steward.[20] Hugh Phillips, who was appointed in 1696 as steward to John Caryll of West Harting in Sussex, had come from Warwickshire where he had served for nine years in the household of Francis Lord Carrington. His new employer (who had gone into exile with James II) was related to his former employer and both men were Catholics.[21]

Catholic squires had a need for stewards who were trustworthy in a religious as well as a financial sense. Some of their stewards were recusants, others may often have been conforming Catholics. Sir Philip Constable of Everingham in Yorkshire and his son Sir Marmaduke employed a kinsman, George Constable, who was presented for recusancy in 1664. In his will, which was drawn up in 1672, he left a considerable number of legacies. Among other things, he bequeathed his great grey mare to Sir Marmaduke; his dun colt to Lady Constable; his little grey mare to his young master Philip Constable; his new cloak to the Catholic chaplain, Christopher Bankes; and £1 to his good friend Mr Poskett who may be identified as Nicholas Postgate, another seminary priest. Nor did he forget his fellow servants: legacies of £3 each were bestowed on two female servants while the other fifteen servants received 10s each. At the same time he gave sums of money to several persons, including Sir Marmaduke's daughter Anne who was a nun at Louvain, with the intention that masses should be said for the 'comfort of my soule'.[22] In the reign of Charles II many of the leading Catholic families sought refuge abroad to escape the persecution which was being waged or threatened and

in these circumstances the position of steward assumed even greater importance. In 1678 Sir Charles Shelley of Michelgrove in Sussex obtained a
licence authorising him and his son John to travel to the Continent, ostensi-
bly for health reasons, and in his absence the steward, William Jackson, was
in effect the family's chief representative in England. Shortly before his master's death in 1681 Jackson explained in an affidavit that Sir Charles could not
possibly be guilty of recusancy as he was living in France.[23]

As illustrated in the following table[24] the salaries paid to estate stewards in
the seventeenth century varied widely but were mainly in the £20 to £40 a
year range:

£ a year	number of stewards
100	2
90	1
80	1
70	1
60	4
50	5
40	8
30	8
20	18
10	6
5	1
	55

Now and again a man of wealth might specify a particular salary level in his
will. In 1682 a Norfolk squire, William Windham of Felbrigg, gave direction
to his executors that during his son's minority they should employ 'some
knowing person' to manage the estate, allowing him not more than £40 a year,
while in 1690 Sir John Maynard of Gunnersbury in Middlesex stipulated that
his steward Thomas Bradford, 'whome I have allwayes found diligent and
faithfull', should be paid a salary of £80 a year.[25] Although it was not unusual
for a steward to serve the same family for a considerable period the award of
a pay increase appears to have been a comparatively rare event. For reasons
which remain obscure Robert Constable, who served as steward to the
Pelhams of Halland House in Sussex, found himself in the unhappy position
of having to accept a pay cut. For some years he received a salary of £20 a year
but this was reduced to £15 a year as from 25 March 1624 when the accounts
contain the cryptic entry 'my owne wages now abated'.[26]

At the same time a steward's income did not necessarily consist only of his
salary and some associated perquisites. Not infrequently his employer was
prepared to grant him a lease of property on favourable terms. In 1693 Sir
John Lowther of Whitehaven in Cumberland appointed William Gilpin, a
lawyer, as his steward in succession to Thomas Tickell who had recently died
and one of Gilpin's first actions was to ask his master to allow him to take over
the leases which had been made to his predecessor: 'And for the lands and
tyths that Mr Tickell held, because they will be necessary for me, I shall be
your farmer for them (if your honour pleases) upon his terms'.[27] In addition,
there was the possibility that a steward who was highly regarded might

receive a handsome legacy under the provisions of his master's will. In this respect the gentry appear, on the whole, to have been more generously inclined after the Civil War period than before, perhaps because they were becoming more heavily dependent on their stewards. In 1659 Sir Henry Lee of Ditchley in Oxfordshire bequeathed £500, together with a chestnut mare, to John Cary (who was described as one of the few persons he could trust) and £200 to his wife Jane. After Sir Henry's death Cary continued to serve the Lee family in the dual capacity of steward and trustee at a salary of £30 a year.[28] In 1663 Edward Scott of Scot's Hall in Kent gave his steward William Hartridge a number of legacies: £220 in cash, some lands at Lympne, a quantity of silver plate and all his printed books.[29] When John Every of Cothay in Somerset drew up his will in 1679, shortly before his death, he made provision for the payment of £500 to Edward Ford 'for and in respect of the faithfull service which he . . . hath as my steward heretofore done and performed for me'. In doing so he took into account the fact that he had not previously rewarded him apart from the grant of a tenement in reversion. In 1685, however, the Court of Chancery was informed that the legacy was still unpaid even though Ford had been appointed as one of the trustees.[30]

Some stewards acquired sufficient wealth, not necessarily from fraudulent practices, to enable them to purchase freehold property for themselves. In 1663 John Kendall, who had served for over 30 years as steward to the Barringtons of Hatfield Broad Oak in Essex, bought the neighbouring manor of Bassingbourn and settled there with his family. The following year he signalled his emergence as a country gentleman by having his pedigree registered at the heraldic visitation of the county.[31] Another of the Barrington stewards, Tobias Hewitt, does not appear to have had the same kind of aspirations but he was nevertheless a man of some substance who was able to lend his master, Thomas Barrington, a total of £1100. Hewitt died in 1686 while still employed as steward and in his will, which was drawn up two days before his death, left £1000 to his wife and a number of legacies to his relatives and friends and his servants John Reynolds and Diana Pettit.[32]

About the beginning of 1634 Sir William Savile, who was seated at Thornhill in Yorkshire, received a letter from his uncle Lord Deputy Wentworth in which he offered comprehensive advice on the management of his affairs. Among other things, he told him that he considered his steward, Henry Cookson, to be an honest man, though churlish and proud natured, but that it would be prudent to examine his accounts on a weekly basis.[33] While such close monitoring might have been necessary in the particular circumstances it was a highly unusual procedure. As a general rule the steward submitted his accounts of income and expenditure either once a year or at six-monthly intervals. If his master was satisfied he annotated the accounts to that effect and appended his signature alongside that of his steward. If, however, there was a deficit or the revenue was less than anticipated the steward's performance would inevitably come under scrutiny, though he could often invoke extenuating factors. Sir Henry Slingsby the Yorkshire diarist wrote of his steward Thomas Richardson that he was

> a man of great integrity and of indefatigable pains and industry who formerly had serv'd my father. I do trust him with the receiving of all my

rents, and what monys he pays to me I give him an acquittance of it, and but once a year receive his accounts. I never yet had cause to doubt of any false deeling: for he always would make his accounts streight to a farthing: if he did misreckon he tooke the loss to himself.

After Sir Henry's execution in 1658 Richardson continued as steward. In December 1668 we find him presenting a revenue account for the year 1667 on which he subsequently noted that there was a surplusage of £12 8s 5d due to the accountant (that is, himself) 'which is payd to him'.[34]

In discharging his responsibilities a steward often felt obliged to seek directions from his master before committing himself to a particular course of action; and if his master was absent for any significant length of time he was usually expected to keep him fully informed of developments at home.[35] In a letter dispatched from London in March 1687 a Devonshire squire, William Cary of Clovelly, left his steward, John Tawton, in no doubt that he took it amiss that he had heard nothing from him for five weeks: 'I should have thought myself very happy If I could have had the favour of a lyne or two in a month's tyme. But I hope 'tis your over zeale for my service that keeps you soe much employed that you cannot afford one Letter in Answeare.'[36] During the 1680s Sir John Reresby of Thrybergh in Yorkshire was frequently in London where he kept up a regular correspondence with his steward Thomas Robotham, mainly but not exclusively on estate matters. On one occasion Robotham informed him that he had been very ill but hoped to have the arrears of rent cleared by the next rent day; on another that he had turned the miller out of his house. In May 1684 he thought it worth mentioning that he and his wife were proposing to call their baby John, clearly as a gesture of respect to his master. From time to time he was involved in the recruitment of servants: in March 1686 he was writing that he had found a suitable person for the position of butler who was willing to do everything he could 'to give Content' but that he was still looking out for a new keeper for the park.[37]

During the 1660s Sir Andrew Henley of Bramshill in Hampshire was continually dispatching written instructions to his steward, Thomas Rawlinson, who was based in the West Country. Rawlinson was not only responsible for managing his large estates there but was also assigned the task of superintending a building programme at Henley House in Somerset and other houses belonging to the family. Sir Andrew, who often styled himself 'your loving master', issued directions on a variety of matters but was sometimes dissatisfied with the replies which he received. In May 1660 he told Rawlinson that there was not a line in his most recent letter 'in answeare of my last to yow, soe that I understand not what is done or not done of what I writt last. I pray make up the accompt with the Tennants . . . without more adoe, and send mee a coppie of it forthwith'. On another occasion he was fussing about the materials for the building work at Henley House: 'in your next acquaint me how the bricks are served against the weather at Henley and get them all brought into the great new seller and buttery, that roome will hold them and keep them dry; let all the Hamden stone about the House bee brought together.'[38]

Despite his exalted status within the household the steward usually took care to display all the deference and respect which was considered to be due from a servant to his master. In 1641 Nicholas Denham, who was steward to the Cokes of Melbourne in Derbyshire, wrote in a letter to Sir John Coke that 'I am not negligent in your buisines nor will be, but shall be ever redy to use all diligence in your affaires soe long as you shall thinke me worthy of your service and imployment'.[39] In normal circumstances, however, the relationship between a steward and his master was often harmonious and even cordial, particularly when a mutual feeling of confidence developed in the fullness of time.

In a few households it was the squire's wife who exercised an oversight of the activities of the steward, either because she was the dominant partner or because her husband was incapacitated or heavily engaged in other matters. During the 1630s Dame Judith Barrington, the strong-minded wife of Sir Thomas Barrington, signed the accounts kept by the steward, John Kendall, and other servants. Instructions which she issued to Kendall before his departure for London in 1632 covered such matters as the receipt of rents and the payment of debts and interest. In addition, she considered that there was a need for legal action: 'I think', she told him, 'it wear very fitt you gott your Master to begin a suite with John Smyth about his spoyling Cottingham Woods'. Besides all the business which Kendall was required to transact in London he was entrusted with the task of buying a new suit for one of the Barrington children. In the course of a subsequent legal dispute in which Kendall was involved Lady Barrington commented that he 'may Challenge all the money he laid out for my husband; I being the manager of all things and usually what he did was by my Command as from my husband'.[40] In Suffolk Dame Priscilla D'Ewes, the wife of Sir Willoughby D'Ewes of Stowlangtoft, also took on responsibility for clearing the steward's accounts. During the years 1676 to 1678 John Colby was submitting accounts of his disbursements on a monthly basis for her inspection.[41]

In the main the gentry appear to have been satisfied with the performance of their stewards even though it could prove difficult to get in all the rents when economic conditions were unfavourable. Many stewards served for periods of twenty years or more and few were dismissed except for gross misconduct. In a Chancery case of 1627 Sir Edward Baynton of Bromham in Wiltshire alleged that the sacking of Michael Tidcombe, 'who had bin a long tyme employed and trusted' by his father 'in his estate and affayres', had been engineered by Sir John Danvers and others in order to further their plans for depriving him of part of his inheritance.[42] Some testators lavished praise as well as material rewards on their stewards. In a codicil which he added to his will in 1659 a Suffolk landowner, James Calthorpe of Ampton, commended the honesty and fidelity of his steward Ralph Newman who for many years had been responsible for managing his estate and had always given him a just and faithful account of the rents, issues and profits which he had received.[43] Not infrequently a steward was nominated by his master as one of the executors or trustees of the estate or alternatively was employed by them as their manager. On the other hand, it was sometimes claimed in litigation that a steward had been lax or inefficient. When Sir Robert Bolles of Scampton in Lincolnshire drew up his will in 1663 he made generous provision for his steward Thomas Smith (who was a kinsman of his) and appointed him as one of the trustees of his estate. In a Chancery case which was heard the following year Sir John Bolles the son took a very different view of Smith's capabilities. Smith, he related, 'had not beene soe good a Steward for his . . . father in his life tyme as he might have beene'. At the time of Sir John's marriage he had certified that the manor of Scampton was worth £1000 a year but in his accounts for the period 1657 to 1663 the receipts which he had recorded had fallen far short of this. Sir John was anxious to take on responsibility for managing the trust estate himself in order to pay his father's debts and raise marriage portions rather than 'leave it to so loose a way of management'. In one of the depositions which were taken it was alleged that Smith had been entertaining his friends rather too lavishly while his master was living in London but there were others who maintained that Sir Robert had regarded him as completely trustworthy. Mary Watkinson, who had formerly been a servant at Scampton Hall, testified that she had heard Sir Robert say that 'I beleeve my Cozen Smith is as just and carefull in my bussines as any man can bee'.[44] As we have seen, John Every the Somerset landowner thought very highly of his steward Edward Ford and named him as a trustee. In 1686, however, his record as steward came under attack: it was said that the estate revenue had suffered from his 'ill management' and that in particular he had granted leases and copyhold tenancies at low rates.[45]

More serious even than the issue of managerial competence was the spectre of the corrupt steward whose sole or primary objective was self-enrichment. During the course of the seventeenth century there were at least a dozen lawsuits in which stewards employed by gentry families were accused of dishonesty and in some cases of associated offences of graver import. Christopher Danby of Farnley in Yorkshire was a Catholic squire who had inherited an estate worth some £1500 a year. During his minority a Catholic kinsman who was also called Christopher Danby was appointed steward and he continued to hold this position until dismissed in 1608. Two years later his former employer complained in a Star Chamber bill that he had defrauded him of £7000 by misappropriating most of the rents and profits of his estate and that he had allowed his houses 'to decaie and to fall to utter ruin'. In addition, he and his assistant William Clarke had attempted to break up his marriage by inventing stories of adultery and projected murder. As a result of these insinuations he and his wife had lived apart for a time but had eventually been reconciled. For good measure the hapless squire claimed that there had been a plot to murder him and that one of the confederates was a seminary priest.[46] According to a Chancery bill of 1662 William Bockenham had behaved no less ruthlessly as steward to Thomas Lake of Great Stanmore in Middlesex, a young man of weak judgment who could easily be 'wrought upon'. Bockenham, it was alleged, had conspired with others to strip him of his estate and in order to further their aims they had encouraged him to indulge himself in heavy drinking. Even worse he had provided him with rooms and bedding 'where severall persons had lately before bin sicke of the small pox'; and in the event Lake himself had died of the disease.[47]

In 1668 Sir John Howe of Little Compton in Gloucestershire was involved in litigation with his steward Thomas Wolley. Wolley, he told the Court of

Chancery, was a person of lowly origin who had initially been taken into his household as a menial servant but who had managed to acquire considerable knowledge of the law. As his steward he had been responsible for keeping some of the manorial courts, gathering in all the rents, issues and profits of his estate (which amounted to over £4000 a year) and negotiating leasehold and copyhold tenancies. It had been agreed that Wolley should submit his accounts once a year but when Sir John began to grow old and infirm he was no longer able to scrutinise them in detail. Seizing his opportunity, Wolley had embezzled large sums of money and falsified the accounts in order to conceal the nature of his activities. In his response Wolley denied that he had behaved improperly and offered to make his accounts for the years 1650 to 1667 available for independent examination.[48]

From 1670 until his death in 1676 Sir John Armytage of Kirklees Hall in Yorkshire employed Walter Curwen as his steward and relied upon him 'to receave his rents and to sell his woods, corne and Cattle and to receave the mony for the same'. In 1683 his son Sir Thomas began legal proceedings against Curwen. After his father's death (he related) he had asked him to make his books and accounts available for scrutiny but before they had been fully examined he had insisted on taking them away. From this partial inspection it had appeared that Curwen had received £8628 19s 5d and disbursed £8577 7s 3d; in fact there was much more due from him 'for that he hath omitted to charge himself with several summes received, and hath charged more in his disbursements then he really disbursed as would plainely appeare by the said books and Accountts if produced'. Although Curwen maintained that he only owed £52 15s 4d he was ordered to deliver up all the relevant documents to a Master in Chancery.[49]

Given the nature of his responsibilities it was never likely that the estate steward would be a popular figure and indeed he could sometimes find himself in physical danger. Among the papers of the Court of Star Chamber there are a number of cases which shed some light (admittedly only from one angle) on the relations of stewards with fellow servants, tenants and others in the wider community. In 1610 Sir Richard Brooke of Norton in Cheshire informed the Court that some of his Catholic tenants had boycotted his manorial courts at Acton; that his steward, Richard Rydgate, had therefore fined them; and that as an act of revenge Rydgate had been attacked and wounded.[50] In 1614 Sir George Savile of Thornhill in Yorkshire submitted a bill about deer poaching in Emley Park which sparked off a bitter tirade against his steward and brother-in-law William Vernon. One of the defendants, Robert Hare, considered that he had been unfairly dismissed from his position as keeper of the park and put all the blame for this on Vernon whom he described as Sir George's 'Steward or Cheife Comaunder in his affaires' and a gentleman of a very greedy disposition. Vernon, he alleged, had become displeased with him for no good reason and through his backbiting had persuaded Sir George, a 'kinde and worshipfull Maister', to dispense with his services to his great prejudice and loss.[51] In 1618 the Attorney General narrated a story of mob violence which had been occasioned by the farming activities of a Catholic squire, Sir Ralph Lawson of Brough Hall in Yorkshire. On Sir Ralph's orders some of his demesne lands at Scremerston in Durham had

72. Memorial to
Thomas Grenhill
in Beddington
parish church,
Surrey.

been ploughed up and this had resulted in an armed riot by men who claimed
that their pasture rights had been extinguished. When Sir Ralph's steward
James Lawson (who was one of his sons) had pleaded with them to desist they
had assaulted him and left him for dead.[52]

In 1622 Robert Constable, who was employed as steward by the Pelhams
of Halland House in Sussex, presented a Star Chamber bill in which he
described himself as a gentleman of an ancient blood. By way of background
he explained that in July 1619 Thomas Jefferies and others had unlawfully
entered Halland Park and poached deer and rabbits. They had then proceeded to take legal action against him in the Court of King's Bench and at
the Lewes quarter sessions, alleging that he was a common barrator and dis-
turber of the peace. As a result he had been arrested by the under-sheriff but
had managed to obtain his release by entering bail in the Court of King's
Bench. Subsequently, however, his adversaries had assaulted him at Lewes
and threatened to kill him. In response the defendants claimed that

Constable was a most troublesome and contentious person who had 'afflicted and oppressed' not only them but others in the neighbourhood; that he had been busily engaged in fabricating evidence; and that in the incident at Lewes (which had taken place in the Red Lion) he had been the first to draw his sword. In addition, Jefferies told the Court that at a meeting at Halland House, when Sir Thomas and his wife were present, Constable had spoken out against him and attempted to provoke him. This, he affirmed, had so angered Sir Thomas that he had sharply reprimanded Constable for his insolence.[53]

Many stewards remained in post until death or sickness cut short their labours. In March 1671 the Yorkshire steward Thomas Richardson wrote to his master, Sir Thomas Slingsby, that he was afraid that his illness would 'hinder for ever seeing yow to take my last farewell of yow' unless he was willing to visit him at Knaresborough. This, he hastened to assure him, 'may be done without any danger to yor person'.[54] Occasionally a steward was accorded some kind of church memorial though it was appropriately modest in comparison with the monuments of his master's family. Following the death of Thomas Grenhill in 1634 his brother and sister arranged for a brass plate in his memory to be set up in the parish church of Beddington in Surrey (Pl. 72). Among others things they put it on record that he had been educated at Magdalen College, Oxford and had been steward to Sir Nicholas Carew of Beddington House. In another Surrey church, the parish church of Battersea, two of the stewards employed by the St John family were commemorated: Charles Chappell, the son of a prebendary of Salisbury cathedral, and William Foote who had served the St Johns for no less than forty-seven years by the time of his death in 1713.[55] Samuel Renault (who was presumably of French stock) was steward to both Sir Ralph Hare and his son Sir Thomas at Stow Bardolph in Norfolk. In 1678 he was buried in the church there and the following inscription was placed on his gravestone:

> Here lys buried underneath this stone,
> A willing friend to all, a foe to none,
> A steward, true and faithfull, husband kind,
> A father tender, one of right Christian mind,
> His days consum'd with labour, care and pain,
> His body rests in hopes to rise again.

No steward could have desired a better epitaph.[56]

CHAPTER EIGHT

Coaches and Coachmen

Writing in the reign of Charles II, John Aubrey observed that 'the Gentry of the Nation is so effeminated by Coaches they are soe far from managing great horses that they know not how to ride hunting horses'.[1] The private coach was the seventeenth-century equivalent of the motor car. Besides the benefits which it offered in terms of comfort and convenience it was also a status symbol which proclaimed that its owner was a person of wealth and social position. From the evidence provided by expenditure accounts, wills, inventories and correspondence it is clear that most squires with an income of £1000 a year or more felt obliged to purchase coaches and that after the Restoration other gentlemen with smaller estates were following their lead in increasing numbers. Coaches were to be seen not only in the counties around London but in every county of England. During his extensive travels in the reign of Charles II Thomas Baskerville noted, apparently with some surprise, that in Nottingham there were 'many coaches rattling about'.[2] In Cornwall, which was even more remote in every sense, many of the leading gentry owned coaches, among them the Boscawens of Tregothnan, the Bullers of Shillingham, the Carews of Antony House, the Corytons of Newton Ferrers, the Godolphins of Godolphin House and the St Aubyns of Clowance.[3] On the other hand, coaches were probably of limited value in the bleak and mountainous regions of northern England. In a letter addressed to a royal official in January 1670 Sir Philip Musgrave of Hartley Castle in Westmorland told him that there had been heavy snow in the mountains and he considered it impossible to pass over Stainmore common with his coach until there was a thaw.[4]

The coach had particular attractions for women and perhaps especially for those who (unlike Celia Fiennes) had little enthusiasm for travelling on horseback. Above all, it opened up the prospect of greater mobility. Often a well-to-do squire included a coach and horses in the testamentary provision which he made for his wife. In his will, which was drawn up in 1677, Sir Roger Burgoyne of Sutton in Bedfordshire left his wife, Dame Anne, both his coaches and his four coach horses together with four other horses which were presumably intended for her servants. During her widowhood, when she was living at Wroxall in Warwickshire, Lady Burgoyne travelled to London,

Cambridge and Yorkshire (where she had relatives) as well as to Sutton Hall and the houses of neighbouring gentry. In May 1680 her journey to London took the best part of four days: on the first night she lodged at Banbury, on the second at Aylesbury and on the third at Uxbridge.[5]

Slow journeys were usually a reflection of the poor state of the roads which could be particularly hazardous in bad weather. On one occasion Sir Edward Harley was informed by his wife, Dame Abigail, that she had been travelling in their coach from Oxford to Ludlow in Shropshire and the roads had been so deep in mud that it had not been possible to exceed thirteen miles a day for the last three days.[6] While menservants who accompanied a coach on horseback did so primarily for security reasons they had an additional function to perform when it slid into a ditch or became embedded in mud.

In the early seventeenth century the private coach was still a relatively primitive type of conveyance. After the Restoration, however, there were new technological developments which ensured increased comfort for the passengers: in particular, improvements in the suspension and the introduction of glass windows in place of the leather flaps or curtains which had hitherto served as protection against the elements.[7] In 1676 an Essex squire, Sir John Barrington of Hatfield Priory, paid £44 10s 0d for a new coach 'with whole glasses in the doores'.[8] During the later Stuart period it was also common practice for a wealthy family to own two or three coaches, including perhaps a workaday 'travelling coach' and a more elegant model which was clearly meant to impress. Following the death in 1678 of Sir Richard Powle of Shottesbrooke in Berkshire his trustees sold a pair of coach horses for £20, a postillion horse for £5, the best coach for £50 (out of which they paid £6 3s 0d for parking fees in the city of London), a travelling coach for £30 and an old coach 'past useing' for £5. Sir Richard had served for a time as master of the horse to the Duchess of York (an office which he had bought) but according to Andrew Marvell he had been unable to ride because of a venereal infection.[9]

During this period two types of light carriage, the chariot and the calash, were becoming fashionable, though not to the extent of superseding the more robust and capacious coach. Probably one of the main attractions of these new variants of the coach for a country squire was that they provided him with the means to drive himself around the estate where he lived or on short journeys in the general neighbourhood. At the time of his death in 1681 Sir John Lenthall of Bessels Leigh in Berkshire had a coach which would be valued at £60, a calash and a chariot which together would be appraised at £13, two coach geldings and four coach mares.[10] Similarly, the personal effects of Sir Thomas Hesilrige of Noseley Hall in Leicestershire, who died in 1698, included a coach, a chariot and an old calash.[11] In the last decade of the century it was borne in on the government that the profusion of coaches and carriages (which were particularly numerous in and around London) had worthwhile fiscal possibilities. Under the provisions of poll tax measures which were enacted in 1692, 1694 and 1698 anyone owning a coach, chariot or calash was required to pay 20s a quarter over a period of one year unless he was already meeting or contributing to the cost of a horse and horseman for military purposes.[12]

In the seventeenth century there were coachmakers in York and other provincial towns. The accounts of Sir Simonds D'Ewes, who was seated at Stowlangtoft in Suffolk, reveal that in 1641 he bought a new coach in the nearby town of Bury St Edmunds.[13] The main coach-building centre, however, was London and in particular the parish of St Martin-in-the-Fields in Westminster. The Smyths of Hill Hall in Essex were one of many gentry families in the counties around London which drew on the services of metropolitan coachmakers and harness makers. Writing from London in 1665 James Smyth told his stepmother, Dame Beatrice, that in obedience to her commands he had been to see her coachmaker, Mr Bridges. The new coach was now virtually ready but Mr Bridges wanted to know 'what coller the tassels and poynts shall bee of, and with all, what culler the carridge of the coach must be painted with all, which will be quite fenished in two days' time after he hath received your Ladyship's order'.[14] Over the years another Essex family, the Barringtons, had a number of coaches built for them in London. Shortly after the Restoration Sir John Barrington found it necessary to commission a herald painter to draw, paint and gild his coat of arms, together with all the quarterings, on a new coach which he had bought as this work had been 'ill done' by the coachmaker.[15] While many of their customers lived in south-east England the London coachmakers were also receiving orders from gentlemen whose estates were situated in more distant counties, though in some cases they also had town houses in the capital. Among their clients were Sir William Lower of St Winnow in Cornwall, Sir John Hele of Wembury in Devon, Sir Roger Townshend of Raynham Hall in Norfolk, Robert Coke of Holkham in Norfolk and Sir William Clifton of Clifton in Nottinghamshire. At the time of his death in 1679 Robert Coke, who was one of the most substantial landowners in England, owed his coachmaker, Edward Hooper, no less than £966 5s 9d.[16]

Besides their primary role as manufacturers the coachmakers also undertook repair and painting work. On the death of a well-to-do squire it was customary to make arrangements for the 'blacking' of the family coach as a sign of mourning. In 1688 William Bassett, a coachmaker whose workshop was in the parish of St Martin-in-the-Fields, instituted legal proceedings against Philip Boteler of Watton Woodhall in Hertfordshire whose family had been making use of his services for many years. Boteler, he claimed, owed him £36 15s 0d for work which had been carried out following the death of his father. At the request of one of the trustees a coach belonging to the family had been put into mourning (a process which had included the application of black paint to the undercarriage and wheels) and had then been driven back to Watton Woodhall in time for Sir John's funeral. A year later, after the period of mourning was over, the coach had been painted red and a new set of wheels had been fitted.[17]

The price of a coach naturally varied according to its size and standard of finish which were often a reflection of the purchaser's social rank. In 1694 a Dorset landowner, Sir John Hanham of Dean's Court in Wimborne Minster, observed in the course of legal proceedings that during his minority he had been prevailed upon to 'buy horses and equipage Suitable to the quality of a Barronet'.[18] On the evidence of their accounts and other sources of information the gentry usually paid between £30 and £60 for a coach

73. A coach and six at Sherborne House, Gloucestershire, the seat of the Dutton family. Engraving by Johannes Kip (Sir Robert Atkyns, *The Ancient and Present State of Glocestershire*, second edition, 1768).

both before and after the Civil War. Writing from London in 1665 Sir Edward Harley told his wife that "I have bought a Coach, the cheapest I could, yet the price of Coach and harness is £38'.[19] On the other hand, it was possible to spend much more than this if the purchaser was untroubled by financial constraints. When Sir William Drake of Shardeloes in Buckinghamshire, a man of great wealth, died in 1669 he was succeeded by his nephew (young Sir William Drake) who immediately bought himself a coach with money given to him for that specific purpose. In his accounts the steward noted that Mr Calthorpe the coachmaker had been paid £85 for the new coach and 'all things belonging' by which he presumably meant the harness and fittings but not the coach horses which were the subject of a separate transaction.[20] Sometimes a coachmaker might be willing to accept an old coach in part exchange and adjust his price accordingly. In 1640 the accounts of Sir Thomas Barrington's steward contain the entry 'for a new Travelling Coach besides the old given in Exchange' and record a net cash payment of £30.[21]

Coach horses could be bought for between £10 and £20 each, though some cost considerably more: in 1654, for example, Sir John Pelham of Halland House in Sussex paid £60 for a pair of horses.[22] The number of horses used depended on such factors as the size and weight of the coach and the condition of the roads in the general area. A team of six horses might be regarded as a little ostentatious but it could sometimes be a matter of practical necessity (Pl. 73). In December 1689 Peter Legh of Lyme Hall in Cheshire received a message from his sister Lettice Bankes, who lived at Winstanley

Hall in Lancashire, about the arrangements for a visit she would shortly be making. In this letter she asked him to send his coach horses to Manchester and

> if you please bring the saddle and Harness for the 2 foremost Horses and a Postillian, we being forcs't to put 6 Horses unto the Coach and have but harness for 4, soe desire you to lend us yours; we have noe boy that knows how to ride postillian . . . Our Coach is so heavy and the ways so ill that 4 they say can never bring us to Manchester; our ways hereabouts are the worst.[23]

Many of the gentry, however, considered a team of four horses to be sufficient for normal purposes (Pls 74 and 75). According to a Chancery report of 1676 which concerned the financial affairs of a minor, William Kingsmill of Sydmonton in Hampshire, the keeping of four horses for his coach involved expenditure of £30 a year.[24]

Some gentlemen kept their coaches in the stables built for the horses while in 1633 Sir George More of Loseley in Surrey was using a barn for the same purpose.[25] On the other hand, the coach-house as a building specifically designed for the function was already beginning to make its appearance in the early part of the seventeenth century. When a Yorkshire squire, John Kaye of Woodsome Hall, undertook a major building programme at Denby Grange in Charles I's reign it seemed perfectly natural to him to provide himself with a coach-house.[26] An inventory which was carried out at Hatfield Priory, the Essex mansion of the Barrington family, in 1632 refers both to a coach-house and a 'Coaches Horses stable'.[27] In the latter part of the century many gentry families had purpose-built coach-houses, among them the Cottingtons of Fonthill Gifford in Wiltshire, the Fishers of Great Packington in Warwickshire, the Leightons of Wattlesborough Hall in Shropshire, the Walpoles of Houghton in Norfolk, the Heaths of Cottesmore in Rutland and the Lowthers of Lowther in Westmorland. In the journal which he kept Sir John Lowther noted that in 1663 he built a coach-house and stable at a total cost of £80.[28]

The extent of coach ownership among the propertied classes meant that there was a very substantial demand for coachmen who were both proficient and reliable. An obvious source of recruitment was London with its superabundance of private coaches and growing numbers of commercial vehicles available for hire. In 1623 there was a report that the proclamations directed against the practice of sojourning in the capital had led to the departure of 7000 families and with them 1400 coaches, though some of these families were already returning; and subsequently, in 1636, it was estimated that in London alone there were over 6000 coaches.[29] Licensing arrangements governing the use of hackney coaches were first introduced in the reign of Charles I while from the 1650s onwards stagecoach services were being operated on all the main routes out of London.[30] When the Scotts of Scot's Hall in Kent were in need of a coachman it was to their metropolitan contacts that they turned for assistance. In a letter which can be assigned to the reign of Charles I one of these contacts, James Bush, informed Lady Scott that 'I haply chanced on a very honest man that will

74. A coach and four in front of the Pleydell mansion at Ampney Crucis, Gloucestershire. Engraving by Johannes Kip (Sir Robert Atkyns, *The Ancient and Present State of Glocestershire*, second edition, 1768).

undertake the office of a coachman with your Ladyship, whose sufficiency therein your nobleness need not doubt, or for his demeanour, otherwise is so well known unto me that it doth encarage me to commend him to your Ladyship.'[31] Although Sir Edward Harley had a servant who was very keen to be appointed as his coachman he appears to have discounted the possibility of finding a suitable candidate in his own county of Herefordshire or

TONG. *The Seat of the Hon.ble S.r George Tempest Bar.t near Bradford in the West-Riding of y.e County of YORK.*

75. A coach and four at Tong Hall, Yorkshire which belonged to the Tempest family. Engraving by Johannes Kip (British Library, Lansdowne MSS 898, fol. 62).

any of the adjoining counties. Writing from Westminster in April 1662 he communicated to his wife the good news that he had been offered a likely coachman.[32]

On occasion a coachman was acquired without the need for any special recruiting effort. When Sir John Fortescue of Salden House in Buckinghamshire married Elizabeth Wintour in 1663 it was decided that her coachman, John Pello, should be taken into his service. In 1675 Sir John added a codicil to his will in which he acknowledged that there was £20 owing to Pello for his wages and made provision for the grant of a lease to him.[33]

Besides his primary function it was also the coachman's responsibility to take care of his horses, clean the coach and ensure that it was in good working order, though the specialist services of a coachmaker were usually required for any major repairs. At home he often had the support of a groom and stable boy; and *en route* he was sometimes assisted by a postillion who rode one of the leading horses. If asked about the attractions of his job he would conceivably have referred to the varied nature of the journeys which he undertook and the sense of freedom which they imparted. At one extreme, he might convey the family to church on Sundays if it was not immediately adjacent to the house; at the other, he might transport them on lengthy journeys, possibly spread over several days, to such places as London or Bath. Some coachmen who were employed by wealthy landowners with London town houses might spend at least as much time in the metropolis as in the country. It was on one of these protracted visits that a bizarre incident occurred at the town house belonging to Hugh Boscawen of Tregothnan in Cornwall: in July 1693 his coachman shot and killed a fellow servant with a blunderbuss after mistaking him for a burglar.[34]

As a general rule the coachman was the most highly paid of the outdoor servants with the exception of the gardener. In the second half of the century a wage of £6 a year was often considered appropriate which meant that for pay purposes he was broadly equated with the butler. In his accounts Richard Hale of King's Walden in Hertfordshire recorded the appointment in 1687 of Henry Bacon as his coachman, John Davis as his butler and John Collings as Bacon's successor and noted in each case that a wage of £6 a year had been agreed upon.[35] Although, as we have seen, Sir Cecil Bishop of Parham was a hard master he was willing to pay his coachman rather more, perhaps because Sussex had a notorious reputation among men of their profession as a county 'full of mud and myre'. John Venter, who left his service in 1690, received a wage of £9 a year. His immediate successor, who is described only as Richard in the accounts, was also paid £9 a year at the outset but this was later increased to £10 a year. In March 1693 the steward put it on record that in accordance with his master's directions he had given the coachman the sum of £1 'which hee had to Bett at the horse Race'. During the course of 1694 there was a particularly high turnover of coachmen. James Wood, John Holden and John Haynes were all dismissed though in August 1694 the latter was taken back into Sir Cecil's service. In the closing years of the century John Lawton was employed as coachman and appears to have been satisfied with a wage of £8 a year.[36]

Besides his wage the coachman was provided with livery clothes and boots or shoes and could expect to receive gratuities from visitors who travelled in his coach. In addition, he was reimbursed for the expenditure which he incurred during his journeyings. The accounts kept by Thomas Noble, who was steward to the Carylls of West Harting in Sussex in the reign of Charles I, record payments to the coachman (and in some cases to the postillion) for food and drink, for the stabling and feeding of the four coach horses, for a pot of oil bought at London and for a charge of 2s 4d which had been levied for the ferrying of the coach and horses across the Thames at Putney.[37] Now and again a coachman's standard of performance earned him a place among those servants who were individually named as legatees in his master's will. In such cases he was usually given £5 or £10 but in 1648 Sir Edmund Bacon of Redgrave in Suffolk left his coachman John Nestlyn the handsome sum of £80.[38]

In common with a number of his fellow servants the coachman was allowed his own bedchamber. At Clovelly Court in Devon, however, his room was also used for the storage of equipment and other items associated with his work. When George Woodyer left the service of his master, William Cary, on 15 October 1700 he was paid the remainder of his wages, which came to £5, together with 18s for his disbursements. At the same time he handed over an inventory of 'things in his Chamber' which included the coach harness, four collars for the coach horses and another four for saddle horses, two seats for the coach and one for the calash, five saddles, a pillion, two pairs of curry combs and brushes and two water pails.[39]

On the evening of 12 February 1682 a Wiltshire squire, Thomas Thynne of Longleat, was travelling in his coach along Pall Mall when he was intercepted by three horsemen in the pay of Count Königsmarck who had designs on his estranged wife. Thynne was shot five times and died the following morning. The funeral was held in Westminster Abbey where the monument which was erected offers a dramatic portrayal of his murder (Pl. 76).[40] Assassination

76. The relief on Thomas Thynne's monument in Westminster Abbey.

was not the kind of danger which was commonly associated with coach travel but there were more obvious hazards. The activities of highwaymen could not be lightly disregarded, though they varied in intensity over the course of the century. In July 1687 a Cumberland baronet, Sir George Fletcher, and his travelling companions, who included two of his sons, had a narrow escape while journeying through the forest of Windsor. The horsemen who had been escorting their coach had been sent on ahead to the house they were visiting on the assumption that there was no danger on this final section of the route. Suddenly, however, the coach was confronted by two highwaymen. One of them ordered the coachman to stop and when he refused to do so fired twice but missed him. His companion then shot and killed the postillion; the coachman drove his horses at a furious pace; and the two marauders hurriedly departed from the scene.[41]

A matter of no less concern was the problem of the drunken coachman. In an age when heavy drinking was common at all levels of society this was no mere hypothetical possibility. When Sir Simonds D'Ewes expressed his disgust at the antics of those who had plied his coachman with strong drink we may assume that this had not only offended his Puritan susceptibilities but aroused fears about his own personal safety.[42] In July 1654 John Evelyn visited Sir Edward Baynton of Spye Park in Wiltshire and wrote in his diary that 'our Coachmen made so exceedingly drunk that returning home we escaped incredible dangers. Tis it seemes by order of the Knight that all Gentlemen's servants be so treated: but the Custome is barbarous, and much unbecoming a Knight, much lesse a Christian.' In March 1669 he relates that he went with Henry Howard (later Duke of Norfolk) on a visit to his friend Sir William Ducie at Charlton House in Blackheath and that the servants there 'made our Coach-men so drunk that they both fell-off their boxes upon the heath, where we were faine to leave them'. In the event they were driven to London by two gentlemen belonging to Howard's entourage.[43] A Northamptonshire squire, William Tate of Delapré Abbey, had a hair-raising experience in February 1690 when travelling in a coach which Lord Hatton had lent him

77. A detail of the memorial to Sir Miles Hobart in Great Marlow parish church, Buckinghamshire showing the frieze depicting his fatal accident.

after he had enjoyed his lordship's hospitality. Writing to Hatton on his return to London he told him that he had arrived home safely, 'though wee escaped often narrowly through the coachman's being extraordinarily in drink, which he gott by the way'.[44]

Whether through a coachman's negligence or for other reasons there were frequent mishaps both in town and country. In a recital of the misadventures which had befallen him in the course of his life Sir James Harrington of Ridlington in Rutland thought it worth recording that in his youth he had been involved in an accident in his father's coach. As a zealous Puritan he was at pains to stress that such episodes demonstrated that his life had been spared through the benevolent working of divine providence.[45] In a similar autobiographical account Sir William Waller the parliamentarian general recalled that his coach mares broke their reins while he was journeying to Hickleton Hall, his sister's house in Yorkshire.[46] In February 1627 Sir Gilbert Gerard of Harrow on the Hill in Middlesex was summoned to appear before the Privy Council after failing, in his capacity as high sheriff of Buckinghamshire, to welcome the Duke of Buckingham on his arrival at Aylesbury. Sir Gilbert's explanation (which was apparently accepted) was that his coachman had fallen out of his box during the journey to Aylesbury; that this had happened so suddenly that he had been led to think that it was due to some contagious disease; and that he had therefore decided that it would be prudent to absent himself in the interests of all concerned.[47] In July 1660 his relative Sir John Barrington was travelling along Fleet Street in his coach when the wheels fell off. According to his accounts the sum of 1s 6d was spent on the purchase of nails for emergency repairs and the payment of gratuities to the bystanders who came to his assistance.[48]

Occasionally a coach accident proved fatal. In June 1632 Sir Miles Hobart, the former Speaker of the House of Commons, was killed when his coach overturned while going down Snow Hill in Holborn. Sir Miles was buried in his parish church of Great Marlow in Buckinghamshire and a crudely executed monument depicting the accident was subsequently erected in his memory (Pl. 77).[49] In September 1687 a similar accident occurred at York when Sir Gilbert Gerard of Fiskerton in Lincolnshire 'dyed by A bruise in his head by the over turning of his coach'.[50] Nothing, however, could dent the enthusiasm displayed by the gentry for coach travel, though they might complain about the traffic congestion in London.

CHAPTER NINE

Chaplains and Tutors

In the seventeenth century few gentry families were legally entitled to employ private chaplains. Under the provisions of statutes dating back to Henry VIII's reign this was a privilege confined to archbishops, bishops, peers, knights of the garter, judges and senior officials of the Crown.[1] In the reign of James I these severe restrictions were largely disregarded but from 1629 onwards William Laud, first as Bishop of London and then as Archbishop of Canterbury, sought to ensure, with the backing of Charles I, that they were rigorously enforced.[2] Reports on the situation in the Provinces of Canterbury and York indicated that there were a considerable number of gentry who were circumventing the law by one means or another, though Bishop Morton of Durham commented that he had no knowledge of anyone not legally qualified who wanted to keep a chaplain.[3] In an annual report which he submitted to the king in January 1640 Laud singled out Sir John Cutts of Childerley in Cambridgeshire as a prime suspect. The Bishop of Ely, he related, had told him that Sir John had a private chaplain but was claiming that he was a curate though he had no parochial responsibilities; and that the household only attended services in the domestic chapel adjoining Childerley Hall.[4] After Laud's downfall no further attempt was made to control the employment of chaplains on any systematic basis. On the other hand, there were many country squires for whom this was a matter of no more than academic interest. In a pamphlet which was published in 1655 as a response to his critics Sir George Sondes of Lees Court in Kent acknowledged that he had no chaplain in his house but stressed that he performed that office himself and that he prayed with his family at least once a day.[5] More generally, it is unlikely that the services of a chaplain were much in demand in those great houses which Sir William Waller described in a work published in Charles II's reign as 'Theaters of debauchery and viciousness'.[6]

In the course of the century there were at least 220 Protestant gentry who had private chaplains at one time or another. Some may have taken the view that this was what was expected of men of their standing in society; others desired the company of a university graduate whose interests ranged well beyond such matters as cattle prices or the prospects for the harvest. In April

1668 Sir Edward Nicholas, the former Secretary of State who was now retired, was seeking to recruit a chaplain who would reside with him at West Horsley Place in Surrey. While the search was under way his son John wrote to him that the President of St John's College, Oxford would do him a great kindness if he could find him 'a pious civill Chaplain' for he would 'receive great contentment in his conversation'.[7] Often, however, the presence of a chaplain in a gentleman's house was a sign of genuine religious commitment. Many Puritan gentry kept chaplains, among them such families as the Boscawens, Hampdens, Drydens, Barringtons and Gurdons.[8] In 1630 Sir Erasmus Dryden of Canons Ashby was involved in negotiations with another Northamptonshire landowner, Sir John Isham of Lamport, over a possible match between his grandson John and Isham's daughter Elizabeth. Writing to Sir John on 22 April he told him that he was gratified to hear that 'your purpose is to lay a sound foundacion, namely that you will constantly keepe in your howse such a faithfull mynister as they shall like of, to instruct and governe your howse'.[9] Besides the Puritan gentry there were other devout Protestants who employed domestic chaplains. One of the most notable of these men was Sir Norton Knatchbull of Mersham Hatch in Kent who sometimes preached sermons on private occasions and was the author of a commentary on the New Testament which went into four editions between 1659 and 1692.[10]

Throughout the century the universities represented a major source of recruitment. Many of those appointed as chaplains were young men who had recently graduated and since as a rule their duties were not particularly onerous they had an opportunity to continue their studies if they were so minded. Unless they had strong nonconformist convictions they were usually hoping to obtain benefices in due course, not least through the patronage or influence of the men who were employing them. The Barringtons of Hatfield Priory in Essex had some kind of understanding with their chaplains that they would put them into one or other of their Yorkshire livings of Rowley and Walkington as and when a vacancy occurred; and they apparently regarded this as a necessary inducement.[11] In his will, which was drawn up in 1635, Sir John Hare of Stow Bardolph in Norfolk not only left his chaplain, Thomas Martin, a legacy of £20 but gave direction that he should have the next spiritual living in his gift which should fall vacant.[12] Similarly, it was reported in 1677 that Sir William Drake of Shardeloes in Buckinghamshire had given the living of Amersham to his chaplain, Josiah Smith, 'a very worthy person'.[13]

In 1679 William Windham, who was seated at Felbrigg in Norfolk, persuaded his brother-in-law Horatio Lord Townshend to confer the living of Stiffkey on his chaplain, William Harmer. As his successor Lady Townshend recommended a Mr Gurnele who had once served as chaplain to Sir Lestrange Calthorpe of West Barsham. According to another of Windham's relatives she had commented that 'he is the best Man that ever came in a House and minds nothing but his studyes'; that he was about thirty years of age and as good a preacher as Mr Harmer; and that he was 'modestly speaking' and (as she had heard) 'a Man of great piety'. In fact her only reservation concerned his periwig which in her view was too fair and in the light of her testimony Windham was fully prepared to take him into his service.[14]

78. Henry Jessey
(Samuel Palmer,
*The Nonconformist's
Memorial*, 1775).

The chaplains in Puritan households included ministers who had forfeited their livings on account of their refusal to conform and young graduates who for reasons of conscience were reluctant to enter the ranks of the parish clergy. On leaving St John's College, Cambridge in 1624 Henry Jessey (Pl. 78) became chaplain to one of the leading Puritan squires in Suffolk, Brampton Gurdon of Assington Hall. Although he was ordained in 1627 he declined several offers of livings since human ordinances and ceremonies in public worship 'had gotten more footing than he could comply with'. In 1633, however, he was finally prevailed upon to take up a position as assistant to William Alder, the vicar of Aughton in Yorkshire, but his rejection of the Laudian innovations ensured that the appointment was short-lived. He then found shelter in the house of another Puritan landowner, Sir Matthew Boynton of Barmston, who was so concerned about the trend of events in England that he eventually went into temporary exile in the Netherlands.[15] Following the Restoration the Puritan gentry (who were now mainly termed Presbyterians) took into their houses a considerable number of ministers who were forced to relinquish their livings as a result of the Act of Uniformity of 1662. While this significantly increased the supply of godly chaplains it was a once-for-all accession but in the last decades of the century the newly established dissenting academies were becoming an important source of recruitment.

In some parishes the incumbent or a stipendiary curate also acted as the squire's domestic chaplain and indeed would usually live with him if there was no parsonage house. When Richard Lowe was appointed vicar of the

Derbyshire parish of Melbourne in December 1639 it was on the recommen-
dation of Sir John Coke, the Principal Secretary of State, who had approached
the ecclesiastical authorities on his behalf. Melbourne Hall was the Coke
family's country seat and there was a prior understanding that he would serve
as their chaplain. In January 1640 Sir John told his son and namesake that he
was 'exceedingly comforted' that Lowe 'gives you al so good contentment
and specially to your self and my daughter, who shal enioy his ministerie
most'. However, he went on, 'let mee advise you not to cry him up too loude,
that the eys of our churchmen bee not cast uppon him, who can not indure
any confluence to those that go not in their idle way'. The following month
his daughter Elizabeth expressed her satisfaction that God had sent to
Melbourne 'so godly a minister of his word'.[16] During the years 1633 to 1652
Christopher Elderfield was the rector of Burton in Sussex. Since, however,
Burton was a depopulated village he was actually employed as the private
chaplain of his patron, Sir William Goring, and resided with him at Burton
Place where for much of his time he was immersed in scholarly activities.
When a work of his was published shortly after his death the editor dedicat-
ed it to Sir William and in doing so observed that Elderfield 'lived as deep in
your affections, as you lived high in his devotions. His great studie was to
advance you in Spirituals, yet he was willing to return some considerable
Retributions to you, so far as he was intrusted by you, in Secular affairs'. In a
strange twist of fate Sir William's son and heir married a devout Catholic and
from the latter part of Charles II's reign there was a Jesuit chaplain at Burton
Place.[17] Writing about the situation in Cheshire following the Restoration a
nonconformist divine, Adam Martindale, named several gentlemen who kept
chaplains: Sir Willoughby Aston of Aston, Sir Peter Leycester of Nether
Tabley, Sir Thomas Mainwaring of Over Peover and Thomas Cholmondley of
Vale Royal. Their chaplains, he noted, were single men and conformists who
either had a benefice, a public chapel or a fellowship.[18]

A chaplain in a Protestant household was usually paid a salary of £20 or £30
a year. This was significantly more than the kind of wage which most household servants received though on the other hand his emoluments were modest compared with those which some of the parish clergy enjoyed. Roger
Williams, who served as chaplain to Sir William Masham of Otes Hall in Essex
during the years 1627 to 1630, wrote in a letter addressed to Dame Joan
Barrington that it was well known 'how A gracious God and tender
Conscience . . . have kept me back from honour and preferment'. Besides
many earlier offers, he went on,

> I have had since 2 severall livings proffered me, each of them £100
> p.annum: but as things yet stand among us I see not how any great
> meanes and I shall meete that way. Nor do I seeke nor shall I be drawne
> on any tearmes to part . . . from Oates so long as any Competencie can be
> raised, or libertie afforded.

Not long afterwards, however, he departed for New England.[19] During the
reign of Charles II the Morleys of Glynde Place in Sussex had a succession of
nonconformist chaplains, including Joseph Swaffield and Zachary Smith the
former vicar of Glynde. As recorded in William Morley's expenditure

79. Simon Patrick. Portrait by Sir Peter Lely, *c.* 1668 (National Portrait Gallery, London).

accounts Swaffield was paid £10 for his services in the half-year ending on 28 May 1676 while in March 1678 there is an entry indicating that Smith had so far received £15 since his appointment as chaplain and that at Lady Day the sum of £30 would be due to him for a whole year.[20] Occasionally, however, a more generous spirit prevailed. In his autobiography Simon Patrick (Pl. 79), who was eventually made a bishop, describes how he became chaplain to Sir Walter St John of Battersea in Surrey. His appointment in 1656 followed an initial meeting at which he created such a good impression that Sir Walter offered him £60 a year 'and his lady privately told me she would give ten pound a year (which she did) rather than not have my service'.[21]

In November 1672 a Hampshire squire, Richard Norton of Southwick, offered Henry Newcome (the son of an ejected minister) the position of household chaplain at a salary of £40 a year. A former parliamentarian, Colonel Norton had a preference for ministers of the Independent or Congregational persuasion. The young man considered that the proposed salary was a 'noble allowance' but decided to accept another offer even though it was not so financially attractive. In coming to this conclusion he was heavily influenced by his father who advanced a number of reasons for declining the invitation from Southwick House. In the first place, he was not sure that his son would be able to satisfy Norton's requirements, 'the Colonel having had an able nonconformist to go before'. Secondly, Norton's family was 'great, and so temptations more, and the attendance greater', which his son's weak constitution 'might not be so well able to answer'. Finally,

Southwick was a long way from Manchester where the Newcomes were then living.[22]

The basic function of a Protestant chaplain was to conduct the regular prayer sessions at which the whole household was present. Depending on the kind of family he was serving he might also be called upon to preach, catechize, instruct the children and servants or repeat the sermons which had been delivered in the parish church; and in the case of some Puritan families he preached in the general neighbourhood as well as in the privacy of the squire's house. John Ball, who served as curate of Whitmore in Staffordshire from 1610 until his death in 1640, had an additional role as chaplain to Edward Mainwaring, 'a pious and much esteemed Gentleman'. For some years he lived with the Mainwarings at Whitmore Hall and during that time was heavily engaged in their service 'for every evening he expounded a portion of Scripture, which was read in course, and many mornings also was helpfull in Catechizing of the Family'.[23] In the ecclesiastical canons of 1604 it was stipulated that except in times of necessity no minister should preach or administer holy communion in any private house unless it had a chapel which could lawfully be used for divine service.[24] Many of the gentry had their own chapels but the activities of the chaplains whom they employed did not usually extend as far as the Church's sacraments. During the Commonwealth period, however, children were often christened and the eucharist administered in private houses in defiance of the ban on Prayer Book services. In December 1655 Michael Edge, a young graduate who had recently been taken on as Sir Francis Burdett's chaplain at Foremark Hall in Derbyshire, asked the celebrated Richard Baxter whether and in what circumstances the administration of the sacraments was lawful. This was an issue, he told him, 'which I do the rather put to you because with some Ministers private Babtismes are as ordinary as Babtisme it selfe almost'.[25]

In discharging their religious duties some chaplains felt under no obligation to exhibit the kind of deference which social convention required. During the reign of James I Richard Sedgwick was employed as chaplain by Sir Edward Onslow, 'a person of eminent virtue and piety' who was seated at Knowle in the Surrey parish of Cranleigh. In this capacity it was his practice 'to catechize the Family by turne, wherein he used no respect of persons, the meanest not being left out, and the chiefest not forborn'. Since there was no preaching minister at Cranleigh he regularly delivered two sermons in public each Sunday and later on in the day 'called the whole Family in private to render an account' of what they had heard.[26] Another Puritan divine, Thomas Cawton, served as chaplain to Sir William Armyne at Orton Hall, which was situated in the Huntingdonshire village of Orton Longueville, during the years 1633 to 1637. His son testifies that he 'would neither smother faults nor smooth them over in the greatest but would so sweetly reprove and admonish all sorts according to their qualities that though he were so honest as to be plain yet he was so discreet as to be pleasing in his reprehensions'.[27] In practice much clearly depended on whether the chaplain enjoyed the full support and confidence of the head of the household and his wife. In some families there was a considerable turnover of chaplains which suggests the possibility of strains and tensions but in others the relationship was extremely close.

Simon Patrick, who was the son of a Lincolnshire squire, writes of his period of service with the St John family that

> never was any man, I have often thought, more beloved in any family than I was; especially by the lady of it, who was very pious, and so delighted in my conversation that she desired to contract a friendship with me; and I hope they received no small benefit by me, particularly my lady who told me she never understood religion till she knew me.

Another of Sir Walter St John's chaplains who was highly regarded was Nathaniel Gower; in 1695 he married Johanna Foote, a daughter of the steward William Foote.[28]

Besides his attributes as a preacher or spiritual counsellor a chaplain sometimes possessed other talents which were considered valuable. In the reign of Charles I the Whitelockes of Fawley Court in Buckinghamshire had a chaplain who, in the words of Bulstrode Whitelocke, 'was very rare, both for vocall and intrumentall musicke, and was not the worse preacher, butt a well bred man, a schollar and a travayler'. After the Restoration, when he was living at Chilton Foliat in Wiltshire, Whitelocke employed a nonconformist chaplain, James Pearson, who also acted as tutor, physician and land agent. In 1671 Pearson had an important role as go-between in the marriage negotiations in which Whitelocke was then engaged.[29]

For the Catholic gentry the practice of keeping a chaplain was far more hazardous. Under the provisions of the Elizabethan penal legislation the offence of receiving and assisting Jesuits and seminary priests was punishable by death (though in practice it was rarely treated as a capital offence) while anyone attending Mass could be sentenced to a year's imprisonment.[30] In 1610 Father James Sharpe, who had been serving as chaplain to the Babthorpes of Osgodby Hall in Yorkshire, wrote that the devotion of the Catholic gentry of the East Riding 'in making their houses common to all who come even with the danger of themselves and their whole estate' and in 'the maintaining of priests in their houses, some one, some two, is memorable among them'.[31] According to Dame Grace Babthorpe her family was never without the comfort of priests and often there were three or four at a time.[32]

During the course of the seventeenth century at least 120 gentry families in England had Catholic chaplains while many more received periodic visits from mission priests. Of the families with chaplaincies there were thirty-five seated in Yorkshire and eighteen in Lancashire. These included a number of prominent families such as the Vavasours of Hazlewood Castle, the Constables of Everingham, the Stapletons of Carlton, near Snaith, and the Tempests of Broughton in Yorkshire and, on the other side of the Pennines, the Towneleys of Towneley Hall, the Shireburns of Stonyhurst and the Cliftons of Lytham. At the other extreme there were some counties where only one or two major families had Catholic chaplaincies. Among these families were the Welds of Lulworth Castle in Dorset, the Throckmortons of Coughton in Warwickshire, the Nevills of Nevill Holt in Leicestershire, the Bedingfelds of Oxburgh Hall in Norfolk and the Heneages of Hainton and the Thimblebys of Irnham in Lincolnshire.[33]

A list of Catholic provenance which was compiled in 1692 contains some revealing comments on a number of missioners who were residing with gentry families. At Tichborne House in Hampshire Sir Henry Tichborne had a Franciscan chaplain, Augustine Hill, and there was also another missioner, John Churcher, who was very old and ill and 'past labour'. Andrew Bromwich, who was serving Thomas Giffard at Chillington Hall in Staffordshire, was 'much commended for his prudence and diligence'. For Yorkshire there are numerous references to chaplains and in some cases a few details are supplied. Dr George Witham had recently settled at Naburn Hall, near York, with his sister and her husband, George Palmes. Francis Hodgson, who was about forty years of age, had been living with George Witham of Cliffe Hall for several years. This George Witham was the father not only of Dr Witham (whose abilities were recognised by his appointment as the Northern Vicar General) but of Christopher Witham who is described in the following terms: '. . . he is but young and been about 7 or 8 years in the mission. He halts a little but very pious and regular and preaches often. He resides at Cliffe with his father and mother and is a help to many poor people that come thither.' Among the rest Paul Stevenson, who was Sir Walter Vavasour's chaplain at Hazlewood Castle, was considered to be 'an able, witty man' while John Baites, who lived with Sir Miles Stapleton at Carlton, was characterised as 'a sober vertuous man'.[34]

The private papers of Catholic families rarely contain any information about the stipends of their chaplains, perhaps because it was felt that this might be potentially incriminating. In December 1684 Sir Robert Throckmorton drew up a list of the annual charges on his estate. For the most part he named the recipients, including his steward and housekeeper, but there is a more cryptic item which is almost certainly a veiled reference to his chaplain: this relates to the payment of £60 a year to 'the gentleman' at Coughton Court and his other house at Weston Underwood in Buckinghamshire.[35] In contrast, the accounts of Sir Francis Radcliffe of Dilston in Northumberland reveal that in 1686 his long-serving chaplain Ferdinand Ashmall was only being paid £12 a year.[36] The chaplain's stipend, however, was not necessarily his only source of income. Many of the missioners were younger sons of gentry families and some at least would have been granted portions or annuities by their fathers. On occasion a Catholic squire might bequeath money to a group of priests within a particular county or region. In January 1681 John Caryll of West Harting in Sussex prepared a schedule of legacies which was clearly not intended to be a formal codicil to his will. Among other things, he left £50 to all Catholic priests 'as well Regulars as Seculars residing in Sussex, Hampshire, Wiltshire, Dorsetshire to be equally devided amongst all'. In addition, three named priests were given legacies totalling £20 over and above their share of the £50.[37]

While it was a wise precaution on the part of Catholic landowners to provide their houses with priest-holes these were not generally designed for anything but emergency use (Pl. 80).[38] During periods when there was little or no religious persecution the chaplain would often live quite openly as a member of the household, though he would usually dress in ordinary clothes and use an assumed name. How far his presence was advertised beyond the limits of the household clearly depended on the personal inclinations of the

80. A priest-hole at Sawston Hall, Cambridgeshire where the Huddleston family was seated.

squire but according to Gregory Panzani, a papal emissary who visited England in 1632, many wealthy persons were prepared to allow their poor Catholic neighbours to hear Mass in their houses.[39] The Eyres of Hassop in Derbyshire, who were one of the leading Catholic families in northern England, had a succession of Jesuit chaplains residing with them. In the 1680s they were involved in a legal dispute and some of the evidence which was collected in the course of these proceedings offers us a glimpse of the domestic arrangements at Hassop Hall. In the reign of Charles II Rowland Eyre and his family followed the ancient custom of dining in the great hall, along with the servants, in preference to the now general practice of taking meals in the privacy of a separate dining-room. A tenant of the Eyre family,

Thomas Alkin, testified that on one occasion when he was dining at the squire's table his uncle Edmund Hurd (who was employed as a bailiff) whispered to him that the man sitting opposite Mr Eyre was a priest; in fact it was the chaplain, John Weedon.[40] A painting commissioned by Sir Henry Tichborne in 1670 faithfully captures the more relaxed mood which was in evidence among the Catholic gentry before the Popish Plot crisis. In recording the ceremony involving the distribution of the Tichborne dole the artist depicted the whole household, including Sir Henry's chaplain (Pl. 81).[41] During the years of persecution, however, there was a very different atmosphere in Catholic manor-houses, particularly in view of the threat presented by surprise searches. Sir John Yorke was a Church Papist who lived at Gouthwaite Hall in a remote part of Yorkshire, the moorland region known as Netherdale or Nidderdale. In 1613 he and his wife, Dame Julian, were arraigned in the Court of Star Chamber following allegations that a seditious play had been staged at Gouthwaite Hall. Witnesses who were examined deposed that most of the servants and tenants were 'popishelie affected'; that there had been mysterious comings and goings; that some guests had taken their meals in private and, apart from the family, had been seen only by the steward, Marmaduke Lupton, and two or three other servants; and that searches which had been carried out had led to the discovery of various secret places and passages and such items as Catholic vestments and books. A mason, Robert Joy, testified that he had made two secret rooms adjoining the bedchamber where Sir John and his wife slept and that this work had been done at the direction of Lady Yorke.[42]

During the reign of James I many Yorkshire Catholics had their houses searched for priests. In a Star Chamber case of 1619 it was alleged that Thomas Waterton of Walton Hall had been so incensed by a search which had

81. The dole ceremony at Tichborne House, Hampshire. By Gillis van Tilborch, 1670

been made two years earlier that he had declared that for the future he would become an open and professed papist and that he had a secret place in his house where he could hide a seminary priest without any fear of discovery.[43] There were other Yorkshire squires, however, whose security arrangements proved less effective. In 1609 two priests were taken in Richard Cholmley's house at Brandsby but he managed to obtain a pardon for himself and his wife through the assistance of Philip Earl of Montgomery.[44] While William Vavasour of Hazlewood Castle was in prison for refusing the oath of allegiance a search which was made of his house resulted in the arrest of his chaplain. In spite of this episode he 'continued to live according to his old manner, very devoutly, always keeping a priest in his house', as indeed did his successors. For many years his son Francis, who was a Franciscan, served as his chaplain and in the latter part of his life he himself was a brother of the Third Order of St Francis, 'wearing publickly the habit and cord'.[45] When two priests were found at Osgodby Hall the squire, Sir William Babthorpe, drew his sword and held the pursuivants at bay while they made a rapid departure. As a result he was imprisoned for a time and had such a heavy fine imposed on him that he was forced to sell his whole estate.[46]

In the persecution which followed the discovery of the so-called Popish Plot in 1678 a considerable number of missioners were arrested, including the chaplains who resided with Sir Charles Shelley of Michelgrove in Sussex, William Massey of Puddington Hall in Cheshire and Richard Shireburn of Stonyhurst in Lancashire. When Edward Petre was captured at Michelgrove another priest, Thomas Churchill, was celebrating Mass in the private chapel there but managed to escape. In December 1678 Shelley obtained a licence to travel abroad and in April 1679 Massey followed his example, three months before his chaplain, John Pleasington, was executed.[47]

Sometimes a Catholic chaplain also acted as tutor to the children but many families had resident schoolmasters whose religious loyalties coincided with their own. An inventory of Everingham Hall (Pl. 82), the Yorkshire mansion of the Constable family, which was drawn up in 1637 reveals the existence of two school-rooms, the 'Lowe schoole house' and the 'upper schoole house'.[48] When another Yorkshire squire, William Langdale of Langthorpe Hall, was presented for recusancy in 1615 it was alleged that one of his servants, Thomas Jackson, had been teaching in Langdale's house without a licence. During the court proceedings which followed, however, the need for a licence was challenged on the dubious grounds that Jackson was 'a butler and no schoolman'.[49]

Most Protestant gentlemen in seventeenth-century England sent their sons away to school at some stage in the educational process. This might be a school such as Eton or Winchester which enjoyed a national reputation; a local grammar school such as Hertford, Bury St Edmunds or Repton which attracted pupils from beyond the immediate neighbourhood; or one of the many private schools which were often run by clergymen as a means of supplementing their income. Nevertheless the employment of a resident tutor was far from uncommon, particularly among the wealthier families. Some parents may have felt that there was no adequate substitute for personal tuition or they may have thought it prudent to keep their sons at home until

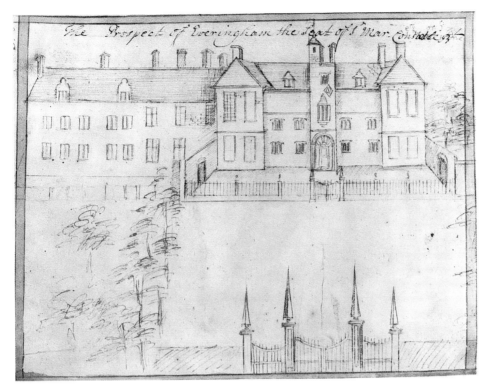

82. Everingham Hall, Yorkshire. An early eighteenth-century drawing by Samuel Buck (British Library, Lansdowne MSS 914, fol. 15).

they were old enough to be admitted to university or the Inns of Court. On the other hand, this type of education was sometimes no more than the initial phase of a child's schooling: during the reign of Charles I, for example, William Leigh, one of the sons of Sir Francis Leigh of Addington in Surrey, was educated at home for two years and then spent five years at Eton.[50]

In terms of their provenance and status private tutors and domestic chaplains had much in common. Many of those engaged as tutors were fresh from university and in some cases were hoping that they would eventually obtain either a benefice or a fellowship. When John Bolles, the son and heir of Sir Robert Bolles of Scampton in Lincolnshire, was admitted to Gonville and Caius College, Cambridge in 1656 it was noted in the register that for a period of seven years he had been educated at home under Mr Gelsthorpe. This was Edward Gelsthorpe, the son of a Norfolk gentleman, who had graduated from Gonville and Caius in 1647 and was a fellow of the college during the years 1655 to 1677.[51] Others who became resident schoolmasters included nonconformist ministers who had been forced to give up their livings in the purge which followed the Restoration. Occasionally a dissenting minister exercised the dual function of chaplain and tutor. James Calvert, a Presbyterian divine, was employed in both capacities first by Sir Thomas Strickland of Boynton in Yorkshire and then by Sir William Middleton of Belsay Castle in Northumberland. At Belsay Castle he preached constantly in the private chapel, taught his son John and, following Sir William's death in 1690, assumed the further role of guardian to the new baronet.[52]

As in the case of household chaplains the tutor would normally take his meals with the squire and his family and was generally paid a salary of £20 or

£30 a year. In 1623 Sir Henry Baker of Sissinghurst in Kent gave direction in his will that Arthur Brickenden, who was teaching his eldest son, should be allowed £20 a year for nine years 'to the end he shall by his best endevors assist my . . . Executors as they shall have occasion to imploy him'.[53] During the course of Chancery proceedings in 1683 the Court was informed that Sir Fulwar Skipwith of Newbold Hall in Warwickshire, a baronet who was then about eight years old, was receiving tuition from Robert Jefferson, a Cambridge graduate, in the house of a relative. In return for his services Jefferson had 'his dyet and £20 p.annum . . . And a horse allowed him to ride abroade' with his pupil. In what was a clear acknowledgement that this form of education had potential drawbacks it was further stated that Thomas Jackson, a youth of about the same age as Sir Fulwar, had been brought into the household 'purposely to Learne with him to induce him to have the better Love and Likeinge to his booke'.[54]

    In some cases a tutor was appointed when the children were mere infants. In 1640 Sir Henry Slingsby of Red House in Yorkshire recorded in his diary that he had taken on a schoolmaster (Robert Cheyne, a graduate of Emmanuel College, Cambridge) to teach his son Thomas who was then only four years old. It was his intention (he went on) that Thomas should begin to spell and read Latin as well as English and to learn to speak it 'more by practise of speaking than by rule'. In this respect he was following the example of Montaigne whose essays had inspired him to keep a diary.[55] Among the more substantial gentry there was a tendency to put a very high value on the learning of languages, in particular Latin and French. When Sir Edward Carr of Aswarby in Lincolnshire drew up his will in 1618 he made provision for the payment of an annuity of £30 to Louis Minguest on the basis that he would instruct his sons Robert and Rochester in the French and Latin tongues. At the end of the century the sons of Jonathan Cope of Ranton Abbey in Staffordshire had two private tutors: an English schoolmaster who had a salary of £10 a year and a French schoolmaster who was paid at the rate of one guinea per month.[56]

    Some private tutors failed to earn unqualified approval. About the end of June 1641 Thomas Smyth, a Somerset squire who was then in London, received a disturbing letter from John Edwards, his steward at Ashton Court. Edwards reported that he had spoken to Mr Foster, who was tutor to his nine-year-old son Hugh, and gave him an account of their discussion about his charge:

> hee saith that hee loyters as much . . . as hee did whilest you weare at home, and seldome comes to praiers at nighte. I see Mr Foster is troubled at it, the childe's good and his engagement soe much being at stake, and there being as much tyme spent in play as there is in followeinge the booke . . . instead of goeinge forward it's well yf hee keepe that which hee hath already lerned. Mr Foster conceaves the way to remidie this is to have the childe kepte to his booke as in a tender and lovinge way, soe in some discrete awe too, and yet without any correction, for he affirmeth hee enclynes not that way.

Shortly afterwards Florence Smyth, the wife of Thomas Smyth, informed her husband that Mr Foster had left the house and it was not clear whether he would return. In fact, she went on,

> he is grone so dopish and discontented a man as I know not what that I think he rather discorages the child than the child him . . . when you com home wee most think of some other tuter for the boy who I beleve to be as tracktable as ever he was to one that will keep him in hart.[57]

Aside from the resident tutor the wealthier gentry often enlisted the services of music and dancing masters, usually on a monthly basis, to enable their children to acquire the requisite social accomplishments. Dancing skills were considered necessary for both sons and daughters but it was mainly the female children who were taught to sing and perform on musical instruments. Between 1670 and 1685 Sir Daniel Fleming of Rydal Hall in Westmorland periodically employed a music master, William Hutchinson, who provided his daughters with instruction on the harpsichord, the manichord and the virginals. From time to time a dancing master was also engaged: Mr Leak in 1674 for Katherine and Alice and Mr Tinkler in 1680 for Barbara and Mary.[58] During the minority of Sir John Harpur of Calke in Derbyshire his guardians ensured that detailed accounts were kept of the expenditure which they incurred. For the year beginning on 25 March 1695 there were various payments on behalf of his sister Anne, including £5 6s 0d to Mr Lambe for the purchase of a spinet; further sums amounting to £9 10s 0d which he received for giving her tuition on the instrument; and £3 17s 0d to Mr Porter for teaching her to dance. Sir John himself had a governor whose salary of £50 a year suggests that his responsibilities were considerably greater than those of a mere tutor.[59]

CHAPTER TEN

Domestic Activities

From the reign of Elizabeth onwards there were frequent expressions of concern about the decay of hospitality in England. So far as the country gentry were concerned a number of factors contributed to this process: in particular, the growing practice (at least among major county families) of sojourning for long periods in London or one or other of the major provincial towns, either because of the attractions of an urban life or because of a pressing need for retrenchment; the sale of estates to moneyed men whose social aspirations were not necessarily accompanied by any great respect for the traditional obligations associated with landed wealth; and changing attitudes to the old style of housekeeping with its emphasis in culinary matters on quantity rather than sophistication. Even so, there were many squires in the seventeenth century who had a reputation for dispensing what was termed great or noble hospitality, though this could vary considerably in its scope. Sir Ralph Delaval of Seaton Delaval in Northumberland, who entered into his inheritance in 1607, 'kept an open, great and plentifull house for entertainment, his owne family consisting dayly in his house of threescore persons and above . . . He delighted much in the company of his kinsmen and friends and entertayning of strangers'.[1] According to Robert Thoroton the Nottinghamshire historian Sir Gervase Clifton of Clifton Hall, who was one of the first men to be granted a baronetcy, 'generously, hospitably and charitably entertained all, from the King to the poorest Beggar'; indeed his port or general lifestyle and his hospitality 'exceeded very many of the Nobility'.[2] Richard Evelyn of Wotton in Surrey was described as 'a lover of hospitality' while his son George, who succeeded him in 1640, had such a hospitable nature that he excelled all other landowners in the county in maintaining 'that antient Custome of keeping (as it were) open house the whole yeare'. On occasion George Evelyn had as many as twenty guests staying at Wotton House, some of whom remained there all summer 'to his no small expense'.[3]

John Popham of Littlecote House in Wiltshire (Pl. 83) had a published work dedicated to him in 1635 by a minister who thoroughly approved of his munificent housekeeping:

And for Hospitality you have ever bin so mindfull to intertain neighbours and strangers that few great Houses in our parts can contend or compare for free, frequent and magnificent intertainment with your Litle-coate . . . you not only . . . entertaine, yea invite and entreat into your house your neighbours, friends and strangers but also daily at your gates breake your bread and open your almes basket to the poore of the Parishes round adjoyning, and refresh their hungry bowelles.

83. Littlecote House, Wiltshire. Painting by Thomas Wycke, late seventeenth century.

As John Aubrey testifies, Popham was a spendthrift who was heavily in debt at the time of his death. In a Chancery suit of 1649 Alexander Popham, who was now the head of the family, told the Court that his late brother had 'wasted his Estate in Hospitalitye', though in fact the bulk of the family's extensive landed possessions had survived the crisis.[4] Richard Legh, who was one of the richest landowners in Cheshire, was praised for his constant hospitality at Lyme Hall in the sermon preached at his funeral in 1687. It appears, however, to have been a highly selective form of hospitality which may have been politically motivated. In expatiating on this subject the minister laid stress on the splendid and magnificent entertainments which Legh had provided and the great resort of persons of quality and offered the opinion that 'his House might very well be styled a Country-Court, and Lime the Palace to the County-Palatine of Chester'.[5]

Whatever the scale of hospitality it would hardly have been feasible for a country gentleman to maintain a large household, with all that this meant in terms of food and drink, without drawing heavily on the resources of his estate. In 1641 Zachery Hillard, who served as steward to Edward Phelips of Montacute in Somerset, commented in a letter to his master that 'I find by experience that noe gentleman in the Countrye can well keepe his house without he use some husbandry and keepe a good parte of his demeasnes in his hands, for Corne and other necessaries'.[6] Even the wealthiest landowners considered it important to engage in both livestock and arable farming. The farming operations of John Savile, a Yorkshire squire with an estate revenue of £3000 a year, were recorded in an inventory which was drawn up after his death in 1659. At Methley, where he was seated, he had 8 acres of wheat and barley and 9 acres of peas and beans while the livestock consisted of 40 cattle and calves, 87 sheep and lambs and 10 pigs. In addition, similar farming activities were being undertaken at Whitwood, not far from Methley, and Adwick le Street which was rather further away. In total there were 58 acres under cultivation and 212 farm animals.[7] While demesne farming was a key element in the economics of household management the gentry often had many other sources of food within the ambit of their estates. The deer park, the rabbit warren, the fish ponds, the dovecote, the kitchen garden and the orchard all made their contribution to the provisioning of the country house. Bulstrode Whitelocke relates in his autobiography that in 1637 he created a park of about 20 acres at his Buckinghamshire seat, Fawley Court, and stocked it not only with red and fallow deer but with rabbits, hares, pheasants, partridges and pigeons.[8] In the orchards and gardens belonging to Richard Legh at Lyme Hall there were apples, pears, apricots, peaches, plums, nectarines, herbs, peas, artichokes, cabbages, turnips and potatoes.[9] Arthur Onslow of West Clandon in Surrey had carp and tench in his fish ponds while in 1692 a traveller in Westmorland noted that at Burneside Hall, the seat of Thomas Braithwaite, there was 'a large pond stored with tench, trout and eels' (Pl. 84).[10] Hopyards whose produce was used for the flavouring of beer were to be found not only in Kent, where they were particularly numerous, but in many other counties, including Devon, Norfolk and Yorkshire. There are also occasional references in accounts and inventories to the practice of bee-keeping. At the time of his death in 1670 Sir John Cutts of Childerley Hall in Cambridgeshire had twenty-seven hives of bees which were valued at £8.[11]

Most gentry households brewed their own beer and produced their own butter and cheese. Cider-making was well established in Devon, Dorset,

84. Burneside Hall, Westmorland.

Worcestershire and the counties bordering Wales, though it was not wholly confined to these regions. In some places honey was converted into mead as another alternative to beer. In February 1698 the contents of Edmund Wyndham's mansion at Kentsford in Somerset included two dozen pint bottles and one dozen quart bottles of mead.[12]

In his memoirs Sir Christopher Guise of Elmore in Gloucestershire wrote that 'Elmore is a fitt place for fish ponds, for pleasure boates, and intertaynments on the water, for foule, for fruite . . . and is very well and cheape accomodated with all things for house keepinge'.[13] In practice, however, the country house could never be completely self-sufficient in matters of food and drink unless its owner had particularly austere tastes. In an account of the family mansion at Wotton in the Surrey hills John Evelyn the diarist tells us that the market town of Dorking, which was only three miles away, served it abundantly with provisions 'as well of land as Sea'.[14] Among other things, it was necessary to purchase wine, sugar and spices. Sir William Waller, a man with strong Puritan beliefs, had serious reservations about the practice of using spices in cookery:

> people affect an ingenuity in luxury . . . It is not enough to have good meat if it have not a rellish of the East-Indies; it must be so spiced that an Aegyptian would think it were rather imbalmed to be buried and kept for Mummy then seasoned to be eaten; it must be so diversified and so disguised in the dressing that every dish must be a riddle.[15]

The kind of supplies which were bought in may be judged from the correspondence which took place in the years 1637 to 1641 between Sir William Calley of Burderop Park in Wiltshire and his son William on the one hand and Richard Harvey, a servant of Endymion Porter, on the other (Pl. 85). Harvey had formerly been employed in Sir William's household and was now acting as his London agent with responsibility for the supply of clothes, provisions and newsletters. Although the Calleys sent their servants to Marlborough to buy some of their groceries they also found it necessary to order many items from London. In 1638 these included wine, currants, pepper, nutmegs, ginger, cinnamon, mace, cloves, a barrel of sugar, Jordan almonds, olives, salad oil, Danzig sturgeon and wine corks or bungs. On one occasion Sir William asked Harvey to obtain for him twenty or thirty pounds of very good lump sugar or Metville sugar; on another his son reminded their agent that he wanted him to procure four pounds of green ginger when Mr Courteen's ships arrived at Milford Haven.[16] In 1659, following the death of Sir Henry Lee, a list was drawn up of the provisions remaining in his house at Ditchley in Oxfordshire. Among the groceries were refined ginger, lump sugar, brown sugar, currants, raisins, prunes, rice, dates, almonds, cinnamon, cloves and nutmegs. In the cellar there were 68 bottles of claret and 34 bottles of Canary wine, together with $34\frac{1}{2}$ hogsheads (or approximately 1760 gallons) of beer and $4\frac{1}{2}$ hogsheads of strong beer.[17] In October 1675 the Newdegate family's wine cellar at Arbury Hall in Warwickshire contained French, Spanish and German wines. In checking the stock Richard Newdegate noted in his pocket book that there were twelve dozen quarts of claret, a dozen quarts and 34 pints of sack, 8 quarts of Frontignac, 12 quarts of old Rhenish wine, 10 quarts

85. Letter of Sir
William Calley to
Richard Harvey, 19
May 1638 (Public
Record Office,
State Papers
Domestic, Charles
I, S.P.16/cccxc/122).

of Hochheimer, 6 quarts of white muscadine and 30 quarts of old sherry.[18] Depending on their quality such large amounts of wine could involve a considerable outlay. Between May and September 1693 Sir Edward Leighton of Wattlesborough Hall in Shropshire ran up a bill of £209 7s 0d for supplies of wine which included many bottles of champagne.[19]

In a memorandum drawn up in 1604 Sir William Wentworth of Wentworth Woodhouse in Yorkshire advised his son Thomas (the future Earl of Strafford) to be frugal in his housekeeping and suggested that 'if yow spend but a third parte of your revenewe in your house yow shall doe the wyser and better'. Similarly, Sir Richard Grosvenor of Eaton Hall in Cheshire told his son in 1636 that 'The third part of a man's certaine revenue (mee thinks) were a fitting proportion to bee spent' on housekeeping.[20] For most families the costs involved in housekeeping were a major element of expenditure. In the early part of James I's reign Sir William Paston of Oxnead in Norfolk gave direction that after his death the feoffees whom he had nominated should allow his heir £800 a year (out of an estate revenue of £3300 a year) 'to keepe A standinge howse dureinge his life'.[21] In a codicil to his will Sir Thomas Coningsby of Hampton Court in Herefordshire commented that in the matter of hospitality he considered it advisable that his son Fitzwilliam should continue to live in a secondary house with an establishment of proportionate size and that he should spend no more than £1000 a year. At his death in 1625 Sir Thomas left an estate worth £3000 a year but it was charged with the payment of legacies.[22] In 1638 Sir Henry Slingsby of Red House in Yorkshire wrote in his diary that he spent £500 a year on housekeeping 'if the demesne grounds which I keep in my own hands be reckon'd according to the Rent it would give, and the charges in getting it'. His accounts indicate that the expenditure on provisions for the household averaged £300 a year during the period 1635 to 1641 while his rent-roll amounted to some £1600 a year.[23] Thomas Smyth of Ashton Court in Somerset, who was reported to be a man worth £2000 a year, estimated that in 1641 his household expenses would be of the order of £548 a year, including £100 for wages, £60 for bread, £40 for wine and £15 for coal.[24] Richard Winwood, who was seated at Ditton Park in Buckinghamshire, had an estate revenue of £2500 a year and a reputation for open-handed hospitality which receives ample confirmation in the diary of his friend Bulstrode Whitelocke. When Whitelocke and some members of his family paid a visit to Ditton Park on 28 December 1663 they found no fewer than 300 people at dinner. On 1 January following he noted that Winwood again laid on a dinner for a large number of persons who had come to Ditton Park 'without invitation' and added that 'there was good order, no debauchery nor swearing and they had good cheer'. Winwood died without issue in 1688 and five years later his widow, Anne Winwood, testified in the course of legal proceedings that he had spent around £1000 a year on housekeeping (including about £170 for wages) and charitable activities (Pl. 86 for the Winwood memorial).[25]

Although some gentry began the day with breakfast it appears to have been no more than a light repast which was served without any measure of formality. Generally, there were two set meals a day: dinner at 11 a.m. or noon and supper at 5 or 6 p.m. Sir Hugh Cholmley, whose mansion was situated on the south cliff at Whitby in Yorkshire, writes that during the reign of Charles I the gates 'were ever shut up before dinner . . . and not opened till one o'clock, except for strangers who came to dinner, which was ever fit to receive three or four besides my family'.[26] The servants, for their part, usually sat down for their meals an hour or so later than the family when they would partake of the food and drink which remained. At the funeral of Sir John Norton of Rotherfield in Hampshire which took place in 1687 the preacher touched on this progression in commending him for his generous hospitality. His table, he recalled, was 'always found loaded with such substantial Provisions, as having serv'd the Parlour, afterwards feasted the Hall, and plentifully reliev'd the Poor at his Gates'.[27]

The food served in gentry households included beef, pork, mutton and lamb, veal, rabbits, venison, pigeons, poultry, game, wild-fowl, fish and oysters. Sir William Calley criticised his son's liking for venison which he

86. Monument
with effigies of
Richard Winwood
and his wife Anne
in Quainton parish
church,
Buckinghamshire.

described as 'a mechanic taste' but many of his fellow gentry enjoyed venison pasty.[28] For the dessert course, when a sweet wine was often served, there might be a variety of dishes ranging from fruit and cheese to puddings and cakes.

The household accounts kept by Thomas Noble, who served as steward to Sir John Caryll of West Harting in Sussex during the years 1638 to 1643, tell us much about the scale and nature of housekeeping among the wealthier gentry. The Carylls, who were a Catholic family, had recently sold a substantial amount of property but Sir John was still a major landowner with a rent-roll of some £1700 a year. Now and again Noble referred to the visits of relatives and friends of the family who were usually of the same religious persuasion. In the week beginning 12 January 1639 they included Sir Charles Smyth and his wife, Sir Garret Kempe and Sir John Shelley while on another occasion he annotated his accounts 'everie daye straingers in this weke also'. Over the Christmas period (when it was customary to provide a dinner for the tenantry) there was naturally a great upsurge in the consumption of food and drink. In the week beginning 22 December 1638 he noted that nine pigs (or porkers as he called them) and eight sheep had been killed and listed a large quantity of poultry, game and other birds which had been drawn from the estate (or perhaps in some cases received as gifts): 12 geese, 7 woodcock, 2 snipe, 3 swans, 4 ducks (including mallard), 12 widgeon, 10 teal, 23 turkeys, 15 capons, 10 hens, 16 pullets, 17 chickens, 34 'tame ducks' and 7 cocks. In addition, the sum of £100 19s 2d was spent on the purchase of provisions in this week and the following two weeks. Occasionally there was a delivery of oysters which probably came from Whitstable in Kent: 1400 in December 1638 and 2600 in March 1639. In some years the brewhouse was a hive of activity. During the year ending on 24 September 1641 there were twenty brewings which produced 236 hogsheads of beer and ale while in the same period 200 hogsheads were 'spent' in the buttery. When recording this information Noble also made the point that fewer candles had been used 'this yere then the last yere by 9 dossen'. In presenting a general account for the year ending on 30 September 1642 he informed his master that three hogsheads of sack had been bought for £42 4s 2d and six hogsheads of claret for £31. He further reported that the expenses of his table in that year had amounted to £692 2s 3½d and that when certain extraordinary disbursements were added in 'the whole expenses' of his house came to £744 4s 4d, excluding such cost items as the dairy, the husbandry and the stables.[29]

For many of the country gentry the feeding of the poor was a moral duty which went with the ownership of estates. In an account of some of his private meditations which was published in 1647 a Lincolnshire squire, Sir John Monson of Burton Hall, declared that

> we are but the poore men's Stewards who have an interest both in our wealth and increase, so as their propriety lieth in our possessions, which we ought at least weekly to account for . . . and to make our ability the gage and size of our bounty, justice or charity to them, with relation to our families, condition, quality and other circumstances . . . let us give with a large heart and an open hand, knowing that we should receive God's blessings like the ground that drinketh in the rain, but to make it more fruitfull.[30]

Sir Richard Grosvenor took a similar view but was not in favour of indiscriminate giving and urged his son to drive away all lusty rogues and sturdy beggars.[31] While Richard Winwood might open his doors to the neighbouring poor it was more usual for them to be fed at the gates. 'Twice a week', wrote Sir Hugh Cholmley, 'a certain number of old people, widows and indigent persons were served at my gates with bread and good pottage made of beef'.[32] Shortly before his death in 1676 Sir Robert Worsley of Appuldurcombe in the Isle of Wight expressed the wish that the 'constant weekly Alms att his doore' should be continued during his son's minority both there and at his other residence in Chilton Candover on the mainland. According to the testimony of persons who knew of the arrangement the value of these alms amounted to £50 a year.[33]

Following the death of Sir John Shuckburgh in 1661 an inventory was made of the contents of his house and demesne lands at Over Shuckburgh in Warwickshire and among the items listed was 'a bell to ring to Prayers'.[34] In the seventeenth century many, perhaps most, country houses had a daily routine of household prayers, whether or not there was a domestic chapel or a resident chaplain. In 1635 the minister who preached at the funeral of Sir Francis Pile of Compton Beauchamp in Berkshire told the congregation that 'for the week-dayes, God was daily and duly, ever since he was an housekeeper, called upon in his family two or three times a day, evening, morning, and at noone'; and that in the latter part of his life he had kept a chaplain 'to doe the divine office'.[35] At Kirklington Hall in Yorkshire it was Christopher Wandesford's practice to have family prayers at 6 a.m., 10 a.m. and 9 p.m. and this kind of schedule was also favoured by Sir Edward Onslow of Knowle in Surrey: at 6 a.m. the husbandmen assembled for prayers and at 10 a.m. there was a more general session at which the family and the household servants were present.[36] In some houses, however, it was customary to have prayers immediately before or after dinner and supper. At Lees Court in Kent there were prayers before dinner and after supper and at the evening session Sir George Sondes insisted that his sons should take it in turns to read a chapter from the Bible.[37]

In households where there was genuine spiritual fervour the amount of religious activity tended to be far greater than in Sir George Sondes's household at Lees Court. Family prayers in such households often involved catechizing and psalm singing as well as scripture readings. Unless there were urgent matters requiring their personal attention the squire and his wife might be engaged for several hours a day in private prayer and meditation and in studying the Bible and published sermons and other religious works. According to the minister who preached at her funeral Lady Mary Jolliffe, the wife of William Jolliffe of Caverswall Castle in Staffordshire, considered this earthly world to be vile and despicable and made religion 'her great Business and Employment'. This was reflected in 'the constant frequency of her private Devotions, which she perform'd three times a Day at the least', her regular practice of fasting, her diligent reading of the scriptures and her meditating on the Word of God.[38] For godly families Sunday, or the Lord's Day as they called it, was the most important day of the week. It was a day which was given over almost entirely to the performance of religious duties, not only in the parish church but at home. If there was a domestic chaplain he would usually be expected to preach a sermon for the benefit of the whole household. Alternatively, a visiting minister or, exceptionally, the head of the household might take on this task while it was not uncommon for a sermon which had been heard in the parish church to be repeated and opened up for general discussion. In addition, some Puritan families such as the Gells of Hopton Hall in Derbyshire and the Harleys of Brampton Bryan in Herefordshire had special days of humiliation when they prayed and fasted and sought forgiveness for their sins.[39]

In its own way the regime of corporate activities in Catholic houses was no less intensive as we learn from Father James Sharpe's account of life in the Yorkshire mansion of the Babthorpe family during the early years of James I's reign. On Sundays at Osgodby Hall the chaplains had a substantial programme of sermons, catechizing and spiritual lessons besides the celebration of Mass. On 'work days' there were usually two Masses: one for the servants (who were all Catholics) at 6 a.m., which was often attended by members of the family and the other at 8 a.m. for the rest of the household. In the afternoon the household assembled for evensong at four o'clock and this was later followed by matins which in accordance with Catholic practice would have been held at midnight.[40]

In a sermon published in 1610 John Dod emphasised, in relation to Protestant households, that 'It is not sufficient for us to be religious our selves but our families must also be religious. Not only the heads and governours but the whole household must be addicted unto God's service'. Servants must learn to know their duty 'and be ready to ioyne with their governours in all godly and Christian exercises'.[41] Other Puritan authors such as his friend Robert Cleaver and William Gouge were equally adamant that it was incumbent on the master to ensure that his servants received a proper grounding in the principles of religion, that they fully participated in the corporate worship of the household and that they also went regularly to church.[42] Occasionally a godly squire took on personal responsibility for instructing and catechizing the servants but more often this task was performed by his wife[43] or a domestic chaplain. At Cockfield Hall in Suffolk Dame Elizabeth Brooke, the widow of Sir Robert Brooke, arranged for 'a grave divine' to visit her house for the purpose of expounding the principles of religion and catechizing the servants, functions which she had formerly entrusted to her chaplains. She also attached great importance to the repetition of sermons which she used as the subject matter for discourses aimed at improving the understanding of her household.[44]

In some gentry households it appears to have been the practice to encourage rather than to command the servants to attend family prayers or church services, though in such cases the moral pressure must have been considerable. Dorothy Hanbury, the wife of Edward Hanbury of Kelmarsh in Northamptonshire, was described as 'a religious governour of her servants' who was 'a good example unto them, and in cold winter mornings would rise betimes and come to prayers, to draw them on to be present at this exercise'.[45] On the other hand, it is unlikely that Sir Edward Harley's servants at Brampton Bryan enjoyed any freedom of choice. Someone who clearly knew him well wrote after his death in 1700 that it was delightful

> to see morning and evening his whole family from the meanest servant to the Eldest child worshipping God with great seriousness and sobriety, with good order and decency; his constant method was, he read a chapter . . . both in the old and new Testament, sung a psalm and pray'd; and each servant had a bible, and were instructed in what was read, and in the principles of the Christian faith, from the poor postboy to the waiting Gentleman.[46]

A mandatory approach was certainly favoured by the Popham family of Littlecote in Wiltshire before the time of the Civil War. In 1635 a clerical acquaintance observed that Sir Francis Popham and his son John had always been determined to serve God with their whole household and to ensure that all their servants were present at the set times of prayer, 'yea to compell them to come on the solemne dayes and times unto God's house that it may be full'.[47] Compulsion, whether open or implied, was probably commonplace but Robert Cleaver for one considered that all was far from well. Cooks and butlers in great houses rarely went to church; and even if they deigned to appear it was usually for only part of the service. More generally, a large household often made its way to church in a piecemeal fashion: first the husband arrived, then the wife a quarter of an hour later and finally the servants (some of whom had no doubt been hard at work). In fact the minister could be half-way through the service before they were all present. In Cleaver's view the master should take steps to ensure that the whole household came to church together.[48]

87. Hawking
(Richard Blome,
*The Gentleman's
Recreations*, second
edition, 1710).

As a leisured class the country gentry had ample time at their disposal for field sports and other forms of recreation. Not infrequently a godly divine publicly denounced what he regarded as their hedonistic way of life. When a Northamptonshire minister, Thomas Burroughs, preached a funeral sermon in 1657 the presence of his patron, Sir John Langham of Cottesbrooke, did not deter him from pursuing this theme:

> How many Gentlemen be there, of whom when they die, all that can be said is this, They were born, they did eat, and drink, and play, and hunt, and hawk, and lived like so many wild Ass-colts, never minding any thing that concern'd God's glory, or their own salvation . . . and so died, and dropt into hell?[49]

In the main the gentry were impervious to such criticism, even if they were aware of it. Sir Edward Peyton, a Puritan squire who was seated at Isleham in Cambridgeshire, described hunting and hawking as 'most commendable exercises'. Hunting, he stressed, was a manly and heroic sport which helped to promote bodily health.[50] In a memorandum which he drew up for the edification of his grandson William Higford of Dixton in Gloucestershire offered a rather wider perspective. 'Hunting', he told him, 'is usefull, to know the situation and distance of places, and to enure your Body to labour . . . So also is the Gentile exercise of Hawking, more especially at the River, to see the Falcon lessen her self, and to fall down upon the Foul like a Thunderbolt'.[51] Another Gloucestershire squire, Sir William Guise of Elmore, would have

been considered by many to have been a typical representative of the landed gentry. According to his grandson he was 'never a lover of bookes, butt of all corporall exercises and pleasures, as dancing, hunting, hauking, and such country sports, which made him of a robust complexion'.[52] Some men preferred hawking to hunting (Pl. 87). A wealthy landowner would often employ a full-time falconer and this continued to be a common practice for two or three decades after the Restoration. By the end of the century, however, hawking was falling out of favour, largely because of the growing popularity of shooting.

Throughout the seventeenth century the gentry hunted deer and hares (Pls 88 and 89). After the Restoration they also began to engage in fox-hunting, though the eclipse of deer-hunting only became fully apparent in the early years of the eighteenth century. In 1674 it was reported that some of the Sussex gentry around Chichester had spent seven or eight days hunting foxes which would have involved lengthy forays across open country.[53] Many well-to-do squires kept packs of hounds which were often a source of great pride. In 1638 Sir John Sedley of Southfleet in Kent stipulated in a codicil to his will that 'my next male heire male forever shall keepe tenn couples of hounds att the least in his own custody' and settled a rent-charge of £20 a year to cover the cost of maintaining the pack.[54] A generation later John Strangways of Melbury Sampford in Dorset bequeathed his pack of hounds, together with a horse called Northumberland and a bay gelding, to John Every of Cothay in Somerset who clearly shared his love of hunting.[55] When hunting parties were

88. Deer hunting (Richard Blome, *The Gentleman's Recreations*, second edition, 1710).

89. Hunting the hare (Richard Blome, *The Gentleman's Recreations*, second edition, 1710).

90. Shooting game (Richard Blome, *The Gentleman's Recreations*, second edition, 1710).

91. Fishing (Richard Blome, *The Gentleman's Recreations*, second edition, 1710).

organised gentlemen were often prepared to travel considerable distances with their hounds. In the early part of James I's reign we find Sir Henry Savile of Methley inviting guests to a gathering of Yorkshire landowners at Hickleton Hall, the seat of his brother-in-law Sir John Jackson, for the purpose of enjoying a few days of hunting and hawking. In a letter addressed to his kinsman Sir Richard Beaumont of Whitley Hall he described the arrangement which had been agreed upon as 'every one but one man besides his huntesman or faulconer' and urged him to bring 'the creditt of your kennell'. On a different but related matter he added that 'I would nowe gladly send houndes into Leicestershire yf you can sende me worde howe'.[56]

Other outdoor activities which were considered to be fitting pastimes for a gentleman included shooting (Pl. 90), fishing (Pl. 91), horse-racing and bowling. Inventories of the contents of country houses often contain references to such items as fowling guns or pieces, birding guns and fishing nets. One of the most important consequences of the Game Act of 1671 was that the landed gentry henceforth had an exclusive right to shoot pheasants, partridges and other game.[57] Some landowners had small boats which they used for fishing, either in their own lakes or pools or in neighbouring rivers. An inventory drawn up in 1683, following the death of Sir Clement Fisher of Packington Hall in Warwickshire, refers to the 'Great Pool' where there were two rowing boats and a storage box for fish; another boat in the park pool; and fishing nets which were kept in a garden house.[58] At the time of his death in 1687 a Shropshire squire, Richard Fowler, had two fishing boats moored in the River

Severn, a few miles from his house, Harnage Grange. Within the house there were fishing nets and six fowling pieces.[59]

In some counties, at least, the sport of horse-racing was already well established in the early part of the century. In a memorandum book Thomas Meynell, a Catholic squire seated at North Kilvington in Yorkshire, recorded a number of races held in the years 1621 to 1624 at such places as Hambleton, Bagby, Thirsk, Knaresborough and Richmond. In April 1623, he noted, 'ther was seaven horses which rune at Richemond for a Bowle worth £12, and a salte worth six, the first horse to have the best, the second, the next. Sr William Gascoigne did win the first. I myselfe did win the second'. In the same week his son Richard won the best cup at Thirsk.[60]

In the seventeenth century football and cricket had little or no appeal for the gentry but they displayed a great deal of enthusiasm for the more exclusive sport of bowling (Pl. 92). Bowling greens or alleys were to be found at many of the larger country houses, among them Montacute House in Somerset, Sydmonton Court in Hampshire, Halland House and Slaugham Place in Sussex, Stoke Court in Herefordshire, Clifton Hall in Nottinghamshire and Burton Agnes Hall in Yorkshire.[61] An inventory of the household goods at Sir Thomas Barrington's Essex mansion, Hatfield Priory, which was drawn up in 1632 includes a reference to twelve pairs of bowls and two jacks. His son John shared his love of the game: in a book of expenses covering the years 1651 to 1654 one of his servants recorded a number of occasions when he played bowls with his uncle Sir William Masham, both at Hatfield Priory and at the latter's house, Otes Hall.[62] In some counties such

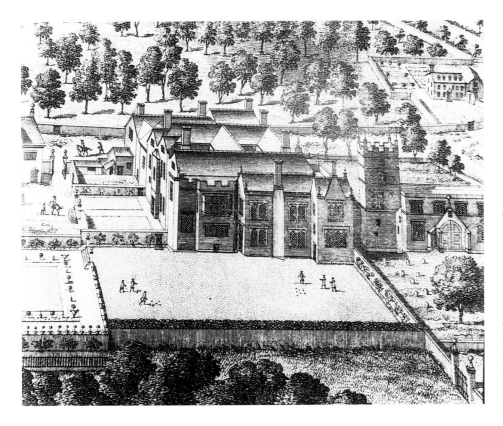

92. Men playing bowls at the mansion of the Bray family in Great Barrington, Gloucestershire. Engraving by Johannes Kip (Sir Robert Atkyns, *The Ancient and Present State of Glocestershire*, second edition, 1768).

as Suffolk, Dorset and Berkshire there were bowling clubs which served as convivial meeting-places for the neighbouring gentry. During his travels in the reign of Charles II Thomas Baskerville noted that within half a mile of Faringdon in Berkshire there was a 'delicate' bowling green where in the summertime the gentry of those parts met to divert themselves in the pleasant air.[63]

Godly divines not only deplored the amount of time devoted to field sports but also expressed strong reservations about some of the recreational activities which went on indoors. In particular, they considered it sinful to take part in games of chance or to play for money.[64] Here and there a pious gentleman such as Sir Ralph Delaval of Seaton Delaval in Northumberland or Sir Samuel Rolle of Heanton Satchville in Devon refused to allow card-playing or dicing in his house[65] but this kind of attitude was far from common. Card games, dicing, backgammon and shovelboard were all popular pastimes in the houses of the gentry and as a rule were played for small stakes. In 1654 Dorothy Osborne spent some months with her brother-in-law Sir Thomas Peyton at Knowlton Court in Kent and during her residence there wrote in a letter to her future husband that 'the sun was up an hower before I went to bed to day . . . wee goe abroade all day and Play all night, and say our Prayers when wee have time'.[66]

In many country houses there was a pair of playing tables which were usually to be found in the hall or one of the parlours. Shovelboard tables also appear in inventories: in 1679, for example, two tables of this kind were listed among the contents of the hall at Grey's Court, the Oxfordshire mansion of the Knollys family while in Sir Robert Wingfield's house at Easton in Suffolk there was a room which was described in 1671 as 'the shovell board roome'.[67] Some gentlemen had a liking for chess which as a game of genuine skill was largely immune from Puritan censure. In 1670 the great parlour at Childerley Hall, the Cambridgeshire seat of Sir John Cutts, contained a pair of playing tables, a chessboard and two sets of chessmen.[68]

The game of billiards was not unknown to Shakespeare: in *Anthony and Cleopatra* the Queen says to a reluctant Charmian 'let's to billiards'.[69] In the latter part of the seventeenth century a number of country squires owned billiard tables, among them William Morley of Glynde in Sussex, Sir John Shuckburgh of Over Shuckburgh in Warwickshire, Sir William Halford of Welham in Leicestershire, Sir William Clifton of Clifton in Nottinghamshire and Sir Ralph Assheton of Whalley in Lancashire. In January 1675 Morley noted in his account book that he had lost £2 10s 0d at billiards; and that he had paid Mr Foxe 2s 6d for 'turning' the billiard table legs. Assheton kept his billiard table in the gallery at Whalley Abbey while Shuckburgh's table had been set up in the banqueting house in the garden. In a few cases, however, there was a separate billiard room. An inventory which was drawn up in 1686 following the death of Sir Arthur Harris of Hayne in Devon contains references both to a billiard room and what was termed 'the Sportinge Chamber'. A Leicestershire squire, Sir Thomas Hesilrige of Noseley Hall, also had a billiard room: in 1698 its contents were described as a billiard table, two old tapestry hangings, five old maps, a press and two old pictures.[70]

In all ages, wrote William Higford, 'Musick hath been esteemed a quality becoming a noble personage'; and he assured his grandson that 'you will be most compleat when you joyn the vocal and instrumental both together'.[71] When Sir John Fortescue of Salden House in Buckinghamshire drew up his will in 1669 he referred in a supporting document to 'the least parlour commonly called the singing roome'.[72] In the larger country houses the contents often (though by no means in all cases) included musical instruments and in particular virginals, harpsichords and viols. Virginals and harpsichords belonged to the same family of keyboard instruments and indeed their names tended to be interchangeable. References to the harpsichord occur more frequently after the Restoration, possibly reflecting its further technical development. We learn from a Chancery suit that shortly before the death in 1664 of Sir Christopher Wray of Glentworth in Lincolnshire his wife had received a pair of harpsichords which had been sent down from London on approval; and according to his steward's accounts Thomas Lake of Canons in Middlesex had a harpsichord bought for him in 1689 at a cost of £25.[73] The viol was a stringed instrument which was played with a bow. Usually a gentleman would have a chest of viols which contained a number of instruments ranging from treble to bass. A few families had organs installed in their houses, among them the Shireburns of Stonyhurst in Lancashire, the Dudleys of Clopton in Northamptonshire and the Slannings of Marystow in Devon.[74]

The 'home-delights' of Sir Thomas Wodehouse of Kimberley in Norfolk were described in a verse chronicle of his family as 'Musiq and a booke'. In 1658 the contents of his music room at Kimberley Lodge included an organ, a harpsichord and a chest of viols. His enthusiasm for music was inherited by his son Sir Philip who was said to have been 'a man of good learning, ready wit, and exceedingly skilled in Music'. In the latter part of his life the composer John Jenkins was a member of Sir Philip's household at Kimberley Lodge.[75] Sir Peter Leycester, a Cheshire baronet, was also an accomplished musician. In 1667 his music room at Tabley Hall contained a variety of instruments: 'One Complete Chest or Set of Violes, beinge seaven in number, Two Trebles, Two Basses, Two Tenours, and one Lyra-Viole, with all the Viole-Stickes thereto belonginge; also one payre of Virginalls, one Psittyrne enlayd with mother of Pearle, one Gittyrne with Wyre-Strings of a Triangular fforme, one old Lute, one Violin with all their appurtenances.'[76] From time to time the squire and his family might be entertained by a troupe of actors or a band of musicians who would generally provide an accompaniment for dancing. During the reign of James I the Shuttleworths of Gawthorpe Hall in Lancashire were visited by two drama companies under aristocratic patronage, Lord Stafford's players and the Earl of Derby's players, and their accounts also include a number of payments to pipers, fiddlers and other musicians.[77] In the latter part of the century the accounts kept by Sir Daniel Fleming of Rydal Hall in Westmorland record several occasions when plays were put on in his house by more homespun actors from Kirkby Lonsdale and the hamlets of Troutbeck, Long Sleddale and Applethwaite. The choice of plays was not unambitious: in December 1661 the Flemings were treated to a performance of Thomas Heywood's comedy *The Fair Maid of the West* while the following year the Long Sleddale players presented the sombre tragedy *Ferrox and Porrex*, or *Gorboduc* as it was more commonly known, which had first been staged a century earlier.[78]

CHAPTER ELEVEN

Intellectual Pursuits

In the seventeenth century a country gentleman of any standing would have had at least a few books in his house. As a general rule such books as he might possess were kept in his private study or closet where, among other things, he would deal with his correspondence, take stock of his financial situation and, if he was a pious man, spend some time each day in prayer and meditation. An inventory of Ripley Hall in Yorkshire which was drawn up in 1618 reveals that the books which had belonged to Sir William Ingleby (and which he had bequeathed to William Ingleby his nephew and heir) were distributed between the new study, the old study and the dining parlour. In the old study they were stored along with such prosaic items as a sparrow net, a lark net, horse collars and bridles.[1]

The idea of a separate library room which was given over more or less entirely to the display of books shelved in elegant cases only gradually took hold even among the wealthier gentry. One of the earliest references to this type of room occurs in an inventory of Bramshill House in Hampshire which was prepared in 1634 following the death of Sir Edward Zouch. In this large Jacobean mansion which had only recently been completed the room described as the library contained 250 books together with 'certaine Mathematicall Instruments'.[2] After the Restoration the picture begins to change. In the reign of Charles II there were a number of major families which housed their books in libraries, among them the Springetts of Broyle Place in the Sussex parish of Ringmer, the Hobys of Bisham Abbey in Berkshire, the Yelvertons of Easton Mauduit in Northamptonshire, the Digbys of Stoke Dry in Rutland and the L'Estranges of Hunstanton in Norfolk.[3] In an account of his friend Ralph Sheldon, a Catholic squire whose principal residence was in Warwickshire, Anthony Wood describes how he established his magnificent library at Weston Park. After his wife's death in 1663 Sheldon 'spared not any mony to set up a standing library in his house at Weston'. In 1667 he travelled to Rome where he 'furnished himself with many choice books, as also with medalls and coines for the setting up a closet of rarities'. On returning home in 1670 he purchased manuscripts and more printed books. During the period 1675 to 1679 Wood devoted a good deal of time and effort to the task of organising his library and drew up two detailed catalogues of its contents. This library, writes Wood, 'he setled in a large square wainscot roome over the kitchin, and his medalls and rarities and pictures in a little roome over the entrie into the hall; which continuing there until 1682, and then Mr Sheldon causing the room at the north end of the gallery to be waincoted, translated them thence'.[4]

As the following examples illustrate,[5] the size of book collections varied widely:

owner (with date of inventory/catalogue)	*house*	*number of books*
Sir Thomas Knyvett (1618)	Ashwellthorpe Hall, Norfolk	1407
Sir Peter Leycester (1672)	Tabley Hall, Nether Tabley, Cheshire	1332
Sir Ralph Bovey (1679)	Stowe Hall, Long Stowe, Cambridgeshire	176
William Lygon (1681)	Madresfield Court, Worcestershire	554
Sir John Drake (1684)	Ashe House, Musbury, Devon	340
Brome Whorwood (1684)	Holton House, Oxfordshire	100
Sir William Glynne (1692)	Ambrosden House, Oxfordshire	800

Sir Ralph Bovey's collection at Stowe Hall was kept in three closets. In 1679 there were forty-one small books and about twenty play books in a closet near the gallery; five folio volumes in one of the closets adjoining his lodging chamber; and sixty books, together with fifty play books and sermons, in another closet there. In addition, he had 269 books in his town house in Gray's Inn Lane, Holborn. At Madresfield Court the library consisted of 127 folio volumes, 111 quarto volumes, 272 octavo volumes and 44 smaller books, together with 236 pamphlets.[6]

The literary tastes of country gentlemen found expression in their library catalogues, the references to book purchases in their expenditure accounts and the itemised bills which they received from London booksellers who were generally their main source of supply. The abundance of religious works (Pl. 93) (which were often dedicated to members of the gentry) is a testimony not only to the spiritual values of some families at the upper levels of society but to the kind of ethos which prevailed in the field of education and the profusion of biblical commentators and exponents of what was termed 'practical divinity'. Among the most popular books of this kind (at least in Protestant households) were John Foxe's *Book of Martyrs*, Bishop Lewis Bayly's *The Practise of Piety*, the collected works of Bishop Joseph Hall and the published sermons of two other men who became bishops, Edward Stillingfleet and John Tillotson. During the early seventeenth century the libraries of Puritan squires such as Sir Robert Harley of Brampton Bryan in Herefordshire, Sir Thomas Barrington of Hatfield Priory in Essex and Sir Simonds D'Ewes of Stowlangtoft in Suffolk contained the works of a considerable number of godly divines, in particular William Perkins, John Dod, John Preston, William Gouge, Robert Bolton and Richard Sibbes. Even a zealous Puritan, however, might take an interest in other forms of literature. Sir Robert Harley's library catalogue of 1637 includes Shakespeare's sonnets, the

93. Some examples of seventeenth-century religious works.

plays of Ben Jonson and Bacon's essays; and about the same time Sir Thomas Barrington's book dealer was supplying him with the Second Folio edition of Shakespeare's works, a verse translation by George Sandys of Ovid's *Metamorphoses*, the poems of Thomas Randolph and a book on falconry. Sir Simonds D'Ewes owned law books, books by classical authors and an assortment of other works, among them Chaucer's *Canterbury Tales*, William Camden's *Britannia*, John Speed's *The History of Great Britain*, Fynes Moryson's *Itinerary*, Gervase Markham's treatise on horsemanship and Machiavelli's *The Prince*. He also had a large quantity of manuscripts: in his will he referred to 'my pretious librarie, in which I have stored upp for divers yeares past with great care, cost and industrie divers Originalls or Autographs, Ancient coines of gold, silver and brasse, Manuscripts or written bookes, and such as are imprinted'.[7]

Sir Robert Harley's library was destroyed or pillaged when his house, Brampton Castle, was stormed by royalist forces in 1644. In assessing his losses he put the value of his study of books at £200.[8] The library of his son Sir Edward, which was catalogued in 1662, also contained many divinity works but its general scope was more extensive and varied. Among other things, it included Bacon's *New Atlantis*, the poems of Margaret Cavendish, Duchess of

Newcastle and Robert Greene's play *Orlando Furioso*; books on chemistry, chess, the art of oratory, the treatment of smallpox and the improvement of vegetables; and pamphlets on the Jews in America and experimental philosophy.[9]

In 1672 Sir Peter Leycester drew up a catalogue of all his books in the study and the parlour at Tabley Hall. In this extensive collection there were books on the law, religion and music; the works of classical authors such as Homer, Horace and Ovid; the plays of Ben Jonson and Francis Beaumont and John Fletcher (but not those of Shakespeare); and the poetry of Chaucer, Edmund Spenser, Michael Drayton, John Donne, George Herbert, Thomas Randolph and Abraham Cowley. Other items in Sir Peter's library included Raleigh's *History of the World*, Henry Peacham's *Compleat Gentleman* and Thomas Hobbes's *Leviathan* and *Behemoth*, his discourse on the causes of the Civil Wars.[10]

When Sir Nathaniel Powell, the owner of Wierton Place in Kent, died in 1675 those responsible for producing an inventory of his personal estate took it upon themselves to list all his books individually. Many of these were law books, including Sir Edward Coke's *Institutes*, Michael Dalton's manual on the office of justice of the peace and a treatise on gavelkind tenure which was particularly widespread in Kent. The rest of his library mainly consisted of religious works by such authors as Joseph Hall, Robert Bolton and Richard Sibbes.[11]

In 1681 a catalogue was prepared of Thomas Lucy's library at Charlecote House in Warwickshire. Since Lucy, a professional soldier, had only inherited the estate in 1677 there can be little doubt that the contents of the library reflected the interests of his predecessors and in particular those of his grandfather Sir Thomas Lucy, a man with a Puritan cast of mind who had spent much of his time engaged in scholarly pursuits. In addition to legal and religious works the catalogue lists many French books, including the essays of Montaigne; the poems of Dante, Petrarch, Chaucer, Edmund Spenser, Ben Jonson and Michael Drayton; William Camden's *Annals of the Reign of Elizabeth*; and Fynes Moryson's *Itinerary*.[12]

The library which had belonged to Sir John Lenthall of Bessels Leigh in Berkshire was catalogued in 1684, three years after his death. Sir John was the son of William Lenthall, the Speaker of the Long Parliament, who may possibly have acquired many of the volumes listed. Aristotle, Virgil, Seneca and Tacitus were represented in the collection, as were Milton and Donne though only through the medium of their prose. Other works included Hobbes's *Leviathan*, Bacon's essays and his *Advancement of Learning*, Camden's *Britannia* and Sir Thomas Browne's *Religio Medici*. There were also several dictionaries: John Cowell's *Interpreter*, the controversial legal glossary which had been condemned by Parliament following its publication in 1607; Randle Cotgrave's French–English dictionary which was the first of its kind; and an Italian–English dictionary which was complemented by an Italian grammar book.[13]

A notebook belonging to Richard Newdegate, the son and eventual successor of Sir Richard Newdegate of Arbury in Warwickshire, contains a list entitled 'A Compleat Catalouge of all my Books' which bears the date 12 December 1696. Altogether he owned 240 books, many of which he had bought himself. Some were the kind of publications which could have been found in hundreds of gentlemen's collections: an expanded version of John Gerard's *Herball*, Nicholas Culpeper's *The English Physician Enlarged*, Michael Dalton's *The Countrey Justice*, works of Joseph Hall and Edward Stillingfleet and *The Practise of Piety*. What is most striking is the wide range of books which testify to his love of English literature: the First Folio edition of Shakespeare's works (which was a highly appropriate item for the library of a Warwickshire gentleman); collected editions of the plays of Ben Jonson as well as Francis Beaumont and John Fletcher; five volumes of plays by John Webster, John Dryden, Thomas Otway and others; and the poetry of George Herbert, Sir John Denham, Edmund Waller and Abraham Cowley. In addition, there are items which suggest the possibility of further interests: John Wilkins's *Mathematical Magick*, two of Robert Boyle's reports on his scientific experiments and Izaak Walton's *Compleat Angler*.[14]

Sir Edward Leighton of Wattlesborough Hall in Shropshire was a man whose love of books was matched by his reluctance to pay for them. His London book dealer, Gabriel Rogers, grew increasingly exasperated over his dilatoriness and on one occasion, when receiving only part of what was due, told him that 'I humbly desire what is A reasonable consideration for the forbearance for the other moneys'. Eventually, in November 1702, there was a final settlement when Sir Edward sent him £50 which brought his total outlay to £144. A composite bill which figured in this settlement lists all the books which had been dispatched since August 1677. These purchases included Samuel Butler's *Hudibras*, John Dryden's play *All for Love* and the sermons of Stillingfleet and Tillotson in 1677 and 1678; Thomas Hobbes's *Behemoth* and Ovid's *Epistolae* 'Englished by the Wits' in 1679; the poems of Andrew Marvell and Shakespeare's *King Lear* and *Richard II* in 1680; and John Locke's *Some Thoughts Concerning Education* in 1693, the year of its publication.[15]

Some gentlewomen had their own collections of books though in their case the evidence is more scanty.[16] Dame Margaret Heath was the wife of Sir Robert Heath who served as Charles I's Attorney General and the mother of Sir Edward Heath of Cottesmore in Rutland. Following her death in 1647 an inventory was drawn up of the books in her closet; they numbered eighty-two in all. These included books of divinity by such authors as Joseph Hall, Robert Bolton and Richard Sibbes but perhaps significantly there were no works by classical writers. Among other items were two copies of John Gerard's *Herball* (a coloured and an uncoloured version), a book on natural history, Henry Peacham's *Compleat Gentleman*, the poems of George Herbert and Robert Cleaver's *A Godlie Forme of Householde Government*.[17] A few of these books were also to be found in the library of Dame Bridget Bennet, the second wife of Sir John Bennet of Dawley in Middlesex, which was catalogued in 1680. This, however, was a much more substantial collection which contained 224 volumes, including no fewer than sixty-three French books; a considerable number of religious works; works of classical authors such as Livy, Seneca and Ovid; Milton's *Paradise Lost* and the poetry of John Donne, Edmund Waller, Abraham Cowley and others; and Raleigh's *History of the World*, Gilbert Burnet's *History of the Reformation* and John Rushworth's *Historical Collections*.[18]

In a work published posthumously in 1680 Sir William Waller offered some waspish comments on the subject of private libraries:

> But among those few persons (especially those of quality) that pretend to look after bookes, how many are there that affect rather to look upon them then in them? Some covet to have libraries in their houses as Ladies desire to have Cupboards of plate in their chambers, only for shew; as if they were only to furnish their roomes and not their mindes.[19]

No doubt there was an element of truth in this criticism yet the fact remains that the gentleman scholar who immersed himself in antiquarian studies or other intellectual pursuits was a not uncommon figure in seventeenth-century England. Sir Richard Worsley of Appledurcombe House in the Isle of Wight was described by a fellow squire, Sir John Oglander, as 'a very pregnant scholler, and verie expert in the Greeke tounge; well seen in all learninge'. He was 'wonderful studious, insomuch as he affected no counterye spoortes, eythor hawkinge or huntinge, but whollie spent his tyme when he wase alone att his booke'.[20] Sir Simonds D'Ewes had such a passion for academic research that in 1634 his friend Sir Nathaniel Barnardiston, who like him was seated in Suffolk, was driven to complain that it was a great pity that their families 'should not have leysure once in two or three yeares to visit one an other'.[21] Sir Henry Yelverton of Easton Mauduit in Northamptonshire inherited a large library of printed books and manuscripts which had been started by his grandfather and further built up by his father. Following his death in 1670 it was valued at no less than £1500 within a total figure of £3047 for his personal estate as a whole. A catalogue which was prepared in 1694 bears testimony to the comprehensive nature of the book collection which was classified under eight heads: Theology, History, Antiquities, Jurisprudence, Miscellanea (which included literary works, both English and classical, dictionaries and grammars), Philosophy and Medicine, Politics, and Geography and Mathematics. Sir Henry was a man of considerable learning who was highly proficient in Latin and Greek and the author of a work entitled *A Short Discourse of the Truth and Reasonableness of the Religion Delivered by Jesus Christ* which was published in 1662.[22]

After Sir William Morice (Pl. 94) resigned as Secretary of State in 1668 he lived in retirement at his country seat, Werrington Park in Devon, 'where he erected a fair Library, valued at £1200, being choice Books, richly bound . . . in the study and perusal whereof was his principal Divertisement, which yielded him the most sensible pleasure that he took during the last Years of his Life'.[23] Sir John Marsham of Whorn's Place in Kent, who was one of the Six Clerks in Chancery, earned the praise of Anthony Wood for his wide-ranging intellectual capabilities. According to Wood's testimony he was 'a person well accomplish'd, exact in histories whether civil or profane, in chronology and in the tongues' and was generally regarded as one of the greatest antiquaries of his time.[24]

Many gentlemen applied themselves to the study of history, heraldry and genealogy. Sir Simon Archer, who was seated at Tanworth in Warwickshire, made a substantial contribution to Sir William Dugdale's celebrated work on the history of his native county. When Dugdale published his *Antiquities*

94. Sir William Morice (Witt Library, Courtauld Institute of Art).

of Warwickshire in 1656 he dedicated it to his friend in acknowledgement of the debt he owed him and described him as a person who had 'a great Affection to Antiquities' and a diligent collector of very many choice manuscripts and other rarities. Sir Simon never lost his enthusiasm for historical research: in 1650, when he was an old man, he wrote that 'If the tymes were quiet . . . I should wholly burye myself in the search of Antiquityes'.[25] Sir Peter Leycester had a wide range of interests, including mathematics, astronomy and theology, but the subject which most took up his time was the history of Cheshire and its landed families. In 1672 his library contained a number of historical and topographical works, among them Camden's *Britannia*, John Speed's *History of Great Britain*, Dugdale's *Antiquities of Warwickshire* and Daniel King's *Vale Royall of England*, a book specifically relating to Cheshire. Sir Peter's *Historical Antiquities*, which was published in 1674 (Pl. 95), begins with a general history of Great Britain and Ireland but mainly consists of an account of the gentry families seated in the Cheshire hundred of Bucklow where Tabley Hall was situated. In his introduction he drew attention to the fact that he had included a transcript of that part of the Doomsday Book which covered Cheshire and added that he had no doubt that this would be 'very acceptable to all the Gentry of that County, and especially to such as love the Study of Antiquities'.[26] One man who would certainly have welcomed the appearance of this work was Sir John Crewe of Utkinton Hall who lived not far away in a neighbouring hundred (Pl. 96). In a manuscript book containing the pedigrees of knights Peter Le

95. The title page
of Sir Peter
Leycester's
*Historical
Antiquities*, 1673/4.

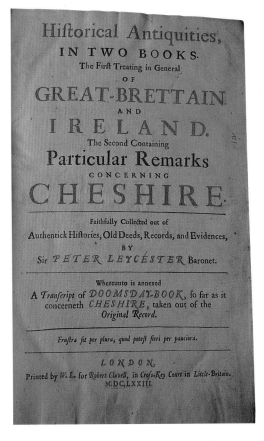

Neve the herald and genealogist inserted the comment that he was 'my spe-
ciall good friend and a great lover of Antiquitys'. At the same time it is clear
that Sir John's interests were not entirely confined to the study of history:
he was also anxious to keep abreast of contemporary affairs and in the early
1690s was ordering books and pamphlets on such subjects as the state of
Europe, William III's proceedings in Ireland and the alleged murder of the
Earl of Essex.[27]

In other counties there were wealthy landowners who displayed the same
kind of zeal and enthusiasm in the pursuit of historical knowledge. In a letter
addressed to Sir Simon Archer in 1638 Dugdale told him that Sir Edward
Dering, who was seated at Surrenden Dering in Kent, was 'a most compleate
gentleman in all respects, and an excellent Antiquarye'. Sir Edward's scholarly tastes were shared by his cousin Sir Roger Twysden of Roydon Hall who was
a friend of both Dugdale and Sir Simonds D'Ewes. Twysden published works
on various subjects and was one of the first scholars to undertake detailed
research on English medieval history.[28] Sir William Pole of Shute in Devon
built up a large collection of manuscripts relating to the history of his county.
Many of them were destroyed during the Civil War but a work which he called
'The Description of Devonshire' was finally published in 1791.[29] In his book
The Historical Antiquities of Hertfordshire, which first appeared in 1700, Sir Henry
Chauncy of Ardeley referred approvingly to several of his fellow gentry who
had similar academic interests. In his estimation William Hale of King's
Walden, who died in 1688, was 'a good Philosopher' and 'a great Historian'. Sir

96. Sir John Crewe. Portrait by Michael Wright (Grosvenor Museum, Chester).

Thomas Brograve of Hamells in Braughing, who had been made a baronet, was a general scholar who was well-read in divinity, law and history and had a particular liking for antiquarian research. His son Sir John, who succeeded him in 1670, 'delighted much in Antiquity, could read most of the old Manuscripts and Records, and sometimes studied the Mathematicks'.[30]

  Autobiographies, memoirs, journals and family histories were other forms of literary activities which became increasingly popular among the gentry though in the main it was never the intention that they should be published. In a manuscript autobiography Sir Simonds D'Ewes traced the rise of his family from the arrival in England of his great-grandfather Adrian D'Ewes, a native of Gelderland, during the reign of Henry VIII to the acquisition of their Suffolk estates and the rebuilding of the mansion house at Stowlangtoft.[31] A similar story emerged when a Hertfordshire squire, Sir John Wittewronge of Rothamsted Manor (Pl. 97), decided in 1664 to prepare an

97. Sir John Wittewronge's house, Rothamsted Manor in Hertfordshire, which he substantially enlarged.

account of his family for (he explained) the satisfaction and information of his sons and daughters and on the understanding that it would be 'transmitted to posterity'. He related that in 1564 his grandfather Jaques Wittewronge had migrated from Flanders to England in order to escape the religious persecution which was being waged by the Spanish authorities. In London he had earned his living as a public notary while Sir John's father had married an heiress, set himself up as a brewer and 'attained unto a very considerable estate'.[32] In some cases the author of a family history came very close to hagiography, at least in describing the characteristics of his immediate forebears. Sir Edward Rodney of Rodney Stoke in Somerset portrayed his father as 'very temperate in his dyet, chaste in wedlock, a good Master to his servants, very hospitable and noble in his port and manner of living'.[33] Others such as Sir Hugh Cholmley, Sir John Reresby and Sir Christopher Guise tended to be more objective in their approach[34]; and Sir Henry Bedingfeld of Oxburgh Hall in Norfolk, writing in the 1690s, was prepared to offer the comment that his uncle Thomas, who had been in the line of succession, 'was a fine Gentleman but a bad husband and had noe cheldren'.[35]

Gentlemen and gentlewomen who took religion seriously often set down their thoughts on particular scriptural texts or on such weighty matters as how their faith should condition personal conduct. Their published works extended across a wide range of subjects within the general context of religion, though they seldom addressed the finer points of theology. One of the most unusual of these works was *The Advise of a Sonne Professing the Religion Established in the Present Church of England to his Deare Mother a Roman Catholike*. The author was Sir Anthony Hungerford of Black Bourton in Oxfordshire who charted his voyage of discovery from the Catholic faith in which he had been brought up to the Protestantism of the Church of England. When his son Sir Edward sought permission to have it printed for the benefit of a wider readership he immediately encountered censorship problems but eventually, in 1639, it was published without the prior knowledge of Archbishop Laud.[36] In other works which appeared during the course of the century Harbottle Grimston extolled the virtues of sobriety in all things and urged his readers to 'use not idlenesse, wanton Books, lascivious Pictures, nor immodest dances'; Sir Roger Twysden mounted a defence of the Church of England during the time of Cromwell's Protectorate when its whole future was in doubt; and Sir Edward Harley attacked the High Churchmen, the deists and the epicureans in expounding his Puritan version of true religion.[37] In 1696 a discourse on religion by Dame Damaris Masham, the wife of Sir Francis Masham of Otes Hall in Essex, was published anonymously. A close friend of John Locke, she had a strong preference for what she termed 'rational religion' which in her judgement was an apt description of the Protestant faith.[38]

Some of the better known literary figures of the seventeenth century were men of gentry stock. Edmund Waller of Hall Barn in the Buckinghamshire parish of Beaconsfield and Sir Charles Sedley of Southfleet in Kent were major landowners while Sir John Denham, the author of the poem *Cooper's Hill*, managed to run through a large estate which his father had left him. Others such as John Evelyn, John Dryden and William Congreve were younger sons or the issue of cadet branches.[39] Richard Newdegate's library at Arbury Hall contained a copy of *The Wonders of the Peak*, a poem by Charles Cotton. Cotton was the squire of Beresford in Staffordshire and a justice of the peace. One of the most versatile men of letters of his generation, he was not only a poet of some distinction but a translator of Montaigne's essays and Corneille's *Horace*, the author of a manual on the growing of fruit trees and a contributor to the most famous work of his friend Izaak Walton for whom he built a fishing lodge in the grounds of Beresford Hall.[40]

Many country squires felt the urge to write verse from time to time, whether or not they had any particular aptitude. During the first half of the century there were a number of occasional poets among the county families of northern England, men such as Sir John Jackson of Hickleton, Sir John Reresby of Thrybergh and Sir Francis Wortley of Wortley in Yorkshire and Sir George Gresley of Drakelow and Sir John Harpur of Swarkeston in Derbyshire. Sir John Jackson is said to have been 'very studious, a good scholar, as also a good poet for Latin'. According to his son, Sir John Reresby was proficient in both the Greek and Latin tongues and 'read and writt much'. Besides his poetical works he left behind him at his death a 'Book of Characters' and some essays which were intended for the guidance of his children.[41] Although Sir Thomas Wroth of Petherton Park in Somerset was an ardent Puritan he mainly exercised his literary talents through the medium of poetry. In 1620 he had two of his works published:

a translation of part of Virgil's *Aeneid* which he called *The Destruction of Troy* and a book of epigrammatic verse entitled *The Abortive of an Idle Houre* in which, among other things, he condemned idleness and 'roaring beggers'.[42] Sir John Beaumont of Grace Dieu Priory in Leicestershire, who was the elder brother of the playwright Francis Beaumont, was the author of a poem on the battle of Bosworth Field in which the heroic couplet was employed for the first time. In 1629 his eldest son and namesake published some of his verse in a collection entitled *Bosworth Field* which also contains poems by his brother and his friends Ben Jonson and Michael Drayton.[43] Sir John Beaumont was one of several Catholic gentlemen who appear among the minor literary figures of the period; others included Sir Aston Cokayne of Ashbourne Hall in Derbyshire and John Caryll of West Harting in Sussex. Anthony Wood writes of Cokayne that 'he was esteemed by many . . . a good poet and a great lover of learning, yet by others a perfect boon fellow, by which means he wasted all he had'.[44] Caryll, who had been a student at the English College in Rome, had two plays put on in London during the reign of Charles II: a tragedy called *The English Princess, or the Death of Richard III* and a comedy, *Sir Salomon, or the Cautious Coxcomb.*[45]

The gentry not only wrote verse: they also had verse written about them, particularly on such occasions as marriages and deaths. In 1636 William Sampson published a book of poems in the form of epitaphs on a number of persons of high social standing in the counties of Derbyshire, Nottinghamshire and Leicestershire. In his account of John Curzon, the late squire of Kedleston in Derbyshire, he depicted him, in his usual high-flown way, as a paragon among men:

> Achilles in thy prime of youth
> Ulysses in thy sager growth
> Lib'rall, yet frugall, soe to none
> Vertue's choise companion,
> Enrich'd with all her sacred partes
> The Muse's friend, and nurse of Artes.[46]

In marked contrast some of the leading Northamptonshire gentry were mercilessly satirised, basically on account of their Puritan sympathies, in an anonymous verse chronicle which was composed in the early part of James I's reign. One of the targets was Sir Christopher Yelverton, a judge of the Court of King's Bench who was seated at Easton Mauduit:

> Yelverton, that Jutting Judge, thinks that
> he is now no Drudge
> And takes Care for a common Good, but
> where Gould flowes as a Flood
> Lord how wold he be precise? But all
> know him that are wise.

Another man who came under the lash was Sir Richard Knightley of Fawsley Hall:

> Richard Knightley, gapinge Dick, never was
> without a Trick
> But it oft faild in Proofe, hurt he did,
> but no behoofe
> Pryvy he was, and paide full well for that
> Sect, as som can tell
> But his Head is farr to greate to worck
> any wyly Feate.

His son Sir Valentine was portrayed as a person who, though outwardly engaging, was in fact guided solely by self-interest:

> Honesty he never knew, nor to his Frend
> how to be true
> For a Puritan he wold passe, yet for
> Gayne wold goe to Masse.[47]

While the gentry were heavily under the influence of classical learning there are signs of a growing interest in such subjects as mathematics, geometry, chemistry and natural history. Scientific works began to appear in their book collections and mathematical instruments were purchased. Sir Edmund Bacon of Redgrave in Suffolk had a laboratory in which he conducted experiments of various kinds. His friend Joseph Hall referred obliquely to his research activities when dedicating one of his Epistles to him in 1624: 'Your philosophicall Cell is a safe shelter from tumults, from vices, from discontentments. Besides that lively, honest, and manly pleasure which arises from the gaine of knowledge in the deepe mysteries of Nature how easie is it in that place to live free from the common cares, from the infection of common evils!' Some of his experimental work seems to have been on the borderline between chemistry and alchemy. His friend and relative Sir Henry Wotton, who was a frequent visitor to Redgrave Hall, was impressed by a technique which he had developed for tinting and colouring stones and pebbles and on one occasion informed him that he was hoping to send him some good flints to be 'agatized' by his 'miraculous invention'. In his will, which was drawn up in 1648, Sir Edmund bequeathed to John Craddock, the minister of Barrow, his 'great grinding stone of Purfere' and two 'perspectives of Saint Marke' which were hanging in the chamber of his laboratory.[48] Another house with a laboratory was Noseley Hall, the Leicestershire seat of the Hesilrige family. In an inventory made in 1698 following the death of Sir Thomas Hesilrige there is a reference to 'the Chimist Roome' which was apparently close to the great hall. This contained a parcel of books, a table, five boxes, glasses, bottles 'and other Instruments belonging to the Chimicall affaires' and two cabinets which were valued in all at £20.[49]

One of the most innovative men of science of seventeenth-century England was a wealthy squire, Francis Willoughby of Middleton Hall in Warwickshire, who was only thirty-seven at his death in 1672. A founding member of the Royal Society, he was highly skilled in mathematics but his main field of interest was natural science. In the course of his researches both at home and on his Continental travels he made drawings and collected specimens of many different kinds of mammals, birds, fishes and plants. His most important work was a book on ornithology which was published posthumously, first in Latin and then in English, through the good offices of his friend and mentor John Ray. As a pioneering study it proved to be a successful publishing venture; among those who owned copies were Sir Edward Leighton and Richard Newdegate.[50]

In their attitude to learning the gentry defy any attempt to indulge in broad generalisations. At one extreme there was the gentleman scholar who was completely absorbed in his studies; at the other, the kind of man who was only interested in hunting and hawking or the accumulation of wealth. As Sir Simonds D'Ewes indicates in his autobiography, the inclinations of father and son could be markedly different. D'Ewes was a close friend of Sir Robert Cotton, a fellow antiquary who allowed him access to his magnificent collection of manuscripts, but he took a jaundiced view of his son Sir Thomas who, he writes, was 'whollie addicted to the tenacious encreasing of his worldlie wealth'.[51]

CHAPTER TWELVE

Scandal

In a Star Chamber case of 1614 John Rashleigh of Menabilly, a former high sheriff of Cornwall, accused two fellow magistrates and others associated with them of circulating libellous material aimed at destroying his reputation. In this material, which consisted of both prose and verse, they had claimed that between 1594 and 1611 he had committed adultery with many women, some of whom were married, and that his wife's death had been occasioned by her distress over his 'lascivious incontinency and filthy course of life'. These insinuations, he assured the Court, were completely false.[1] Whatever the truth of the matter there can be no doubt that sexual promiscuity was relatively common among the landed gentry, both before and after the Restoration, though it is significant that there is little evidence of such conduct in either Catholic or Puritan circles. In 1636 two Lancashire squires, Thomas Hesketh of Rufford Hall and Sir Ralph Assheton of Whalley Abbey, were found guilty by the Court of High Commission of persistently engaging in adultery, the former with no fewer than seven women. Assheton was fined £300 and Hesketh £1000, though this was later reduced to £500.[2] In the same year the Bristol diocesan authorities began proceedings against Sir William Spencer of Yarnton in Oxfordshire and Mary Popley his mistress on a charge of scandalous living. Knowingly or otherwise, his son Sir Thomas followed in his footsteps. Anthony Wood noted that Christiana Hyde, the daughter of a Berkshire squire, was 'concubine to Sir Thomas Spencer of Yarnton in whose house there she now liveth, 1677'; and that she died at Yarnton in 1682. When he drew up his will in 1684 Sir Thomas made generous provision for his illegitimate daughter Margaret Spencer and committed her to the care of his long-suffering wife, Dame Jane, by whom he had four surviving daughters.[3] By this time marital infidelity had reached new heights. In 1666 a nonconformist minister, Oliver Heywood, wrote in his journal that Sir Francis Wortley of Wortley Hall in Yorkshire had died very lately, 'having no child by his Lady, he having turned her off many yeares agoe, but hath left his estate ... to the Earl of Manchester's second son if he will change his name to Wortley and marry a bastard that Sr Francis had by a common whore in London'.[4] In Surrey Sir John Evelyn of Godstone, who had succeeded to a substantial estate in 1664, left his mistress Mary Gittings £500 a year and demolished Leigh Place, the mansion built by his father, in order to spite his brother George who was his next heir.[5]

If much of this irregular sexual activity went on in London or other distant places the country house with its complement of female servants could offer temptations which were not always resisted. In some cases there are no more than hints of impropriety; but in others the evidence is more conclusive. In his historical account of Cheshire families which was published in 1674 Sir Peter Leycester observed in a matter of fact sort of way that Richard Brereton of Ashley Hall, who died in 1649, 'was never Married, but had an illegitimate Son, begot of one Ellin Higginson his Servant, called William Brereton'.[6] George Stonhouse, the eldest son of Sir George Stonhouse of Radley in Berkshire, seduced a kitchen maid and subsequently married her. As a result Sir George disinherited him and in 1669 obtained a new grant of his baronetcy with remainder to his younger sons John and James.[7] Brome Whorwood, a major landowner whose principal seat was at Holton in Oxfordshire, was described by Anthony Wood as clownish and ill-natured and by one of his bailiffs as 'a very passionate man'. For many years his wife Jane lived apart from him 'without', he maintained in a Court of Arches suit, 'any cause or leave by him given'. At an early stage he began what proved to be a lengthy liaison with his servant Katherine Allen who bore him a son. To Whorwood's credit he took care of his son and in 1679 arranged for his admission to Hart Hall, Oxford. In his will, which he drew up in 1682, he made a bequest to 'my naturall or reputed sonne Thomas Whorwood ... whom I hereby enioyne and require to take upon him and bee called by the name of Whorwood, according to a deed or grant to that purpose heretofore by mee to him made under my hand and seale'. To his 'trusty and carefull good servant' Katherine Allen he gave some household goods, together with all his corn, hay, cattle and utensils of husbandry, and appointed her and Dr Edward Master his son-in-law as joint executors. An inventory of Holton House which was submitted for probate purposes in 1684 refers to Mrs Allen's bedchamber, certain items of silver in her possession and a box 'lined with sky coloured Silke said to belong to Mrs Whorwood'.[8]

Marriages between gentlemen of substance and household servants were generally frowned upon, not only because of the difference in station but because no portion was forthcoming. Although such marriages did occur they were very rare. Robert Carr was the son and heir of a Lincolnshire baronet, Sir Robert Carr of Aswarby, who had an estate worth £4000 a year. In the course of proceedings in the Court of Arches which were begun in 1662 he was prepared to admit that he had been engaged in a sexual liaison with Isabella Jones, his mother's waiting gentlewoman, but vehemently disputed her claim that they were married. Some witnesses, however, testified that in February 1659 an ordained minister had married them in a private house at Aswarby; that Carr had been stone cold sober at the time; and that the ceremony had been conducted in accordance with the Book of Common Prayer 'which was then unusuall and very dangerous'. Isabella Carr (as she felt entitled to call herself) was described as a person of good breeding and education whose brother was an esquire with an estate worth £400 a year near Ludlow. She had initially served Lady Carr for four years; had then been employed by Dame

Gertrude Anderson for two years; and had returned to Lady Carr who had promptly increased her remuneration from £8 to £10 a year. According to the evidence provided by Lady Anderson in March 1664 Isabella had told her that her husband had been thinking of sending her abroad but had also been considering the alternative possibility of buying her off. In the event she appears to have received £1000 as the price for abandoning her suit and shortly afterwards Carr married Elizabeth Bennet, the daughter of Sir John Bennet of Dawley in Middlesex.[9]

The mistress of the household, declared Robert Cleaver in his treatise on the ordering of private families, should not make herself too familiar with the servants.[10] Familiarity in a domestic context was one of the major themes of a Star Chamber case begun in 1607 which arose out of a feud between two Leicestershire gentlemen, Sir Thomas Beaumont of Stoughton Grange and Sir Henry Hastings of Braunston who was a suspected papist. A key figure in the proceedings was John Coleman who had served Beaumont for three years as his clerk; had then been dismissed (in a very disgraceful manner, he told the Court); and had immediately secured employment with Hastings. As an act of revenge, it was alleged, he had been circulating libellous reports about Lady Beaumont and her daughters in the counties of Leicestershire, Northamptonshire and Warwickshire. Many of these reports had been couched in the 'most filthye tearmes of ribaldrie' and had depicted them as loose women who had allowed him to indulge himself in excessive familiarity even to the extent of engaging in 'extraordinarye and Carnall Copulacion' with them while Sir Thomas was away from home. A friend of the Beaumonts who came forward as a character witness described Sir Thomas as 'a Gentleman of worthie partes'; referred to his 'wise and religious goverment of his familie, and vertuous bringing up of his Children'; and testified that he had observed at first hand that his wife conducted herself in a sober and modest fashion. In the end the Beaumonts appear to have been vindicated.[11]

Breakspear in the Middlesex parish of Harefield is a late seventeenth-century manor-house incorporating earlier features (Pl. 98). In the reign of James I the house as it then was and its immediate neighbourhood were the scene of some extraordinary happenings which would have provided rich material for the more melodramatic kind of opera. The story emerged in the course of Star Chamber proceedings initiated in November 1619 by Roger Dey who styled himself 'gentleman'. In April Sir Francis Ashby, the youthful owner of Breakspear (Pl. 99), had taken him into his service at a wage of £5 a year. According to his account Dey had performed his duties satisfactorily but for no apparent reason Sir Francis had attempted first to stab and then to shoot him and having failed on both occasions had made use of his authority as a magistrate to have him arrested on a charge of theft. In his response Sir Francis offered a very different version of the chain of events, though one which he must have found acutely embarrassing, and emphatically denied that he had sought to kill him. The plaintiff, he related, was a man of unchaste carriage and lustful conversation who had ingratiated himself with his wife. Through his deceitful behaviour he 'possessed hir hart and had hir Company even at his owne pleasure . . . he would kisse and daly with hir before and in the presence of his fellowe servants'. At first Sir

98. Breakspear House, Harefield, Middlesex.

Francis could not believe what he was told about their conduct but eventually satisfied himself that they were regularly cavorting in the surrounding woods and fields at all times of the night. Although Dey was summarily dismissed he continued his liaison with Lady Ashby, sending her letters and tokens, persuading her to give him money and jewels and frequently arranging assignations with her. In the end Sir Francis decided to lay a trap for his former servant. By means of a fabricated message Dey was lured to a field near the house where he was expecting to meet his mistress but the person awaiting him at the appointed place was in fact a young servant, John Burbury, who had been dressed up in Lady Ashby's clothes. By the time he realised that he had been tricked it was too late: Sir Francis with some of his menservants appeared from their hiding places, seized him and handed him over to the constable. After spending several days in the Marshalsea prison he was bound over to be of good behaviour. Despite the sordid nature of this episode Sir Francis and his wife were reconciled and a year later a daughter was born whom he acknowledged as his own. Sir Francis, however, had no male issue and following his death in 1624 all his estate in Middlesex passed to his brother Robert.[12]

Now and again a manservant captured the affections of one of the squire's daughters or some other female relative. In the early part of James I's reign George St Quintin of Harpham Hall in Yorkshire was dismayed to find that his daughter Alice had eloped with the butler, Robert Frankish, and that they had subsequently married. After Frankish's death her brother, Sir William St

99. The Ashby memorial in Harefield parish church, Middlesex. Sir Robert Ashby and his wife are depicted in the top tier while the effigy of his son Sir Francis is on the extreme right in the lower tier.

Quintin, took pity on her and provided her with material support until she married again.[13] Another Yorkshire family, the Accloms of Moreby Hall, had a similar experience. Shortly before the Civil War, while she was living with her grandfather, Sir Thomas Dawney, at Cowick Hall, Isabel Acclom was secretly married to John Nelson who was one of his servingmen. This so shocked the family that they disowned her.[14]

In 1618 a Puritan squire, Sir Oliver Luke of Wood End in Bedfordshire, brought a Star Chamber suit against Thomas Cockayne, 'a man of a most subtyll and wicked disposicion', whom he had employed as one of his household servants. Cockayne, he alleged, had been well aware that his sister, Katherine Luke, had a marriage portion of £1000 and had been determined to gain possession of it. Disregarding the duty he owed Sir Oliver as his master and 'the disproportion both in quallitie and estate' between himself and Katherine he had pressed her to marry him and, without consulting her brother, she had finally consented. During Sir Oliver's absence he had attempted to abduct her with the assistance of an armed gang. On that occasion the plan had failed but he had since taken up residence in a neighbouring house and was awaiting a favourable opportunity to achieve his objective. In his defence Cockayne argued that he had been living with Sir Oliver as one of his kin rather than as a servant; that Katherine was genuinely in love with him; and that she was old enough to decide for herself.[15]

Five years later the Court of Star Chamber dealt with a case which was not dissimilar in character, though it was concerned with a marriage which had already taken place. In the bill which he submitted Richard Halford of Wistow Hall in Leicestershire told the Court that Richard Bowman, whom he had taken on as an ordinary servingman, had so impressed him by his diligence that he had employed him on weightier matters and for this reason had allowed him access to the most private places in his house. Bowman, however, had taken advantage of this situation to pursue his own base ends. By means of flattery, trifling gifts and fair promises he had wormed his way into the affections of the plaintiff's only daughter, Joan, who was now fourteen years of age. At midnight on 22 June 1622 Bowman and a number of his confederates, all well armed, had entered Wistow Hall and taken Joan away to his father's house at Ratcliffe on Soar in Nottinghamshire where they had been married in a private chamber. A diocesan registrar, John Tibbard, had supplied a marriage licence (which Halford claimed was bogus) and the ceremony had been performed by Thomas Bartram, a poor stipendiary curate. In his response Bartram pleaded that he had already been punished enough by the ecclesiastical authorities for his involvement in the episode.[16]

As the gentry were only too well aware, Stuart England was a country in which violence was endemic even when it was not being torn apart by a civil war. The evidence for this was overwhelming: the destruction of enclosures, the bitter feuds between rival county families, the brawling and duelling, the nefarious activities of highwaymen and footpads, and the frequent incursions into deer parks and assaults on keepers. Against this background the country house offered its occupants a certain feeling of security, perhaps particularly if it had a large establishment of menservants. Even so, there were occasional passages of high drama which thoroughly alarmed the household. At Sutton Scarsdale in Derbyshire a gang of men who had been raiding Sir Francis Leake's deer park reacted angrily when they heard that he was planning to take legal action against them. On 22 September 1609 (he related in a Star Chamber bill) they assembled at a common alehouse and after fortifying themselves with drink marched as far as the gates of Sutton Hall where they assaulted and wounded his servant William Clay. There they remained for about an hour 'in most insolent, bould and presumptuous sorte', calling for Sir Francis to come out and meet them, 'to the great amasemente' of the servants standing by, and demanding that they should be supplied with beer. When he eventually appeared he ordered them to leave but they stubbornly held their ground. As a final resort he decided to exercise his powers as a magistrate and managed to put an end to the siege by the expedient of declaring it to be illegal in the town street of Sutton Scarsdale.[17]

In a Star Chamber bill which he presented in April 1616 Sir George Shirley of Staunton Harold in Leicestershire told the Court that he and his wife, Dame Dorothy, together with all their 'servantes, retinue and famelie, beeinge in number in the whole above fiftie persons', had been living for a time at Faringdon House in Berkshire (which was part of the jointure settled on Lady Shirley by a previous husband). On 3 January (he went on) William Essex, the son and heir of Sir William Essex of Becket House in Shrivenham, Essex Harcourt, his father's servant, and other associates were drinking in the Bell tavern at Faringdon when they became involved in a quarrel with William Underhill who was one of Sir George's servants. As a result Harcourt challenged Underhill to fight him at a time and place to be nominated. Underhill, however, refused to take up the challenge and returned home. At about eleven o'clock that night, when Sir George and his family were either in bed or preparing to retire, William Essex and his party entered Faringdon House and assaulted Underhill and a number of his fellow servants. Dame Dorothy, 'haveinge care and charge of the government of her howse, and beinge tender and carefull of the lyves of her servantes', went downstairs and sought to pacify the intruders, entreating them 'with much earnestnes, and manie plawsable, milde and gentle speeches' to desist. When they responded by redoubling their attacks, putting her in fear of her life, she ordered her servants to disarm them and the instruction was duly carried out. In June 1616 Sir William Essex submitted his own bill in which he narrated a rather different story. According to this account his son decided to pay a courtesy call on the Shirleys and in Sir George's absence was entertained by his wife in the parlour. William Underhill, 'a man that is never satisfied with drinckinge', invited Essex Harcourt to join him in the buttery. After some heavy drinking Underhill took umbrage when Harcourt declined the offer of a flagon of beer and broke a glass in his face. Some of the other servants then appeared and Harcourt was wounded with his own sword. On coming out of the parlour to see what was happening William Essex was confronted by one of the servants, Symon Raleigh, who struck him in the face and ran at him with a pitchfork. In his response to these counter-accusations Sir George refused to comment further on the grounds that Sir William had been outlawed for debt and was not therefore entitled to sue.[18]

The mansion of the Cave family at Bagworth Park in Leicestershire was surrounded by a moat and a strong fence which must have served as a powerful deterrent to would-be intruders. In a Star Chamber suit, however, Sir Bryan Cave described how his adversary Henry Skipwith had managed to circumvent the problem. Skipwith, he intimated, was a man with a very contentious disposition who was always quarrelling with his neighbours and had recently been fined by the Court for various offences. On 24 July 1624 Skipwith called on him and in accordance with the rules of hospitality he invited him to dinner. Afterwards Skipwith persuaded him to travel with him for part of the journey to his own house. Almost immediately he discovered that an ambush had been laid for him and he was set upon by Skipwith and his confederates who included the under-sheriff of

Leicestershire. On hearing the affray some of Sir Bryan's servants rushed to his assistance but came off badly: Anthony Dumbleton was severely injured and Thomas Hyde, John Stoakes, Bridget Tanfield and Ellen Stoakes were also wounded. In the face of these allegations Skipwith maintained that he was under no obligation to put in an answer since the complainant had been outlawed for certain trespasses and contempts of which he had been found guilty in the Court of King's Bench. The causes of the dispute appear to have been financial in nature: Sir Bryan was heavily indebted and Skipwith was one of his creditors.[19]

Occasionally an intrusion had fatal consequences. In 1677 William Waad of Battles Hall in Essex was killed in a field near his house by Robert Parsons, 'a fellow of a debauched life', after he had refused to lend him money while in 1694 Grace Bennet, the widow of a Buckinghamshire magnate, Simon Bennet, was murdered at Calverton House by a butcher from Stony Stratford who had heard of her great wealth.[20] Generally, however, external threats were far less common than the internal dissensions which not infrequently gave rise to domestic violence and cruelty. Sons quarrelled with their fathers or mothers, husbands with wives and brothers with brothers. In some wills there was bitter criticism of an errant son who was described as disobedient or unkind; in others the testator deplored the fact that a daughter had married without his consent. In Norfolk Sir Richard Berney of Park Hall in Reedham settled the bulk of his estate, which was worth £7000 a year, on his second son, though the eldest son inherited his baronetcy.[21] Sir John Offley of Madeley in Staffordshire had similar thoughts but was dissuaded from taking such a radical step by his wife's entreaties.[22]

Shortly before the Civil War Sir Richard Strode of Newnham House in Devon was engaged in a systematic campaign of harassment against his son William and his daughter-in-law Anne whom he claimed had married in defiance of his wishes. His aim was to drive them out of his house and to prevent his son from inheriting the estate to which he was entitled. In a petition which he submitted to the king in 1638 William Strode complained that he was not only 'destitute of present mayntenance' but in danger of losing his patrimony, 'part thereof being alreddy sould and the ancient mansion house alsoe offered to sale'. The young couple continued to live at Newnham House in spite of the fulminations of Sir Richard who often threatened to beat them and have them put in prison. In March 1640 he entered their chamber accompanied by two of his female servants, smashed all the windows and took away their bedding and a cot which had been made ready for the birth of their first child. In October, however, he was obliged as the result of litigation in the Court of Chancery to settle an annuity of £150 on trustees for their benefit and to give an undertaking that he would provide them and their children and two servants at Newnham House with 'sufficient meate, drinke, lodginge, fireinge, washinge, candle light and enterteynment befittinge persons of theire degree and qualitie and . . . alsoe keepe and feede both in winter and summer att howse and abroade two horses of the said William Strode's for his use.' Nevertheless Sir Richard remained convinced that he was more sinned against than sinning. In 1650 he wrote in a letter to Dame Martha Button, the mother of Anne Strode (who had since died), that his son had married the sister of 'my cappitall enemy' and had now twice deceived him in the manner of his marriages.[23]

During the reign of Charles II a relative of Sir Edward Harley informed him that he had recently visited the house of Sir Thomas Stephens at Little Sodbury in Gloucestershire 'where is a divided family, and the poore Lady in a Condition to be Commiserated, being Loaded with too heavy a burden between her affections to her husband and son'. The disagreement appears to have had its origins in the settlement which Sir Thomas made on the occasion of his son's marriage: this involved him in litigation in 1675 and again in 1697.[24] In July 1674 Bulstrode Whitelocke inserted a note in his diary about a bizarre episode which had occurred at Axford House in Wiltshire, the seat of Sir Seymour Pile whose eldest son had married his daughter Frances. According to this account Sir Seymour, 'being druncke, struck his son on the head which so stunned him that he knew not what he did, and struck his father . . . with a small sticke and came away with his wife about 12 a clocke att night' to Whitelocke's house. His daughter, for her part, was frequently illtreated both by her husband and her mother-in-law.[25]

Following the death of Sir Robert Phelips, who was seated at Montacute in Somerset, his widow, Dame Bridget, was engaged in an acrimonious dispute with her son Edward over her jointure lands. 'Ned', she wrote in June 1638, 'ether be licke a sonne, or els hold me as dead and forgotten'. The following month a kinsman of the new squire who had been visiting Montacute House told him that he had found his mother 'extremely out of temper, and would fayne have an ende of all trobles, and for those lands which were questioned she is most willinge that you shall have them'. In October Lady Phelips was complaining to a relative that the rents she was receiving were far less than they should have been and that her son was disregarding his father's wishes; unless he acted honourably she thought it likely that he would die in prison 'for any thing I know'. A few months later she moved out of Montacute House and settled at Redlynch where she continued to vent her feelings about the covetous disposition of her son.[26] In a Chancery case of 1680 Sir Edward Ayscough of South Kelsey in Lincolnshire was accused of maltreating his mother, Dame Isabel, who was claiming a jointure of £400 a year which had been settled on her many years before. In November 1673, it was alleged, Sir Edward had confined her to a 'mean room', pretending that she was melancholy or, in modern parlance, mentally ill. When Sir John Bolles, her nephew, visited South Kelsey Hall in 1678 he had found her 'in a poore and meane Condicion without fitting Clothes or necessaryes'. On the other hand, the Court was informed that Dame Isabel had been so 'distempered' that she had been unable to manage her affairs and that for a time she had been receiving treatment for her illness in London.[27]

More often it was the wives of country squires who were subjected to mental or physical cruelty. In 1639 John Cartwright of Aynho in Northamptonshire found himself exposed as a barbarous husband in a petition which his wife submitted to the king. Katherine Cartwright, who was the daughter of a former Attorney General, William Noy, related that for reasons which remained obscure her husband had banished her to the house of a friend of his, thirty miles away, where she had lived for two years; and that he had subsequently moved her to a farm where she had been kept 'rather as his prisoner than his wife'. Through the intervention of friends she had finally been able to regain her freedom and was now dependent on their support. In conclusion she asked the king to command her husband either to cohabit with her or to allow her maintenance which was commensurate with her marriage portion and his estate.[28] In the latter part of the seventeenth century there is a considerable body of evidence about the abuse of women by their husbands. Francis Tirwhitt of Kettelby House in Lincolnshire was the head of what had hitherto been a staunchly Catholic family. In 1655 he married Elizabeth Lloyd and in return for a portion of £4000 settled a jointure of £500 a year on her. Subsequently he lived in London for about a year with a young gentlewoman who was said to have suffered a miscarriage when he threw her over a chair. In the course of legal proceedings which led to his incarceration in the Fleet prison Stephen Macquene his steward and John Grange, another of his servants, testified that in their presence he had thrown his wife onto a bed, pulled up her clothes above her head so that 'shee lay naked before them her servants' and attempted to strangle her. He had also given order to his servants that if she should return to Kettelby House they should deny her admission; but, as the Court of Arches was informed in 1666, she preferred to live with relatives in view of the threats he had made against her.[29] Lucy Barrington, the only daughter of Sir Thomas Barrington, married twice: her first husband died within two years and her second husband, Sir Toby Tyrrell of Thornton in Buckinghamshire, proved to be such a domestic tyrant that she eventually left him. In a Chancery suit of 1673 Dame Lucy, who by this time was again a widow, declared that for fourteen years she had 'suffered under a very hard usage, severe and ill treatment' by her late husband.[30] Sir Edward Baesh of Stanstead Bury in Hertfordshire managed both to dissipate a substantial inheritance and wreck his marriage. In December 1674, following a marital dispute, he formally agreed that his wife, Dame Anne, could live in his manor-house of Stanstead Bury and that she should have lands worth £130 a year for her separate maintenance. Not long afterwards, however, the Court of Chancery was told that at a time when she was in a very weak and sick condition she had been carried out of his house in her bed and deposited on the ground 'to the great danger of her life'; and that her husband had ceased to provide her with any financial support. The reason for her eviction became clear in 1676 when Sir Edward sold the house and estate. The following year Dame Anne must have concluded that her family was particularly ill-fated when she heard that her brother, William Waad, had been murdered.[31]

In March 1666 Bulstrode Whitelocke twice visited Sir John Reade at Duns Tew in Oxfordshire and on each occasion attempted to effect a reconciliation between him and his wife, Dame Alisimon, 'but in vain, both being willfull'. In August Lady Reade left her husband and before long began proceedings against him in the Court of Arches. Evidence collected from former servants and others contained a range of allegations. Sir John, it was said, was always picking quarrels with his wife and abusing her with foul language and he had denied her any role in the management of household affairs. Nor would he allow her 'such conveniences of Dyet and maintenance and attendance as was agreable and fitt for her'. He had dismissed most of the servants she had brought with her at the time of their marriage and had also dispensed with the services of her chaplain, Anthony Stephens, 'a sober and discreete person' who had been deprived of his Oxfordshire living in 1660. On his instructions the wheels of her coach had been 'taken off and lockt upp least that she should goe abroad'. And while Sir John had been enjoying an intimate relationship with Elizabeth Reade the children's maid his wife had been forced to lodge in inferior accommodation, including a wool chamber at the rear of the house which had no chimney. On the other hand, John Barrett the steward was eager to defend his master's reputation and to put all the blame for the marriage breakdown on Lady Reade. Sir John, he claimed, 'did not thinke any thing too good for her, and did spend very plentifully in housekeeping and other necessaries, And kept as good a house as any Gentleman in the Country'. Lady Reade, for her part, had gone up and down the house singing rhymes or sonnets which she had composed in order to disgrace her husband 'and render him odious in the sight of his servants and neighbours'. On several occasions at dinner and supper he had heard her describe Sir John as 'Divell, Serpent, Tyger, and other vile and hellish denominacions'. She had also been in the habit of calling the maidservants whores and jades and the menservants rogues and pimps; indeed Barrett had grown so weary of her insults that he had seriously thought of leaving. In these circumstances Sir John 'was like a stranger in his owne house' while his servants 'durst not doe their dutyes'. Lady Reade, he went on, had voluntarily moved into the wool chamber so that she could depart without attracting attention. As for the children's maid he considered her to be virtuous and chaste. Another witness backed up the steward's account and made the point that Lady Reade had frequently entertained nonconformist ministers in defiance of her husband's wishes. After weighing up all the evidence the Court of Arches decided that she should receive £30 a month as alimony but Sir John disputed the order and the legal battle continued, first in the Court of Delegates and then in the House of Lords.[32]

Very occasionally the tranquillity of a country house was shattered by a murder, or what was alleged to be a murder, committed by someone living under its roof. When Sir Euseby Andrewe of Charwelton Hall in Northamptonshire died in July 1619 there were suspicions that he had been poisoned by Anne Moyle, a gentleman's wife who had been residing with the family as a guest. When Mrs Moyle was tried at the Northampton assizes one of his physicians, Dr John Cotta, gave it as his opinion, on the basis of an autopsy, that his death was not due to the illness for which he had been receiving medical treatment but to a poison which had been administered to him. He also testified that Sir Euseby told him 'I am not safe, I am not secure in my owne house' and that he believed that Mrs Moyle was seeking to kill him. When his wife, Dame Anne, came into his chamber he ordered her to leave him: 'since yow brave me in my owne house and in this poore distresse wherin I am, get yow from me, and come no more at me untill I sende for yow. Yow make her yowr bedfellow, yowr companion, I wott she is no companion for yow.' Sir Euseby was so angry with his wife that he threatened to cut her out of his will but was dissuaded from amending it. In the end Mrs Moyle was

100. Breamore House, Hampshire.

acquitted, perhaps because of the lack of any obvious motive or because it was felt that Sir Euseby had been delirious on his deathbed. In 1621 Sir Euseby's brother Thomas attempted to re-open the case in the Court of Star Chamber, claiming that there had been a mistrial. Mrs Moyle, he alleged, had conceived 'a secret dislike' of Sir Euseby and had been extremely 'officious' in making broths and jellies for him during his illness. On one occasion she had been seen putting some white powder into a pot of water with meat in it which the cook had left on the kitchen fire; and as a result of her ministrations Sir Euseby's condition had grown much worse. Significantly, Andrewe was careful to avoid any suggestion that his sister-in-law might have been involved.[33]

Other murder cases lacked the aura of mystery which shrouded the Charwelton affair. In 1605 a Yorkshire squire, Walter Calverley of Calverley Hall, killed two of his children and wounded his wife. He then set off with the intention of murdering his other child, Henry, who was at his nurse's house but his horse stumbled and threw him and he was apprehended in time. According to Roger Dodsworth, who witnessed his execution at York, his actions were the product of 'a desperat humour' which had been occasioned by the financial consequences of his own improvidence. The episode gave rise to a number of literary works including the play *A Yorkshire Tragedy* which was performed at the Globe theatre and first published in 1608.[34] In 1629 there was a sensational murder at Breamore House, the Elizabethan mansion of Sir William Doddington in Hampshire (Pl. 100). His wife, Dame

Mary, died from multiple wounds after her son Henry attacked her with a
rapier. Some believed that he was drunk at the time, others that he was
mentally unbalanced. Sir John Oglander observed in his commonplace book
that 'He was crazed in his brains long before that unnatural, abhorred
action'.[35]

After the slaughter of many thousands in the Civil War it might be thought
that a country house murder would have lost its capacity to shock but the
events which took place in August 1655 at Lees Court in Kent proved otherwise (Pl. 101). Sir George Sondes, who had recently completed his rebuilding of Lees Court, was a widower with two sons, George and Freeman. As
Sir Roger Twysden recorded in his notebook, Sir George sided with the heir
in a quarrel with his brother, boxed Freeman's ears 'and longer continued to
discountenance hym then he could endure'. As a result Freeman Sondes
resolved to kill his brother and on the night of 7 August entered his chamber while he was asleep, smashed his skull with a meat cleaver and stabbed
him several times with a dagger. Following the murder he woke up his
father, who was in an adjoining chamber, to tell him what he had done and
Sir George summoned his servants and ordered them to seize him. At his
trial Freeman Sondes pleaded guilty after previously confessing that 'nothing but the instigation of the devil did cause me to attempt this sin'. On 21
August he was hanged and shortly afterwards his father published a tract
in which he defended himself against the aspersions of certain Puritan
ministers.[36]

101. Lees Court,
Kent.

102. Burford
Priory,
Oxfordshire.

In 1697 a murder was committed at Burford Priory in Oxfordshire which was a seat of the Lenthall family (Pl. 102). The victim of this crime was the steward, John Pryor, whose body was found in a garden pavilion close to the house. The Lenthalls were not a family which commanded a great deal of respect: in his usual forthright way Anthony Wood described William Lenthall, the Speaker of the Long Parliament, as a knave, his son Sir John as a beast and his grandson William as 'a fool who married a court-whore'. Shortly before the grandson's death in 1686 his wife (who had recently left him) gave birth to a child fathered by one of his servants. Subsequently she married Charles Hamilton, Earl of Abercorn, a relative of hers who was a man of few scruples. During the long minority of the heir, John Lenthall, he sought to exploit the situation for his own financial gain but Pryor refused to co-operate and it was probably his honesty which cost him his life. The Earl was tried for murder at the Oxford assizes and the gardener (who was mistakenly reported to have been a suspect) appeared as one of the prosecution witnesses. Despite the weight of evidence the jury brought in a verdict of not guilty which gave rise to rumours of bribery. The country people, it was said, were 'much discontented' over this blatant miscarriage of justice.[37]

EPILOGUE

On one occasion when he was returning from London to his Nottinghamshire seat Sir Gervase Clifton received a letter from a young scholar he had befriended in which he wrote that 'The Country breathes a more refined Ayre. The Citties breath like the Citizens' is less sweete though more perfumed . . . the book of nature is as free from deceit as full of recreating delicacyes which speake their Creator.'[1] Country life appears to have had little appeal for those wealthy landed families which sojourned for lengthy periods in their London town houses. For most gentry families, however, the country house with its surrounding estate was the focal point of their world; and indeed there were some well-to-do squires who were reluctant to travel to London except when they had urgent business to transact there or parliamentary duties to perform. In 1631 Sir Edmund Moundeford observed in a letter addressed to another Norfolk landowner, Framlingham Gawdy, that 'I am not sory you Like London no better: I hope we shall sooner have you cam fro' it.'[2] At this time the natural beauty of the countryside aroused little interest, perhaps because it was taken too much for granted, though the more spectacular kinds of landscape could excite feelings of wonder and amazement. In the main the gentry were more likely to enthuse about the splendour of houses and gardens, the purity of the air and water and the opportunities for engaging in field sports.

Not surprisingly, rural life was generally considered to be more salubrious than life in the towns. In 1676 Sir Roger Burgoyne commented in a letter to his friend Sir Ralph Verney, who was then in London, that he was 'very well pleasd that you intend to leave the town because I beleeve the country to be more healthfull'.[3] A considerable number of country gentlemen died of small-pox or other contagious diseases but these were usually contracted in London. In 1640 Sir William Eliott, who lived at Busbridge Hall in Surrey, warned his brother-in-law Sir Simonds D'Ewes 'to be carefull how you receave from London, the sicknes is very daungerous, and a knight of our Country hath therby brought the plague into his howse'.[4] On hearing that an epidemic had spread as far as his own county the owner of a country estate might give direction that his household should remain indoors or at least within the adjacent grounds and impose severe restrictions on the entry of visitors; and in such circumstances the little community usually emerged unscathed.

At its best the world of the country house could be a veritable Arcadia. In *The Worthies of England* Thomas Fuller was moved to insert a panegyric on Mount Edgcumbe, the Devonshire seat of the Edgcumbe family which overlooked Plymouth Sound:

> The hall (rising above the rest) yieldeth a stately sound as one entereth it; the parlour and dining-room afford a large and diversified prospect both of sea and land. The high situation (cool in summer, yet not cold in winter) giveth health; the neighbour river wealth; two block-houses great safety; and the town of Plymouth good company unto it. Nor must I forget the fruitful ground about it (pleasure without profit is but a flower without a root) stored with wood, timber, fruit, deer, and conies, a sufficiency of pasture, arable and meadow, with stone, lime, marl and what not.

When Celia Fiennes viewed Mount Edgcumbe from the outside in 1698 she was equally impressed, describing it as the finest seat she had seen and one which could more appropriately be called 'Mount Pleasant'.[5] Other country seats also attracted admiring comments from seventeenth-century antiquaries and travellers. The mansion of the Portman family at Orchard Portman in Somerset was 'a large faire house . . . neighboured with a parke and all other delights fitting such a place'.[6] Heanton Court in Devon, which belonged to the Basset family, was 'a very handsom Pile, well furnished with all variety of Entertainment which the Earth, and Sea, and Air can afford'.[7] Rydal Hall, the Westmorland seat of the Fleming family, was 'a good old house situated on the side of a little hill'. Surrounding the house were fine gardens, orchards and walks with 'large trees of laurel almost as high as the hall', a row of Scotch firs and a profusion of black cherry trees while further away there were two parks which contained oak, ash and other timber trees.[8]

If many of their country seats offered the promise of an idyllic existence the gentry nevertheless had their share of domestic problems. A number of men and women (including at least nine baronets) suffered from mental illness which often gave rise to lunacy proceedings. In 1621 the Court of Wards was informed that Sir Thomas Musgrave of Norton Conyers in Yorkshire (Pl. 103) was a lunatic who was incapable of managing his estate and in due course a commission was issued for the purpose of determining the facts. According to his relatives he had plunged one of his arms up to the elbow in some boiling liquor; put his bare feet in a fire; stripped himself naked and laid outside his house in frosty weather; and behaved violently towards his wife and children. In a Star Chamber bill Sir Thomas claimed that he was the victim of a conspiracy but it is significant that Lady Musgrave had been forced to take flight because she feared for her life.[9] A gentleman of good estate who was 'distracted', to use a contemporary description of lunacy, might be committed to the care of a London physician or alternatively kept under some degree of restraint in a wing of the ancestral mansion. In 1667 Sir John Fortescue of Salden House in Buckinghamshire stipulated in a legal document that the trustees whom he had appointed should ensure that his son John, who had

103. Norton Conyers, Yorkshire.

been visited with 'Melancholly whereby he became Incapable of manageing himself and his estate', was provided with food, drink, washing, lodging, clothes and all other things 'suitable for his condition and quality'. The son, who inherited the baronetcy on his father's death in 1683, was allocated a suite of rooms in Salden House and allowed £200 a year for his maintenance. In 1695 it was reported that his chamber was situated next to a long gallery where he presumably took some exercise, that his personal servants had adjoining rooms and that two lodging rooms had been set aside for any friends who might visit him. In the course of litigation begun in 1697 John Tipper, a servant who had been acting as his keeper for many years, told the Court of Chancery that Salden House was 'the only place he delights to live in' and that his physicians considered it 'to be the most proper and Convenient place for him to be'. Sir John lived on until 1717 when he was succeeded by his cousin Francis Fortescue.[10]

As we have seen, there was a good deal of domestic strife in country houses which usually involved the squire and his wife as the main protagonists or parents and their children. Such conflicts could severely disrupt the daily life of the household with servants either taking sides or finding themselves in an invidious position. According to one of the defendants in a Chancery case of 1675 Richard Pendarves of Pendarves House in Cornwall had told him that his daughter Anne was 'a Stubborne, undutifull and unruly child both to him and her mother' and that he wished that 'hee could place her abroad because Shee bred disturbance in the family and caused the rest of the Children to bee the more disobedient'.[11]

Many gentry families experienced serious financial difficulties during the course of the seventeenth century. While the Civil War had major consequences for landowners there were other important factors such as extravagance, mismanagement and protracted litigation (though not Crown taxation which was generally light). Estates were mortgaged, servants dismissed and parks denuded of their timber trees. As their situation grew more desperate some gentlemen were outlawed or imprisoned. When Sir William Clifton, a young Nottinghamshire baronet, died in 1686 while sojourning in France he left an estate which was heavily burdened with debt and his executor was forced to embark on the sale of his personal effects at Clifton Hall and his London town house. Among the items sold at Clifton Hall were furniture, bedding, tapestries, curtains, pictures, guns and pistols, a billiard table, a chest of viols, a copy of Francis Bacon's essays, an 'Engine with Leaden pipes', two wheelbarrows, a stone roller, two small boats and fishing nets.[12] The Cliftons managed to survive, though with a reduced estate, but a significant number of families went under. While the minor gentry were particularly vulnerable there were no limits to the damage which a spendthrift could inflict on even the most substantial patrimony. At the height of his prosperity Sir Richard Gargrave of Nostell Priory in Yorkshire enjoyed an income of £3500 a year but he rapidly dissipated his inheritance and died in abject poverty.[13] Following the death of his wife in 1676 Sir George Croke of Waterstock in Oxfordshire 'ran into debt, retired to London, followed women, and ruin'd himself'. The Waterstock estate was sold for £16,000 by his heirs to Sir Henry Ashurst, a London merchant, who pulled down the old hall and built a new house of brick.[14] Alan Bellingham of Levens Hall in Westmorland 'consumed a vast estate' in various northern counties which had been worth £3000 a year. In 1689 his trustees sold the Westmorland property along with the house and most of its contents to his cousin James Grahme, a courtier, for the sum of £24,400.[15] Other families which disposed of large estates included the Knivetons of Mercaston in Derbyshire, the Bickleys of Attleborough in Norfolk, the Chicheleys of Wimpole in Cambridgeshire, the Lingens of Stoke Edith in Herefordshire and the Carys of Cockington in Devon. The fate of Sir Francis Bickley, the fourth baronet, was succinctly recorded by a contemporary: 'the estate sold, he not worth anything, my lady works plain work for her living'.[16]

Financial worries may possibly account for some of the suicides which occurred among the gentry, though there appear in fact to have been various causes. In the course of Charles I's reign a Somerset squire was informed that Sir George Southcote, who was seated at Shillingford in Devon, 'has killed himself . . . the fowrth of the gentility that hath done it this yeare' in this shire.[17] In 1658 it was reported that Sir William Morley of Boxgrove in Sussex, a man of above £3000 a year, had died after cutting his throat.[18] In August 1671 Sir Henry North, who had been serving as a knight of the shire for Suffolk, was found dead in bed at his manor-house in Mildenhall. Although he had been in poor health for some time his death was not due to natural causes: beside him there was a double-barrelled pistol which he had used to shoot himself.[19] In 1694 an Essex knight of the shire, John Lemot Honywood of Marks Hall, hanged himself in his garters at the lodgings he occupied in Fleet Street. In subsequent litigation the authenticity of his will was challenged on the grounds that he was not then 'of a sound mind and of a disposeing memory or judgment.'[20]

Of all the misfortunes which could befall the gentry few were more poignant (certainly in their estimation) than the extinction of a family through the failure of the male line. Such an eventuality was by no means uncommon: for example, some 270 families with an income of £1000 a year or more suffered this fate in the course of the seventeenth century. The Rodneys of Somerset had been seated at Rodney Stoke ever since the thirteenth century. Sir Edward Rodney and his wife Dame Frances had five sons who all died young; a memorial in the parish church records the death in 1651 of George Rodney who is described as the fifth and last son. Not long before his own death in 1657 Sir Edward inserted in his commonplace book the melancholy observation that 'when I dye there will be an end of my family, and the fortunes of my family'. In his will he bequeathed all his lands and goods to his wife and to such of their children as she should think fit. In the event she sold part of the estate and settled the manor of Rodney Stoke on three of their five surviving daughters.[21] In the neighbouring county of Devon Sir Peter Fortescue of Wood Barton in Woodleigh married twice but left no male issue. In 1675, shortly before his death, he made it clear in his will that he was anxious that the estate which had descended to him from his ancestors should continue to be owned by persons bearing the name of Fortescue. Accordingly he gave direction that the trustees he had nominated should convey the property to his eldest daughter Amy if she should marry 'anie person whose propper Surname shall be ffortescue and whoe hath alwaies professed the Protestant Religion now setled in the Church and kingdome of England, being of the degree of Barronett, knight or Esquire, and whoe hath usuallie inhabited and most of his estate lyeing in the Counties of Devon, Cornwall or Somersett.' In practice this requirement does not appear to have been exceptionally demanding since in due course Amy married John Fortescue of Penwarne in Cornwall.[22]

If there were no immediate heirs of either sex a squire would usually settle his estate on a distant kinsman and in these circumstances the family name was often perpetuated. In some cases the fortunate young man had the same surname as his benefactor; in others he was obliged to adopt it, either instead of his own family name or as an addition, under the terms of the settlement. In 1679 Sir Richard Knight, who was seated at Chawton in Hampshire, died without issue, having left the handsome sum of £500 for the erection of a monument for himself in the parish church. His successor was a kinsman, Richard Martin, who in accordance with his wishes changed his name to Knight. The estate which he inherited was worth £1500 a year but Lady Knight claimed that she was entitled to receive a rent-charge of £300 a year for her maintenance and the debts, legacies and funeral expenses which were due to be paid amounted to some £6700. Accordingly it was decided, perhaps not surprisingly, to raise money through the sale of timber.[23]

When there was no direct succession from father to son the death of the squire often gave rise to acrimonious disputes among the squire's kindred over the inheritance of the estate, whether or not he had formally declared his wishes in this respect. These disputes were usually conducted in the Court of Chancery, though occasionally more physical methods might also be employed. In 1670 a young Cambridgeshire squire, Sir John Cutts of Childerley, died unmarried, leaving an estate worth £2500 a year, part of which was settled on trustees for the payment of debts, legacies and funeral expenses. Under the terms of his will the heir was a distant kinsman, Richard Cutts of Arkesden in Essex, who was still a minor. Not long after Sir John's death a quarrel broke out between Joanna Cutts, the heir's mother and guardian, and Edward Pickering and his wife Dorothy (Sir John's aunt) who were acting as administrators of the deceased's goods and chattels. When Mrs Cutts and her son moved into Childerley Hall they met with a hostile reception from Pickering who proceeded to eject them in the most brutal fashion. According to her own account of the incident Joanna Cutts was dragged out of the parlour and dumped in the park.[24]

If death was the great leveller it could nevertheless provide an opportunity for a grand spectacle such as was rare in a country parish. During the first half of the century it was not unusual for one of the heralds from the College of Arms to supervise the arrangements for the funeral of a wealthy landowner with the result that it was conducted with appropriate or even inordinate pomp and ceremony. At the same time there was a substantial demand for the services of herald painters who were responsible for supplying such items as escutcheons or armorial shields, banners and flags which proclaimed the status of the deceased. Among other elements of expenditure were the purchase of mourning clothes for the family and their servants or the material required to make them, the provision of food and drink and the distribution of money to the neighbouring poor who were present at the funeral. In one of his account books Sir Thomas Pelham of Halland House in Sussex noted that in 1624 he had spent £200 on his mother's funeral and over £400 on his father's funeral. His own funeral, which took place in 1654, involved the expenditure of £515 5s 6d. This included £249 16s 6d for black cloth and baize; £23 17s 0d for escutcheons and a velvet horse cloth; £2 11s 11d for the 'blacking' of the coach and horses; £4 for the preacher who also received a mourning cloak; and £10 for gifts of money to the poor.[25]

One of the most impressive funerals in the West Country took place in April 1662 when the corpse of Sir John Stawell, a Somerset magnate whose loyalty to the Crown had cost him dearly, was conveyed from his house at Low Ham to the church at Cothelstone where his principal mansion had been partly demolished by the parliamentarians. The body was carried in a chariot draped in velvet and drawn by six horses with black coverings. Besides Sir John's sons, George and Ralph, the mounted procession included the high sheriff of the county, George Speke, and many other gentry, together with some of their servants; his own male servants, among them the house steward, the cook, the butler and the gardener; the preacher, Richard Meredith, and eight other divines; Norroy King of Arms and three of his fellow heralds who bore the deceased's coat of arms, his gauntlet and spurs, his helmet and crest and his sword and target; two men with pennons or flags, 'one of his single coate, and th'other of his quarterings with the armes of his Lady'; and four trumpeters. From Low Ham the procession wound its way through Langport and Taunton. As the evening drew in the chariot was left in the churchyard at Bishop's Lydeard where it was attended throughout the night by some of Sir John's domestic servants. The following day his body was carried into the church at Cothelstone, placed in a hearse decorated with his armorial bearings and interred near the resting place of his late wife.[26] By this time, however, such a magnificent funeral was wholly anachronistic, at least so far as gentry families were concerned. Even before the Civil War there had been some

Puritan squires whose religious views had led them to express a marked aversion to elaborate funerals and after the Restoration it became increasingly common for the landed gentry to stipulate in their wills that they should be buried privately or without pomp or unnecessary expense. Between these two extremes the demands of social pride meant that there was still a need for the kind of public funeral which accorded with the 'degree and quality' of the deceased. This did not necessarily require the presence of heralds but it ensured that there was continuing work for the herald painters. In 1672 Sir William Twysden of Roydon Hall in Kent recorded the expenditure which had been incurred on the funeral of his father, Sir Roger the antiquary. This included payments for 20 gallons of claret, 12 bottles of sack, 14 taffeta escutcheons which cost 6s 8d each, 2 dozen torches (indicating that the funeral took place at night), 74 yards of black baize for covering the coach, 3 mourning livery suits and coats, and some serge material for the maids.[27] When Sir Francis Throckmorton of Coughton in Warwickshire was buried in 1680 the sum of £60 was paid to a herald painter for banners, flags, escutcheons and other ensigns of honour and the total cost of the funeral amounted to £378 19s 1d.[28]

In June 1684 Anthony Wood was invited to take on responsibility for the funeral of his friend Ralph Sheldon, a Catholic squire seated at Weston in Warwickshire. In the house he arranged for the hall, the staircase and the dining-room and 'the roome of state' to be hung with escutcheons which were supplied by a herald painter who accompanied him. For several days the body lay in state and was viewed, he tells us, by 'above 500 country people' before it was conveyed to Beoley church in Worcestershire which was the family's traditional burial place.[29] Throughout the seventeenth century it was customary on the death of a squire for a number of rooms in his mansion to be decked out with tokens of mourning such as hangings of black baize which remained in place for up to a year. During the course of his travels in the reign of Charles II Thomas Baskerville paid a visit to the home of the Wodehouse family at Kimberley in Norfolk. Sir Philip Wodehouse had recently died and, he noted in his journal, some of the rooms were 'hung with mourning and escutcheons'.[30] When Richard Legh of Lyme Hall in Cheshire died in 1687 his widow's apartments, the nurseries and the bedchamber of his daughter Betty were all fitted up with the accoutrements of mourning. Elizabeth Legh the widow had a 'Mourning Chamber' which contained black hangings for the bed, a black counterpane, two large Spanish blankets of the same colour and four black chairs.[31]

From generation to generation the country house was a silent witness to scenes of joy or sadness and periods of tranquillity or tension. The houses themselves also had their vicissitudes, including damage or despoliation in the Civil War, accidental fires, lack of proper maintenance which contributed to their decay and virtual abandonment in the case of families which spent much of their time in London. As the century reached its end, however, there was a distinct air of permanence about the country house as a gentleman's principal residence and the way of life with which it was associated.

HOUSEHOLDS AND SERVANTS
A NUMERICAL ASSESSMENT

The establishments of servants which appear below exclude all casual labour.

To enable realistic comparisons to be made the heads of households have been grouped within broad income bands which cover all forms of regular income.

£3000 A YEAR AND UPWARDS

1. *Maurice Barrow of Barningham, Suffolk.* In his will (1665) he named 28 servants (male 23, female 5).

2. *Sir John Brownlow of Belton, Lincolnshire.* At the time of his death (1679) he had 31 servants (male 21, female 10).

3. *Sir Edward Carr of Aswarby, Lincolnshire.* In his will (1618) he gave legacies to 45 servants (male 37, female 8). There were also two tutors and a chaplain.

4. *Sir William Clifton of Clifton, Nottinghamshire.* At the time of his death (1686) he had 24 servants (male 21, female 3). The wages bill which this involved amounted to £241 a year.

5. *Sir Thomas Crewe of Steane, Northamptonshire, serjeant at law.* Shortly before his death (1634) he had at least 23 servants.

6. *Sir Francis Englefield of Vasterne, Wootton Bassett, Wiltshire.* In his will (1631) he made bequests to 20 servants (male 16, female 4).

7. *George Evelyn of Wotton, Surrey.* In 1699 he had 17 servants (male 9, female 8).

8. *Sir Harbottle Grimston of Gorhambury, Hertfordshire, Master of the Rolls.* A poll tax assessment of 1678 reveals that his household consisted at that time of 27 persons, including 21 servants (male 16, female 5) and two chaplains.

9. *George Heneage of Hainton, Lincolnshire.* At the time of his death (1692) he had 20 servants (male 14, female 6). In 1682 there was a Catholic chaplain at Hainton Hall.

10. *Sir Robert Henley of Bramshill House, Hampshire.* At the time of his death (1681) he had 21 servants (male 19, female 2).

11. *Sir Henry Hobart of Blickling, Norfolk, Lord Chief Justice of the Common Pleas.* In his will (1625) he gave legacies to 25 servants (male 15, female 10).

12. *Sir John Hobart of Blickling, Norfolk (grandson of the above).* In 1655 he had 27 servants (male 23, female 4). The quarterly wages bill amounted to £41 10s 0d.

13. *Sir John Lenthall of Bessels Leigh, Berkshire.* At the time of his death (1681) he had 21 servants (male 15, female 6).

14. *Thomas Lucy of Charlecote, Warwickshire.* At the time of his death (1684) he had 14 servants (male 9, female 5).

15. *Sir Thomas Pelham of Halland House, East Hoathly, Sussex.* In 1623 he was employing 23 servants (male 18, female 5).

16. *Sir John Pelham of Halland House, East Hoathly, Sussex (grandson of the above).* He had 25 servants (male 17, female 8) at Michaelmas 1682 when the quarterly wages bill amounted to £38 5s 0d. After reaching a peak of 26 the number fell to 15 (Michaelmas 1686) and later to 11 (Michaelmas 1691).

17. *Alexander Popham of Littlecote, Wiltshire.* In 1699 he had 30 servants (male 20, female 10). The wages bill was of the order of £400 a year.

18. *Sir William Portman of Orchard Portman, Somerset and Bryanston, Dorset.* In his will (1690) he named 40 servants (male 30, female 10).

19. *Sir Francis Radcliffe of Dilston, Northumberland.* At the beginning of 1682 he had 29 servants (male 16, female 13). There was also a Catholic chaplain.

20. *Sir John St John of Battersea, Surrey and Lydiard Tregoze, Wiltshire.* In the summer of 1641 there were 14 servants (male 10, female 4) at his house in Battersea.

21. *Sir John Strangways of Melbury Sampford, Dorset.* In his will (1664) he named 23 servants (male 19, female 4).

22. *Peter Venables of Kinderton, Cheshire.* In 1660 (poll tax return) there were 34 persons in the household, including 30 servants (male 17, female 13).

23. *Sir Thomas Wentworth of Wentworth Woodhouse, Yorkshire (subsequently Earl of Strafford).* A list compiled about 1620 shows that the household then consisted of 64 persons, including 50 servants (male 44, female 6). There was also a chaplain.

24. *Sir Henry Willoughby of Risley, Derbyshire.* At the time of his death (1653) he had 48 servants. The wages bill amounted to £200 11s 0d a year.

£1000 A YEAR AND UPWARDS BUT BELOW £3000 A YEAR

25. *Sir Francis Ashby of Breakspear, Harefield, Middlesex.* In his will (1624) he named 12 servants (male 9, female 3).

26. *George Ashby of Quenby Hall, Hungarton, Leicestershire.* In 1618 he had at least 18 servants.

27. *John Ayshcombe of Lyford, Hanney, Berkshire.* An official document of 1642 lists 13 servants (male 8, female 5).

28. *Sir Ralph Babthorpe of Osgodby, Yorkshire.* In the early years of James I's reign he had upwards of 30 servants. There were also two Catholic chaplains.

29. *Sir John Backhouse of Swallowfield Place, Shinfield, Berkshire.* In May 1642 his household consisted of 20 persons, including 17 servants (male 11, female 6).

30. *Sir Edmund Bacon of Redgrave, Suffolk.* In his will (1648) he named 32 servants (male 28, female 4). There was also a chaplain.

31. *Sir Amyas Bampfield of Poltimore, Devon.* In 1625 he and his son John had at least 17 servants.

32. *Sir Thomas Barrington of Hatfield Broad Oak, Essex.* According to his steward's accounts he had 22 servants (male 17, female 5) at Michaelmas 1640 and their wages amounted to £121 16s 8d a year. Usually there was a domestic chaplain.

33. *Sir Henry Bellasis of Newburgh Priory, Coxwold, Yorkshire.* In 1609 he had 51 servants (male 40, female 11). These included a considerable number of farm workers.

34. *Sir John Bellot of Great Moreton Hall, Moreton, Cheshire.* In 1660 (poll tax return) he had 16 servants (male 8, female 8).

35. *Sir Cecil Bishop of Parham, Sussex.* In December 1697 he had 21 servants (male 14, female 7).

36. *Sir John Bolles of Scampton, Lincolnshire.* In 1631 it was reported that there were 30 persons in his household.

37. *Roger Burgoyne of Wroxall, Warwickshire.* In 1612 he had at least 15 servants.

38. *Sir George Cary of Clovelly, Devon.* In 1678 he had 14 servants (male 11, female 3).

39. *William Cary of Clovelly, Devon (brother and successor of the above).* In 1699 he had 18 servants (male 12, female 6).

40. *Francis Charlton of Apley Castle, Shropshire.* An official document of 1642 lists 34 servants (male 23, female 11): 24 at Apley Castle and 10 at Wembridge, Shropshire.

41. *Sir Hugh Cholmley of Whitby, Yorkshire.* In the 1630s there were usually between 30 and 40 persons in his household. These included a chaplain.

42. *Sir George Chudleigh of Ashton, Devon.* In 1660 (poll tax return) his household consisted of 17 persons, including 12 servants (male 8, female 4).

43. *Sir Philip Constable of Everingham, Yorkshire.* At Christmas 1662 he and his son Marmaduke had 26 servants (male 18, female 8). There was also a tutor.

44. *Sir Marmaduke Constable of Everingham, Yorkshire (son of the above).* In 1672 he had 18 servants.

45. *Sir John Corbet of Adderley, Shropshire.* A poll tax return of 1660 records that he had 16 children and servants.

46. *Sir Thomas Danby of Thorpe Perrow and Farnley, Yorkshire.* In 1643 he had 22 servants (male 9, female 13).

47. *Sir William Drake of Shardeloes, Amersham, Buckinghamshire, Chirographer of the Common Pleas.* At the time of his death (1669) there were 19 servants (male 14, female 5).

48. *Sir Walter Ernle of Etchilhampton, Wiltshire.* At the time of his death (1682) he had 13 servants.

49. *Sir John Evelyn of Leigh Place, Godstone, Surrey.* In 1639 he had at least 14 servants.

50. *John Every of Cothay, Somerset.* At the time of his death (1679) there were 11 servants who had lived with him for three years or more.

51. *Sir Clement Fisher of Great Packington, Warwickshire.* According to his steward's accounts he had 12 servants at Michaelmas 1686 and the wages bill amounted to £58 5s 0d a year.

52. *Sir Thomas Fotherley of the Bury, Rickmansworth, Hertfordshire.* An official document of 1642 lists 20 servants (male 11, female 9).

53. *Framlingham Gawdy of West Harling, Norfolk.* According to his accounts he had 13 servants (male 10, female 3) in 1634.

54. *Sir Francis Godolphin of Godolphin House, Breage, Cornwall.* In 1660 (poll tax return) he had 24 servants: 4 married men, 10 single men, 2 widows and 8 single women.

55. *Sir William Goring of Burton, Sussex.* An official return of May 1642 lists 17 servants (male 12, female 5). There was also a chaplain.

56. *Sir Richard Graham of Norton Conyers, Yorkshire.* In the week beginning 7 November 1640 there were 30 persons in the household, including visitors.

57. *Sir Thomas Haggerston of Haggerston, Northumberland.* In the autumn of 1691 he had 14 servants (male 8, female 6).

58. *William Hale of King's Walden, Hertfordshire.* In 1635 he had 10 servants.

59. *William Hale of King's Walden, Hertfordshire (nephew of the above).* In 1688 he had 17 servants (male 10, female 7).

60. *Sir Richard Hawksworth of Hawksworth, Yorkshire.* At the time of his death (1658) he had 24 servants (male 20, female 4).

61. *Sir Thomas Hoby of Hackness, Yorkshire.* In 1600 he had 14 servants (male 10, female 4).

62. *Sir Justinian Isham of Lamport, Northamptonshire.* A document drawn up for poll tax purposes in the early part of Charles II's reign lists 18 servants (male 11, female 7). The wages bill was £80 a year.

63. *Sir John Kaye of Woodsome Hall, Almondbury, Yorkshire.* In 1648 the household consisted of 27 persons. These included 19 servants (male 12, female 7) and a schoolmaster.

64. *Sir Rowland Lacey of Pudlicott, Charlbury, Oxfordshire.* At the time of his death (1690) he had 12 servants (male 8, female 4).

65. *Sir William Leche of Squerries Court, Westerham, Kent.* At the time of his death (1673) he had 13 servants (male 7, female 6).

66. *Sir Francis Henry Lee of Ditchley, Oxfordshire.* At the time of his death (1667) he had 18 servants (male 13, female 5). The quarterly wages bill amounted to £39 7s 6d.

67. *Sir John Lowther of Lowther, Westmorland.* In 1629 he had 20 servants.

68. *Sir John Monson of Burton, Lincolnshire.* In 1631 it was reported that his household consisted of 50 persons.

69. *William Morley of Glynde, Sussex.* According to his accounts he had 14 servants (male 12, female 2) at Easter 1674. There was also a chaplain.

70. *Roger Nowell of Read, Lancashire.* In 1660 (poll tax return) there were 19 persons in the household, including 13 servants (male 10, female 3).

71. *Edmund Parker of Boringdon, Plympton St Mary, Devon.* In 1660 (poll tax return) the household consisted of 19 persons, including 14 servants.

72. *William Pendarves of Roskrow, St Gluvias, Cornwall.* In 1660 (poll tax return) there were 32 persons in the household, including 19 servants (male 13, female 6).

73. *Thomas Pigott of Chetwynd, Shropshire.* In 1660 (poll tax return) the household consisted of 14 persons, including 11 servants.

74. *George Purefoy of Wadley House, Faringdon, Berkshire.* An official return of 1642 lists 26 persons in the household, including 21 servants (male 15, female 6). Purefoy usually kept a domestic chaplain.

75. *Sir Henry Savile of Methley, Yorkshire.* In his will (1632) he named 17 servants (male 13, female 4).

76. *John Shelton of West Bromwich, Staffordshire.* In 1660 (poll tax return) he had 10 servants.

77. *Richard Shireburn of Stonyhurst, Lancashire.* In 1660 (poll tax return) there were 19 persons in the household, including 17 servants (male 11, female 6). There was usually a Catholic chaplain.

78. *Sir John Shuckburgh of Over Shuckburgh, Warwickshire.* At the time of his death (1661) he had 15 servants (male 8, female 7). There was also a chaplain.

79. *Richard Shuttleworth of Gawthorpe, Lancashire.* In 1610 he had 25 servants (male 21, female 4). In 1660 (poll tax return) his household consisted of 27 persons, including 18 servants (male 13, female 5).

80. *Sir Henry Slingsby of Red House, Moor Monkton, Yorkshire.* In May 1628 he had 13 servants (male 9, female 4).

81. *Sir Henry Slingsby of Red House, Moor Monkton, Yorkshire (son of the above).* In 1638 the household consisted of 30 persons, including 24 servants (male 16, female 8).

82. *Thomas Smyth of Long Ashton, Somerset.* In 1641 there were 37 persons in the household at Ashton Court. These included 29 servants (male 22, female 7). The wages bill was £100 a year.

83. *William Stafford of Blatherwick, Northamptonshire.* At the time of his death (1688) he had 17 servants (male 14, female 3). There was also a chaplain.

84. *Sir Robert Throckmorton of Coughton, Warwickshire and Weston Underwood, Buckinghamshire.* At Lady Day 1612 he had 26 servants (male 21, female 5). Of these, 12 were to be discharged.

85. *Sir Francis Throckmorton of Coughton, Warwickshire and Weston Underwood, Buckinghamshire (son of the above).* In October 1672 he had 25 servants (male 17, female 8).

86. *Sir Robert Throckmorton of Coughton, Warwickshire and Weston Underwood, Buckinghamshire (son of the above).* In December 1684 he had 22 servants (male 17, female 5). The wages bill amounted to £120 a year.

87. *Richard Towneley of Towneley, Lancashire.* In 1660 (poll tax return) there were 26 persons in the household, including 22 servants (male 15, female 7).

88. *Sir Henry Vernon of Hodnet, Shropshire.* In 1660 (poll tax return) he had 17 servants (male 11, female 6).

89. *Sir William Waller of Osterley, Middlesex.* In his will (1668) he gave legacies to those servants who by the time of his death would have lived with him for at least two years. These numbered 13 (male 7, female 6) and their wages amounted to £71 16s 8d a year. There was also a chaplain.

90. *Sir Francis Wenman of Carswell, Witney, Oxfordshire.* In his will (1680) he named 11 servants (male 8, female 3).

91. *Sir Peter Wentworth of Lillingstone Lovell, Oxfordshire.* In his will (1673) he made bequests to 20 servants (male 13, female 7).

92. *Sir James Whitelocke of Fawley, Buckinghamshire, Judge of the Court of the King's Bench.* According to his son Bulstrode Whitelocke he had about 20 menservants (this would have been in the years between 1616 and 1632). There was also a chaplain.

93. *Sir John Wyrley of Hamstead Hall, Handsworth, Staffordshire.* In 1660 (poll tax return) his household consisted of 21 persons, including 18 servants.

94. *Sir John Yorke of Gouthwaite Hall, Down Stonebeck, Yorkshire.* In 1613 he had at least 17 servants.

£500 A YEAR AND UPWARDS BUT BELOW £1000 A YEAR

95. *Richard Cholmley of Brandsby, Yorkshire.* In January 1618 he had 25 servants (male 21, female 4).

96. *Henry Coghill of Aldenham, Hertfordshire.* In March 1642 there were 16 persons in the household. These included 11 servants (male 4, female 7) and a chaplain.

97. *William Cotton of Bellaport, Bearstone, Shropshire.* In 1660 (poll tax return) the household consisted of 17 persons, including 14 servants (male 8, female 6).

98. *Dame Elizabeth Craven of Lenchwick, Worcestershire (widow of Sir William Craven).* In 1660 (poll tax return) she had 10 servants (male 7, female 3).

99. *William Dallison of Greetwell, Lincolnshire.* In 1631 it was reported that there were 17 persons in his household.

100. *Sir Charles Egerton of Newborough, Staffordshire.* In 1660 he had at least 12 servants at Newborough Hall.

101. *Richard Erisey of Erisey, Grade, Cornwall.* In 1660 (poll tax return) the household consisted of 20 persons, including 16 servants (male 9, female 7).

102. *Sir John Gore of New Place, Gilston, Hertfordshire.* An official document of 1642 lists 13 servants (male 9, female 4).

103. *Sir Edward Gostwick of Willington, Bedfordshire.* In 1630, when he was a minor, he had 13 servants (male 10, female 3). The half-yearly wages bill amounted to £20 12s 8d.

104. *Sir Richard Hardres of Great Hardres, Kent.* At the time of his death (1669) he had 10 servants.

105. *John Hawtrey of Eastcote House, Ruislip, Middlesex.* An official document of 1642 indicates that the household consisted of 13 persons, including 11 servants (male 7, female 4).

106. *Rowland Hill of Soulton Hall, Shropshire.* In 1660 (poll tax return) there were 17 persons in the household, including 12 servants (male 8, female 4).

107. *John Lane of Bentley, Staffordshire.* In 1660 (poll tax return) the household consisted of 12 persons, including 9 servants.

108. *William Lawton of Church Lawton, Cheshire.* In 1660 (poll tax return) he had 13 servants (male 7, female 6).

109. *Robert Leighton of Wattlesborough Hall, Shropshire.* At the time of his death (1689) he had 15 servants (male 9, female 6).

110. *Sir Peter Leycester of Tabley Hall, Nether Tabley, Cheshire.* In 1647 he had 18 servants (11 male, 7 female) and the wages bill amounted to £42 15s 0d a year. In 1669, however, there were only 12 servants who were paid at the rate of £32 6s 8d a year.

111. *Sir Christopher Nevile of Haddington, Aubourn, Lincolnshire.* In 1692 (the year of his death) he had 12 servants (male 7, female 5).

112. *Alexander Osbaldeston of Osbaldeston, Lancashire.* In 1660 (poll tax return) there were 14 persons in the household, including 12 servants (male 6, female 6).

113. *Sir Thomas Overbury of Admington, Quinton, Gloucestershire.* At the time of his death (1683) he had 12 servants (male 7, female 5).

114. *John Persehouse of Reynolds Hall, Walsall, Staffordshire.* In 1660 (poll tax return) he had 6 servants.

115. *Dame Margaret Pratt of Coleshill, Berkshire (widow of Sir George Pratt).* At the time of her death (1699) she had 14 servants (male 6, female 8).

116. *Robert Sandford of Sandford Hall, Shropshire.* In 1660 (poll tax return) the household consisted of 16 persons, including 13 servants (male 6, female 7).

117. *Sir Geoffrey Shakerley of Hulme, Cheshire.* In 1660 (poll tax return) he had 13 servants (male 8, female 5).

118. *Thomas Stringer of Sharlston, Yorkshire.* In 1641 he had 20 servants (male 14, female 6) and the quarterly wages bill amounted to £10 14s 1d. The following year he was employing 15 servants.

119. *Sir William Strode of Newnham House, Plympton St Mary, Devon.* In 1660 (poll tax return) there were 13 persons in his household, including 6 servants.

120. *Nicholas Toke of Godinton, Kent.* In November 1650 he had 13 servants (male 8, female 5).

121. *Sir John Wittewronge of Rothamstead, Harpenden, Hertfordshire.* At Michaelmas 1648 he had 13 servants (male 8, female 5). The half-yearly wages bill amounted to £29 15s 0d.

UNDER £500 A YEAR

122. *John Arundell of Truthall, Sithney, Cornwall.* In 1660 (poll tax return) his household consisted of 8 persons, including 4 servants (male 3, female 1).

123. *Nicholas Bannister of Altham, Lancashire.* In 1660 (poll tax return) he had 7 servants.

124. *Thomas Barcroft of Cliviger, Lancashire.* In 1660 (poll tax return) there were 9 persons in the household, including 6 servants (male 3, female 3).

125. *Haniball Bogans of St Keverne, Cornwall.* In 1660 (poll tax return) there were 8 persons in the household, including 4 servants.

126. *Mary Bowes of Elford, Staffordshire (widow of John Bowes esquire).* In 1660 (poll tax return) she had 7 servants.

127. *Edward Carew of Littleton, Worcestershire.* In 1660 (poll tax return) he had 7 servants (male 3, female 4).

128. *John Carnsew of Budock, Cornwall.* In 1660 (poll tax return) there were 13 persons in the household, including 7 servants (male 3, female 4).

129. *Thomas Cholmley of Lostock Gralam, Cheshire.* In 1660 (poll tax return) he had 8 servants (male 5, female 3).

130. *Thomas Croxton of Ravenscroft, Cheshire.* In 1660 (poll tax return) the household consisted of 12 persons, including 8 servants (male 4, female 4).

131. *John Dalton of Swine, Yorkshire.* In 1660 (poll tax return) he had 5 servants.

132. *Nicholas Fletcher of Paxford, Worcestershire.* In 1660 (poll tax return) he had 6 servants.

133. *John Fox of Budock, Cornwall.* In 1660 (poll tax return) he had 10 servants (male 5, female 5).

134. *Somerford Oldfield of Somerford Radnor, Cheshire.* In 1660 (poll tax return) he had 8 servants (male 4, female 4).

135. *William Paynter of Antron, Sithney, Cornwall.* In 1660 (poll tax return) he had 8 servants (male 4, female 4).

136. *Richard Pyott of Streethay, Staffordshire.* In 1660 (poll tax return) the household consisted of 10 persons, including 7 servants.

137. *Randle Rode of Odd Rode, Cheshire.* In 1660 (poll tax return) there were 11 persons in the household, including 6 servants (male 3, female 3).

138. *Stephen Thompson of Humbleton, Yorkshire.* In 1660 (poll tax return) the household consisted of 11 persons, including 7 servants.

139. *John Thorpe of Danthorpe, Yorkshire.* In 1660 (poll tax return) there were 9 persons in the household, including 5 servants.

140. *Nicholas Townley of Royle, Lancashire.* In 1660 (poll tax return) he had 8 servants (male 5, female 3).

141. *Henry Winter of Clapton, Somerset.* In 1660 (poll tax return) the household consisted of 7 persons, including 4 servants (male 2, female 2).

ESTATE STEWARDS

This list of seventeenth-century estate stewards does not purport to be exhaustive. Among other things, it excludes stewards on whom there is no information available apart from their surnames.

The following symbols have been used:
* relation (including distant kinsman)
† lawyer

Wherever possible, the list shows how a steward chose to style himself (e.g. gentleman or yeoman).

The annual salary (where known) appears in brackets.

1. *Abdy of Felix Hall, Kelvedon, Essex*   Henry Clarke
2. *Altham of Mark Hall, Latton, Essex*   *Rev. Michael Altham (d.1705)
3. *Archer of Umberslade, Tanworth, Warwickshire*   William Knight gentleman, John Chambers gentleman
4. *Armytage of Kirklees, Yorkshire*   Walter Curwen
5. *Ashburnham of Ashburnham, Sussex*   John Lawrence
6. *Astley of Patshull, Staffordshire*   John Gassaway
7. *Bacon of Redgrave, Suffolk*   John White, †Edward Goate gentleman
8. *Bacon of Shrubland Hall, Barham, Suffolk*   William Minter (£15 a year)
9. *Bagot of Blithfield, Staffordshire*   William Cowper
10. *Bampfield of Poltimore, Devon*   Robert Eastchurch (£30 a year)
11. *Bankes of Kingston Lacy, Dorset*   Matthew Beethell
12. *Barker of Grimston Hall, Trimley St Martin, Suffolk*   Michael Cropley
13. *Barrington of Hatfield Broad Oak, Essex*   *Richard Hildersham, John Kendall gentleman (£10, then £30 a year), John Hawkins, Tobias Hewitt gentleman (d.1686) (£20 a year)
14. *Barrow of Barningham, Suffolk*   Robert Stonham gentleman
15. *Baynton of Bromham and later of Spye Park, Bowden Hill, Wiltshire*   Michael Tidcombe gentleman

(d.1639), Samuel Horsington gentleman, John Clarke, †William Norris esquire (£20 a year)
16. *Bedell of Wood Rising, Norfolk*   *Gabriel Bedell gentleman (£40 a year)
17. *Bennet of Calverton, Buckinghamshire*   Roger Chapman gentleman
18. *Bickley of Attleborough, Norfolk*   Roger Crowe gentleman (£5 a year)
19. *Bishop of Parham, Sussex*   Richard Bradshaw (£30, then £40 a year), John Young (£20 a year)
20. *Bold of Bold Hall, Prescot, Lancashire*   Randle Penington gentleman (£20 a year)
21. *Bolles of Scampton, Lincolnshire*   *Thomas Smith gentleman
22. *Bond of Peckham, Surrey*   James Morrough gentleman (£15, then £50 a year)
23. *Boscawen of Tregothnan, St Michael Penkevil, Cornwall*   Roger Cocke, Thomas Harvey gentleman, Bartholomew Harvey gentleman
24. *Boteler of Biddenham, Bedfordshire*   Michael Wharton
25. *Boteler of Teston, Kent*   Richard Gery
26. *Boteler of Watton Woodhall, Hertfordshire*   Thomas Escourt (£20 a year)
27. *Brooke of Cockfield Hall, Yoxford, Suffolk*   John Wytchingham gentleman, William Betts gentleman
28. *Brooke of Great Oakley, Northamptonshire*   Edward Hun
29. *Brooke of Norton, Cheshire*   Richard Rydgate
30. *Brownlow of Belton, Lincolnshire*   Matthew Aberley gentleman
31. *Calthorpe of Ampton, Suffolk*   Ralph Newman
32. *Carew of Antony House, Cornwall*   John Treis gentleman (d.1697),   †Richard Eare gentleman (d.1707)
33. *Carew of Beddington, Surrey*   Thomas Grenhill (d.1634)

34. *Carr of Aswarby, Lincolnshire*   William Burton gentleman, John Burslem gentleman (£50 a year)

35. *Cary of Clovelly, Devon*   John Tawton, Narcissus Hatherley

36. *Caryll of West Harting, Sussex*   Lawrence Forster, Thomas Noble, Arthur Phillips (d.1695), Hugh Phillips gentleman

37. *Champernowne of Dartington, Devon*   John Furlong, John Rowe gentleman

38. *Cholmley of Whitby, Yorkshire*   George Coward

39. *Clifton of Clifton, Nottinghamshire*   †Robert Leake gentleman, Gervase Holland (d.1673), Samuel Greaves esquire (£30 a year)

40. *Coke of Holkham, Norfolk*   Lawrence Lunn

41. *Coke of Melbourne, Derbyshire*   Nicholas Denham

42. *Constable of Everingham, Yorkshire*   John Archer, *George Constable gentleman (d.1672), Thomas Champney

43. *Corbet of Adderley, Shropshire*   Samuel Dalton

44. *Cottington of Fonthill Gifford, Wiltshire*   Charles Woolmer

45. *Crewe of Utkinton Hall, Tarporley, Cheshire*   Hercules Commander, Richard Smethurst yeoman

46. *Cutts of Childerley, Cambridgeshire*   Thomas Lane (d.1669), John Pearson

47. *Danby of Masham and Farnley, Yorkshire* *† Christopher Danby gentleman (d.1613), Miles Danby gentleman

48. *D'Ewes of Stowlangtoft, Suffolk*   Thomas Downes, Thomas Colby

49. *Digby of Stoke Dry, Rutland and Gayhurst, Buckinghamshire*   Nicholas Hollis gentleman (£20 a year)

50. *Drake of Shardeloes, Buckinghamshire*   James Perrott gentleman (£40 a year), James Boulding (d.1712)

51. *Dunch of Little Wittenham, Berkshire*   Edward Hilliard

52. *Edgcumbe of Mount Edgcumbe, Devon*   William Drinckwater

53. *Egerton of Farthinghoe, Northamptonshire*   James Berry

54. *Eliot of Port Eliot, Cornwall*   *Peter Mayowe gentleman

55. *Ernle of Whetham House, Wiltshire*   William Baily (£47 a year)

56. *Every of Cothay, Somerset*   Edward Ford gentleman

57. *Fairfax of Steeton, Yorkshire*   Ralph Baltrus

58. *Ferrers of Tamworth Castle, Warwickshire*   Nicholas Parker gentleman

59. *Fisher of Great Packington, Warwickshire*   Thomas Harding, William Denston

60. *Fitton of Gawsworth, Cheshire*   Francis Hollinshead gentleman

61. *Fleetwood of Aldwinkle, Northamptonshire*   John Carpenter gentleman

62. *Foljambe of Aldwark, Yorkshire*   Godfrey Somersall yeoman

63. *Fortescue of Salden House, Mursley, Buckinghamshire*   William Simpson (£20 a year)

64. *Fowell of Fowelscombe, Ugborough, Devon*   John Furlong

65. *Fox of Chiswick, Middlesex*   Richard Miller esquire

66. *Frewen of Brickhill, Northiam, Sussex*   George Bishop (£20 a year)

67. *Gage of Hengrave, Suffolk*   William Covell gentleman

68. *Gage of West Firle, Sussex*   George Vaughan, William Eldridge, Thomas Lockier

69. *Garrard of Lamer, Wheathampstead, Hertfordshire*   Christopher Cratford gentleman

70. *Garton of Woolavington, Sussex*   Matthew Young esquire

71. *Gascoigne of Barnbow Hall, Yorkshire*   Robert Carr gentleman (the chief steward)

72. *Gell of Hopton Hall, Derbyshire*   Thomas Parker

73. *Godfrey of Thonock Hall, Lincolnshire*   John Hall gentleman (£20 a year)

74. *Golding of Colston Bassett, Nottinghamshire*   William Richmond (d.1684)

75. *Goring of Danny Park, Sussex*   William Randolph

76. *Grimston of Gorhambury, Hertfordshire*   Thomas Langford

77. *Guise of Elmore and Rendcomb, Gloucestershire*   James Winton (£50 a year)

78. *Guldeford of Hempstead Place, Benenden, Kent*   *John Throckmorton gentleman

79. *Hanham of Dean's Court, Wimborne Minster, Dorset*   Stephen Bowdidge (or Bowditch) (£20 a year)

80. *Hales of Tunstall, Kent*   John Grove gentleman (d.1678)

81. *Harcourt of Stanton Harcourt, Oxfordshire*   Samuel Sandell (d.1695) (£18 a year)

82. *Hare of Stow Bardolph, Norfolk*   Samuel Renault (d.1678)

83. *Harley of Brampton Bryan, Herefordshire*   Samuel Shilton gentleman

84. *Harpur of Calke, Derbyshire*   *John Harpur (£70, then £100 a year)

85. *Haselwood of Maidwell, Northamptonshire*   John Horton

86. *Henley of Bramshill House, Hampshire*   Thomas Rawlinson, Richard Goddard (both men were based in Somerset)

87. *Herris of Woodham Mortimer, Essex*   John Richmond

88. *Hesketh of Rufford, Lancashire*   Edward Bridge

89. *Hobart of Blickling, Norfolk*   Edmund Wise (£30 a year), John Brewster gentleman (£20 a year)

90. *Holman of Warkworth, Northamptonshire*   William Style gentleman (d.1670)

91. *Houghton of Shelton, Norfolk*   †Francis Hill esquire

92. *Howe of Little Compton, Gloucestershire*   Thomas Wolley gentleman

93. *Hungate of Huddleston Hall, Yorkshire*   John Simpson

94. *Hussey of Caythorpe, Lincolnshire* George Rose gentleman, Christopher Noble (£60 a year)

95. *Hutton of Marske, Yorkshire* John Blackburn, Thomas Mudd

96. *Hyde of Aldbury, Hertfordshire* John Hall

97. *Ingoldsby of Lenborough, Buckinghamshire* William Robinson

98. *Ingram of Temple Newsam, Yorkshire* John Mattison (d.1642), John Mattison (his nephew), William Marwood gentleman

99. *Kingsmill of Sydmonton, Hampshire* Richard Colson gentleman, Francis Langton gentleman, John Horton, †Thomas Colnett gentleman

100. *Knatchbull of Mersham Hatch, Kent* Francis Hall

101. *Knyvett of Ashwellthorpe, Norfolk* William Harrison

102. *Lake of Canons, Little Stanmore, Middlesex* †Thomas Franklin esquire

103. *Lake of Great Stanmore, Middlesex* *William Bockenham gentleman

104. *Lawson of Brough, Yorkshire* *James Lawson gentleman

105. *Lee of Ditchley, Oxfordshire* John Cary gentleman (£30 a year)

106. *Legh of Lyme Hall, Cheshire* Edward Thorniley, George Bowdon (d.1659), Thomas Bowdon (his son)

107. *Lenthall of Bessels Leigh, Berkshire and Burford, Oxfordshire* John Pryor gentleman (d.1697) (£13 6s 8d, then £30 a year), John Periam (steward of the West Country estate)

108. *Leveson of Trentham, Staffordshire* John Langley gentleman

109. *Littleton of Hagley, Worcestershire* Ralph Taylor

110. *Lowther of Lowther, Westmorland* Giles Moore, William Atkinson

111. *Lowther of Swillington, Yorkshire* John Cockhill gentleman

112. *Lowther of Whitehaven, Cumberland* Thomas Tickell (d.1692) (£20, then £40 a year), †William Gilpin (£40 a year)

113. *Lucas of St John's, Colchester, Essex* William Nicholson

114. *Lucy of Broxbourne, Hertfordshire and later of Faccombe, Hampshire* *†John Mundy gentleman, †Joseph Garrard gentleman (£10 a year) (both stewards for the Hampshire, Wiltshire and Somerset estates), *†Samuel Eyre esquire (later knighted) (£20 a year)

115. *Lucy of Charlecote, Warwickshire* Nicholas Tue (£10 a year)

116. *Lytton of Knebworth, Hertfordshire* Daniel Lawrence

117. *Maleverer of Ingleby Arncliffe, Yorkshire* Christopher Beckwith

118. *Mallory of Studley, Yorkshire* Geoffrey Adamson

119. *Maynard of Gunnersbury, Middlesex* Thomas Bradford (£80 a year)

120. *Middleton of Belsay, Northumberland* Cuthbert Heron gentleman

121. *Monins of Waldershare, Kent* Edward Fellows

122. *Morley of Glynde, Sussex* Matthew Lownes (d.1678)

123. *Napier of More Crichel, Dorset* Richard Gregory

124. *Newdegate of Arbury, Warwickshire* †Robert Beale esquire

125. *Offley of Madeley, Staffordshire* Christopher Deighton

126. *Owen of Condover, Shropshire* Francis Philipps

127. *Parker of Boringdon, Devon* Francis Collings

128. *Paston of Oxnead, Norfolk* Humphrey Prattant gentleman

129. *Paston of Town Barningham, Norfolk* Robert Billington

130. *Pelham of Brocklesby, Lincolnshire* Richard Benson gentleman

131. *Pelham of Halland House, East Hoathly, Sussex* Robert Constable gentleman (£20, then £15 a year), John Vine, John Newington

132. *Phelips of Montacute, Somerset* Zachery Hillard

133. *Philipps of Stoke Charity, Hampshire* Robert Napier gentleman

134. *Pleydell of Ampney Crucis, Gloucestershire* Thomas Hall, Richard Heffard (joint stewards)

135. *Pole of Shute, Devon* John Freake

136. *Popham of Littlecote, Wiltshire* Henry Rumsey esquire (d.1676), Thomas Leyson

137. *Portman of Orchard Portman, Somerset* Henry Goddard gentleman, John Colby gentleman, Richard Willoughby gentleman, William Crosse

138. *Pratt of Coleshill, Berkshire* John Bond gentleman (£12 a year)

139. *Radcliffe of Dilston, Northumberland* Richard Hayles

140. *Reade of Brocket Hall, Hertfordshire and Duns Tew, Oxfordshire* John Barrett yeoman

141. *Reresby of Thrybergh, Yorkshire* Thomas Smith, Thomas Robotham

142. *Rolle of Shapwick, Somerset and East Tytherley, Hampshire* John Devall

143. *Rushout of Maylards, Havering, Essex and Northwick Park, Blockley, Worcestershire* Edward Crofts

144. *St John of Battersea, Surrey and Lydiard Tregoze, Wiltshire* Thomas Hardyman gentleman (Lydiard Tregoze), Charles Chappell (d.1685) (Battersea), William Foote (d.1713) (Battersea)

145. *St John of Woodford, Northamptonshire* Robert Guy, John Rowlett

146. *Savile of Methley, Yorkshire* Edward Cowper gentleman

147. *Savile of Thornhill, Yorkshire* *William Vernon gentleman, Henry Cookson gentleman

148. *Scott of Scot's Hall, Smeeth, Kent* William Hartridge

149. *Sheldon of Beoley, Worcestershire and Weston, Warwickshire* Thomas Savage

150. *Shelley of Michelgrove, Sussex* William Jackson

151. *Shireburn of Stonyhurst, Lancashire* Gabriel Hesketh gentleman

152. *Shirley of Staunton Harold, Leicestershire*   Anthony Atkinson, Roger Allestry (£66 13s 4d a year), Robert Bennett (£66 13s 4d a year)

153. *Shuttleworth of Gawthorpe, Lancashire*   Edward Sherburn, James Yate

154. *Slingsby of Scriven and Red House, Moor Monkton, Yorkshire*   Robert Burton, Thomas Richardson gentleman (d.1671), Thomas Buckley (£40 a year)

155. *Smyth of Great Bedwyn, Wiltshire*   Thomas Willis (d.1646)

156. *Smyth of Long Ashton, Somerset*   John Edwards

157. *Stanley of Nether Alderley, Cheshire*   Thomas Deane gentleman (d.1695)

158. *Stawell of Cothelstone, Somerset*   Robert Lawrence gentleman

159. *Strickland of Sizergh Hall, Heversham, Westmorland*   Thomas Shepherd

160. *Strickland of Thornton Bridge, Yorkshire*   James Dibble (£20 a year)

161. *Stydolfe of Norbury, Mickleham, Surrey*   William Michell

162. *Tempest of Broughton, Yorkshire*   George Fell, *John Yorke gentleman (1620–78), *Richard Yorke gentleman (his son)

163. *Tempest of Stella, Durham*   George Dunn gentleman

164. *Temple of Stowe, Buckinghamshire*   William Chaplyn gentleman

165. *Throckmorton of Coughton, Warwickshire*   James Waters, James Smyth (£20 a year), Francis Reeve (£50 a year), Robert Grey gentleman, Gyles Poulton (£35 a year)

166. *Tirwhitt of Kettelby House, Wrawby, Lincolnshire*   Stephen Macquene

167. *Tollemache of Helmingham, Suffolk*   John Pulham gentleman, *Ptolemy Tollemache gentleman

168. *Trenchard of Wolfeton House, Charminster, Dorset*   Edward Pye

169. *Turberville of Bere Regis, Dorset*   †Christopher Yonge

170. *Verney of Middle Claydon, Buckinghamshire*   William Roades gentleman (d.1657), John Coleman

171. *Waad of Battles Hall, Essex*   William Cole

172. *Walmsley of Dunkenhalgh, Lancashire*   Adam Bolton (d.1654)

173. *Wandesford of Kirklington, Yorkshire*   Christopher Hunton, Christopher Mitchell (d.1644)

174. *Weld of East Lulworth, Dorset*   Thomas Oakley

175. *Wentworth of Lillingstone Lovell, Oxfordshire*   Peter Saunders gentleman (d.1691)

176. *Wentworth of Wentworth Woodhouse, Yorkshire*   Richard Marris gentleman

177. *Wicks of Haselbech, Northamptonshire*   John Astell (£20 a year)

178. *Wightwick Knightley of Offchurch, Warwickshire*   Henry Webb gentleman (£36 a year)

179. *Wilmer of Sywell, Northamptonshire*   Stephen Gauderne gentleman

180. *Windham of Felbrigg, Norfolk*   Dr Robert Pepper (1636–1700), John Salman gentleman, Joseph Eldon

181. *Wingfield of Easton, Suffolk*   James Slade

182. *Winwood of Ditton Park, Buckinghamshire*   Robert Conway

183. *Wollaston of Shenton, Leicestershire*   Thomas Monck

184. *Worsley of Appuldurcombe, Isle of Wight*   John Bowler gentleman (£40 a year)

185. *Wortley of Wortley, Yorkshire*   *Samuel Wortley gentleman

186. *Wrey of Tawstock, Devon*   John Moon

187. *Wroth of Petherton Park, Somerset*   Andrew Dibble (£30 a year)

188. *Wyndham of Orchard Wyndham, Somerset*   John Wakefield gentleman

189. *Yate of Buckland, Berkshire*   Nicasius Peterson

190. *Yaxley of Yaxley, Suffolk*   Thomas Morphew gentleman

191. *Yorke of Gouthwaite Hall, Yorkshire*   Marmaduke Lupton yeoman

192. *Zouch of Woking, Surrey*   Andrew Conradus

NOTES

ABBREVIATIONS

Al.Cant.	J. and J. A. Venn (eds), *Alumni Cantabrigienses. A Biographical List of all Known Students, Graduates and Holders of Office at the University of Cambridge, from the Earliest Times to 1751*, 4 vols (1922–7)
Al.Oxon.	J. Foster (ed.), *Alumni Oxonienses: the Members of the University of Oxford, 1500–1714*, 4 vols (1892)
BL	British Library
C.3	Public Record Office, Chancery Proceedings, Series II
C.5–10	Public Record Office, Chancery Proceedings, Six Clerks' Series
C.33	Public Record Office, Chancery, Entry Books of Decrees and Orders
C.38	Public Record Office, Chancery, Reports and Certificates
CSPDom	*Calendar of State Papers Domestic*, Public Record Office
DNB	*Dictionary of National Biography*
HMC	Historical Manuscripts Commission
PRO	Public Record Office
PROB 4 & 5	Public Record Office, Prerogative Court of Canterbury, Probate Inventories
PROB 11	Public Record Office, Prerogative Court of Canterbury, Wills
SPDom	Public Record Office, State Papers Domestic
STAC 8	Public Record Office, Star Chamber Proceedings, James I and Charles I
VCH	*Victoria County History*

NOTES TO THE INTRODUCTION

1. The main works relating to the nobility are Lawrence Stone, *The Crisis of the Aristocracy 1558–1641* (1965) and Mark Girouard, *Life in the English Country House* (1980).
2. John Selden, *Table-Talk* (1716), 43.
3. Gregory King the seventeenth-century herald and statistician estimated that in 1688 there were 16,400 gentry families. According to his computation the heads of these families consisted of 800 baronets, 600 knights, 3000 esquires and 12,000 plain gentlemen. The latter figure, however, has been rightly criticised, not least because of King's failure to offer any kind of definition. (G. S. Holmes, 'Gregory King and the Social Structure of Pre-Industrial England', *Transactions of the Royal Historical Society*, Fifth Series, xxvii (1977), 41–68).
4. The main sources from which this table is derived are (1) family estate papers (2) family correspondence, memoirs and diaries (3) the records of the Court of Chancery in the Public Record Office (in particular Chancery Proceedings, Six Clerks' Series, C.5–10, Entry Books of Decrees and Orders, C.33, and Reports and Certificates, C.38) and (4) a number of contemporary lists of the gentry with income figures. There are lists for Berkshire and Wiltshire (Wiltshire Record Office, Seth Ward's *Liber Notitiae Generalis*, D1/27/1/1, fol. 129), Buckinghamshire (Buckinghamshire County Records and Local Studies Service, notebook of Richard Grenville), Derbyshire (PRO, Charles II, S.P.29/lxvi/35), Lincolnshire (*Herald and Genealogist*, ii (1865), 116–26), Northamptonshire (S.P.29/cdxxi/216), Staffordshire (*Staffordshire Record Society, Historical Collections*, Fourth Series, ii (1958), 7–41) and Suffolk (BL, Additional MSS 15,520). In addition there is a general list relating to the abortive proposals for a new order of knighthood, the knights of the Royal Oak, which were put forward after the Restoration (Thomas Wotton, *The English Baronetage* (1741), iv, 363–80).

NOTES TO CHAPTER ONE

1. PRO, Chancery Masters' Exhibits, C.107/112, a particular of Mr Haydon's estate at Cadhay in Devonshire, 1694.
2. PRO, SPDom, Charles I, S.P.16/cxciii/1.
3. Sir Henry Wotton, *Reliquiae Wottonianae* (1672), 49.
4. BL, Additional MSS 53,728, 'Lectures Upon particular Occasions By a father to his family', no pagination. For a general account of hospitality see Felicity Heal, *Hospitality in Early Modern England* (1990).
5. John Howe, *The Whole Works* (1810–22), i, 4, 61.
6. *Camden Miscellany*, viii (1883), 15. George Lipscomb, *The History and Antiquities of the County of Buckingham* (1847–51), iii, 426. Somerset Record Office, Phelips MSS, DD/PH 226, fols 9, 12. John Prince, *The Worthies of Devon*

(1701), 400.

7. Thomas Adams, *The White Devil* (1614), 18–19.

8. *Camden Fourth Series*, xii (1973), 14. HMC, *Various Collections*, ii (1903), 371.

9. *Shropshire Archaeological and Natural History Society*, Series 3, i (1901), 186, 193.

10. Sources include family papers, the older county histories, the Victoria County History series, the volumes published by the Royal Commission on Historical Monuments and Sir Nikolaus Pevsner's *The Buildings of England* series.

11. F. E. Halliday (ed.), *Richard Carew of Antony* (1953), 137.

12. Fynes Moryson, *Itinerary* (1617), part iii, 141.

13. The house was not quite finished at his death in 1625. It was completed by his son Sir John.

14. G. Ormerod, *The History of the County Palatine and City of Chester* (1875–82), iii, 293. P. de Figueiredo and J. Treuherz, *Cheshire Country Houses* (1988), 66.

15. BL, Harleian MSS 570, fol. 13.

16. John Bowack, *The Antiquities of Middlesex* (1705–6), 36–7.

17. BL, Additional MSS 38,599, fols 92–4. West Yorkshire Archive Service, Leeds, MSS of the Earl of Mexborough, MX 77/3.

18. PRO, Court of Wards, Miscellaneous Books, Wards 9/573, no pagination. For the building of Carlton House see J. T. Cliffe, *The Yorkshire Gentry* (1969), 106–7.

19. PRO, SPDom, Charles I, S.P.16/cccxiii/93.

20. PRO, SPDom, James I, S.P.14/xlviii/125A. N. E. McClure (ed.), *The Letters of John Chamberlain* (1939), ii, 30, 415. East Riding of Yorkshire Record Office, Eastoft of Eastoft MSS, DDBE/23/13. *Thoroton Society Record Series*, xxi (1962), 3.

21. H. H. E. Craster and others, *A History of Northumberland*, (1893–1940), ix, 178–9.

22. *Somerset Record Society*, xv (1900), 122. Somerset Record Office, Phelips MSS, DD/PH 127. D. Parsons (ed.), *The Diary of Sir Henry Slingsby of Scriven, Bart.* (1836), 44–5, 51–3. Yorkshire Archaeological Society Library, Slingsby MSS, Box D5, account book.

23. M. Girouard, *Robert Smythson and the Architecture of the Elizabethan Era* (1966), 145–6.

24. E. S. de Beer (ed.), *The Diary of John Evelyn* (1955), iii, 100.

25. Sir William Dugdale, *The Antiquities of Warwickshire* (1730), i, 872.

26. *The Genealogist*, New Series, viii (1892), 150–1. Dorothy Gardiner (ed.), *The Oxinden Letters 1607–1642* (1933), 139–40.

27. John Nichols, *The History and Antiquities of the County of Leicester* (1795–1811), iii, 294. C.10/32/121. C.10/51/150. BL, Lansdowne MSS 914, fol. 151.

28. Nichols, *op.cit.*, iii, 294. *The Genealogist*, New Series, viii (1892), 151. John Aubrey, *The Natural History and Antiquities of the County of Surrey* (1718, 1719), iii, 88.

29. PRO, SPDom, Charles I, S.P.16/cdviii/142. BL, Additional MSS 29,442, fols 46–7. PRO, SPDom, James I, S.P.14/cxc/21. C.33/291/fol. 134. J. W. Morkill, *The Parish of Kirkby Malhamdale in the West Riding of Yorkshire* (1933), 219. C.7/400/45. London Metropolitan Archives, Northwick Collection, Acc.76/791.

30. C.5/192/59. C.7/400/45. C.33/278/fol. 340.

31. PRO, Court of Wards, Miscellaneous Books, Wards 9/95/fols 486–7.

32. *Walpole Society*, vii (1919), 134–5.

33. C.3/415/67.

34. PROB 11/162/91. PRO, Court of Wards, Feodaries' Surveys, Wards 5/1, confession of the estate of Thomas Hillersden.

35. *Cambridge Antiquarian Society*, Octavo Series, liii (1935), 111.

36. Staffordshire Record Office, Bradford Collection, P/1318, no pagination. P. de Figueiredo and J. Treuherz, *Cheshire Country Houses* (1988), 204. J. T. Cliffe, *The Puritan Gentry Besieged, 1650–1700* (1993), 170.

37. PRO, SPDom, Committee for Compounding, S.P.23/189/801, 857. G. Lipscomb, *The History and Antiquities of the County of Buckingham* (1847–51), ii, 10–11. Treadway Nash, *Collections for the History of Worcestershire* (1781–2), i, 351, 537.

38. BL, Harleian MSS 965, fol. 28.

39. E. D. de Beer (ed.), *The Diary of John Evelyn* (1955), iii, 111. PROB 4/10,804.

40. *CSPDom, 1660–1*, 339.

41. House of Lords Library, petition dated 18 October 1644. *Lords Journals*, viii, 306. BL, Additional MSS 21,426, fol. 185.

42. C.8/104/34. *Camden Society*, lviii, 230. BL, Additional MSS 70,130, unbound note by Sir Edward Harley. *Calendar of the Proceedings of the Committee for Compounding*, 3215. Job, chapter 1, verse 21. For a general account of the damage caused to buildings see S. Porter, *Destruction in the English Civil Wars* (1994).

43. Nash, *op.cit.*, i, 351–2, 537.

44. W. Watkins-Pitchford (ed.), *The Shropshire Hearth-Tax Roll of 1672* (1949), 9.

45. BL, Additional MSS 36,996, fols 23–4. J. Throsby, *Thoroton's History of Nottinghamshire* (1790), ii, 338.

46. *Royal Commission on Historical Monuments (England), An Inventory of Historical Monuments in the County of Dorset*, vol. 2, *South-East* (1970), part 1, 163. C. Morris (ed.), *The Journeys of Celia Fiennes* (1949), 14–15.

47. T. Mowl and B. Earnshaw, *Architecture Without Kings. The rise of puritan classicism under Cromwell* (1995). See also G. E. Aylmer, *The State's Servants. The Civil Service of the English Republic 1649–1660* (1973), 280.

48. C.33/218/fol. 762. C.38/164/4 December 1668. BL, Egerton MSS 2983, fols 126–7. Mowl and Earnshaw, *op.cit.*, 123–5 (where the completion date is given as 1660).

49. BL, Additional MSS 70,008, fols 91, 221; 70,010, fols 33, 37, 173; 70,011, fol. 5; 70,123, Shilton to Harley, 14 December 1660; and 70,233, Harley to his son Robert, 2 September 1687.

50. John Prince, *The Worthies of Devon* (1701), 246. PROB 4/10,177.

51. Warwickshire County Record Office, Throckmorton MSS, CR 1998, Large Carved Box, 40. In 1674 Coughton Court had 37 chimneys (Large Carved Box, 26).

52. E. Hughes (ed.), *Fleming-Senhouse Papers, Cumberland Record Series*, ii (1961), 37, 43, 51, 53–5, 59.

53. C.8/419/1.

54. Bodleian Library, Oxford, Rawlinson Letters 51, fol. 200. John Locke, *The Correspondence of John Locke* (ed. E. S. de Beer) (1976–89), iii, 99–100, 122, 197–8, 226, 462–3.

55. Anthony Wood, *The Life and Times of Anthony Wood* (ed. A. Clark) (1891–1900), iii, 313. C.5/100/56.

56. Stebbing Shaw, *The History and Antiquities of Staffordshire* (1798, 1801), ii, 204.

57. Sir Henry Chauncy, *The Historical Antiquities of Hertfordshire* (1826), i, 444.

58. William Shippen, *The Christian's Triumph over Death* (1688), 36.

59. House of Lords Library, Act for settling the Manors of Sir Jacob Astley, 16/17 Charles II, no.19.

60. C.5/52/74. C.33/220/fol. 698 and 324/fol. 457. PROB 11/367/122.

61. PROB 11/370/58. C.33/269/fol. 510. C.38/237/12 December 1690. *VCH, Wiltshire*, xii, 17, 19–20.

62. C. Morris (ed.), *The Journeys of Celia Fiennes* (1949), 58. C.33/274/fol. 95.

63. Lady Elizabeth Cust, *Records of the Cust Family. Series II. The Brownlows of Belton, 1550–1779* (1909), 144–6. C.33/291/fol. 532.
64. BL, Additional MSS 34,164, fol. 88.
65. PRO, Chancery Masters' Exhibits, C.104/54, part 1, maintenance agreement dated 21 March 1698/9, and part 2, bill for repairs, 1685.
66. C.38/256/20 October 1696.

NOTES TO CHAPTER TWO

1. PROB 5/4917.
2. C. Morris (ed.), *The Journeys of Celia Fiennes* (1949), 24–5.
3. Sheffield Record Office, Wentworth Woodhouse Collection, Bright MSS 87. PROB 4/7594.
4. Hull University Archives, Maxwell-Constable MSS, DDEV/66/8.
5. M. Girouard, *Life in the English Country House* (1980), 104.
6. *Yorkshire Archaeological Journal*, xxxiv (1929), 190.
7. PROB 4/17,260.
8. Warwickshire County Record Office, Newdegate of Arbury MSS, CR 136/B571.
9. John Prince, *The Worthies of Devon* (1701), 298–9.
10. PROB 4/20,147. PROB 5/4751. PROB 4/17,255. PROB 4/4192. PROB 4/2355.
11. Sir Hugh Cholmley, *The Memoirs of Sir Hugh Cholmley* (1787), 58.
12. Somerset Record Office, Phelips MSS, DD/PH 226, fol. 3. PROB 4/19,541.
13. PROB 5/4447. For a detailed account of the accommodation provided for servants see below, pp. 101–3.
14. PROB 4/21,822.
15. PROB 4/6582.
16. Sir Peter Leycester, *Historical Antiquities* (1674), 193–7.
17. *Chetham Society*, Third Series, v (1953), 159–64.
18. PROB 4/17,269.
19. D. Parsons (ed.), *The Diary of Sir Henry Slingsby of Scriven, Bart.* (1836), 3, 19.
20. HMC, *Seventh Report*, Appendix, 679.
21. C. Morris (ed.), *The Journeys of Celia Fiennes* (1949), 24.
22. Lambeth Palace Library, MS 943, fol. 293.
23. PROB 4/12,763.
24. Buckinghamshire County Records and Local Studies Service, Claydon House MSS (Letters) (on microfilm), letters of Sir Roger Burgoyne dated 3 May and 15 June 1663, 11 November 1673 and 1 February 1674/5.
25. John Bowack, *The Antiquities of Middlesex* (1705–6), 48.
26. PRO, Exchequer Depositions, E.134/11 William III/Michaelmas 9.
27. H. H. E. Craster and others, *A History of Northumberland* (1893–1940), ix, 176.
28. Sir Henry Wotton, *Reliquiae Wottonianae* (1672), 7.
29. Sir Henry Chauncy, *The Historical Antiquities of Hertfordshire* (1826), ii, 56.
30. PROB 11/338/47.
31. East Sussex Record Office, Glynde Place MSS 199.
32. STAC 8/108/11. *VCH, Gloucestershire*, viii, 72.
33. *Surtees Society*, cxci (1976, 1977), 174, 247.
34. John Bridges, *The History and Antiquities of Northamptonshire* (1791), i, 400. *VCH, Northamptonshire*, iv, 65, 67.
35. Robert Plot, *The Natural History of Stafford-shire* (1686), 337.
36. John Aubrey, *The Natural History and Antiquities of the County of Surrey* (1718, 1719), ii, 160.
37. PROB 4/12,216.
38. C. Morris (ed.), *The Journeys of Celia Fiennes* (1949), 55.
39. BL, Additional MSS 41,308, fols 12, 13.
40. PROB 11/311/60.
41. PROB 4/6201.
42. Lord Francis Hervey (ed.), *Suffolk in the XVIIth Century. The Breviary of Suffolk by Robert Reyce* (1902), 59–60.
43. Morris, *op.cit.*, 28. PRO, Chancery Masters' Exhibits, C.108/225, undated schedule of the goods at Bramshill House to be sold for the payment of debts.
44. PROB 4/16,461.
45. *Walpole Society*, x (1922), 1–37.
46. BL, Additional MSS 33,145, fol. 107.
47. J. T. Cliffe, *The Yorkshire Gentry* (1969), 306–8.
48. PROB 5/1075. PROB 5/3765. Lady Elizabeth Cust, *Records of the Cust Family. Series II. The Brownlows of Belton, 1550–1779* (1909), 160–1. PROB 4/19,541. PROB 4/17,589. PROB 5/4471. PROB 4/12,318. PROB 5/4751. PROB 4/12,379. PROB 5/981.
49. PROB 5/1075. PROB 5/2019. PROB 5/2746.
50. C. Morris (ed.), *The Journeys of Celia Fiennes* (1949), 259. PRO, Chancery Masters' Exhibits, C.108/67, inventory of the goods in Tregothnan House taken 22 and 23 August 1701.
51. G. Ormerod, *The History of the County Palatine and City of Chester* (1882), iii, 546, 659–60, 664. Many of the portraits at Adlington Hall were sold in 1846.
52. *Walpole Society*, xviii (1930), 59; xx (1932), 7; and xxvi (1938), 103.
53. PROB 4/17,834. BL, Additional MSS 39,218, fol. 85.
54. Philip Henry, *Diaries and Letters of Philip Henry* (ed. M. H. Lee) (1882), 235.
55. PROB 4/17,834. For the Pickerings see J. T. Cliffe, *The Puritan Gentry Besieged, 1650–1700* (1993), 3, 16, 62–3, 84–5, 115, 222.
56. PROB 5/4094, part 1.
57. J. Harris, *The Artist and the Country House* (1979), 44, 74, 78–9.
58. PROB 4/4192.
59. *Walpole Society*, x (1922), 29 and xxvi (1938), 55. HMC, *Seventh Report*, Appendix, 481. *CSPDom, 1685*, i, 433. C.7/647/32.
60. Anthony Wood, *The Life and Times of Anthony Wood* (ed. A. Clark), (1891–1900), ii, 420 and iii, 103.
61. PRO, Exchequer Depositions, E.134/26 Charles II/Easter 25.
62. West Sussex Record Office, Parham MSS, account book 1690–2, 63.
63. BL, Additional MSS 33,145, fol. 19.
64. Richard Sibbes and others, *The House of Mourning* (1640), 833. C.38/195/8 May 1676.
65. C.33/254/fol. 46.
66. Anthony Wood, *op.cit.*, ii, 357.
67. W. D. Christie (ed.), *Memoirs, Letters and Speeches of Anthony Ashley Cooper, First Earl of Shaftesbury* (1859), 27.
68. *Surtees Society*, cxci (1976, 1977), 159–61, 248.

NOTES TO CHAPTER THREE

1. Fynes Moryson, *Itinerary* (1617), part iii, 139, 147–8.
2. Sources include the maps of John Speed, the older county histories, E. P. Shirley's *Some Account of English Deer Parks* (1867), the *Victoria County History of England* and the Star Chamber records of deer poaching cases (Public Record Office, Star Chamber Proceedings, James I and Charles I, STAC 8).
3. G. Poulson, *The History and Antiquities of the Seigniory of Holderness* (1840–1), ii, 474.
4. *CSPDom, 1639–40*, 124. *VCH, Northamptonshire*, iv, 14.
5. STAC 8/222/16.
6. STAC 8/200/1.

7. R. B. Manning, *Hunters and Poachers. A Social and Cultural History of Unlawful Hunting in England, 1485–1640* (1993), 117.
8. HMC, *Twelfth Report*, Appendix, part i, 65.
9. Warwickshire County Record Office, Finch-Knightley of Packington MSS, MI 280 (microfilm), account books, vol. 11, 1672–1677, no pagination. R. W. Ketton-Cremer, *Felbrigg* (1962), 61.
10. STAC 8/255/27.
11. East Sussex Record Office, Firle Place MSS, Box 7/6, will dated 3 June 1633.
12. STAC 8/302/3. C. Morris (ed.), *The Journeys of Celia Fiennes* (1949), 117. P. B. Munsche, *Gentlemen and Poachers. The English Game Laws 1671–1831* (1981), 20.
13. Francis Peck, *Desiderata Curiosa* (1732), liber xii, 10.
14. PROB 4/9197.
15. STAC 8/259/4.
16. Fynes Moryson, *Itinerary* (1617), part iii, 148. Tristram Risdon, *The Geographical Description or Survey of the County of Devon* (1811), 6–7. Lord Francis Hervey (ed.), *Suffolk in the XVIIth Century. The Breviary of Suffolk by Robert Reyce* (1902), 35–6. R. B. Manning, *Hunters and Poachers* (1993), 126–7.
17. *CSPDom, 1623–5*, 112. Bedfordshire and Luton Archives and Records Service, Luton Hoo Estates MSS, LHE DW90–2.
18. BL, Additional MSS 38,599, fol. 55.
19. *CSPDom, 1628–9*. 174. *CSPDom, 1634–5*, 523. *CSPDom, 1629–31*, 519. *CSPDom, 1637–8*, 434.
20. *VCH, Cambridgeshire*, ii, 26. John Nichols, *The History and Antiquities of the County of Leicester* (1795–1811), ii, 231–2. PRO, Chancery, Petty Bag Office, Miscellaneous Rolls, C.212/20.
21. *Camden Society*, lviii (1854), 230.
22. John Aubrey, *The Natural History and Antiquities of the County of Surrey* (1718, 1719), iii, 227.
23. *CSPDom, 1660–1*, 400.
24. *CSPDom, 1660–1*, 606. *CSPDom, 1687–9*, 119, 219. C. Morris (ed.), *The Journeys of Celia Fiennes* (1949), 45.
25. Hull University Archives, Maxwell-Constable MSS, DDEV/59/7. *CSPDom, 1686–7*, 402.
26. For a general account of deer poaching see R. B. Manning, *Hunters and Poachers* (1993).
27. STAC 8/198/24. STAC 8/200/29. STAC 8/83/7. STAC 8/284/19. STAC 8/207/14.
28. STAC 8/69/10.
29. STAC 8/226/30.
30. STAC 8/29/2.
31. STAC 8/29/3.
32. STAC 8/210/25.
33. BL, Additional MSS 5682, fol. 280. *CSPDom, 1631–3*, 410. *CSPDom, 1633–4*, 423. *CSPDom, 1634–5*, 308, 471. *CSPDom, 1636–7*. 398. *CSPDom, 1640*, 542. Thomas Birch (ed.), *The Court and Times of Charles the First* (1848), ii, 182. *DNB* (Lunsford).
34. Sir Charles Firth and R. S. Rait (eds), *The Acts and Ordinances of the Interregnum, 1642–1660* (1911), ii, 548.
35. *Surtees Society*, xl (1861), 164.
36. Statute 13 Charles II, cap.10.
37. Lady Evelyn Newton, *Lyme Letters 1660–1760* (1925), 101, 103.
38. Fynes Moryson, *Itinerary* (1617), part iii, 147.
39. *Journal of the Architectural, Archaeological and Historical Society for the County and the City of Chester and North Wales*, New Series, xxiv, part ii (1922), 96–7.
40. A. Browning, Mary H. Geiter and W. A. Speck (eds), *Memoirs of Sir John Reresby* (1991), 73.
41. BL, Additional MSS 33,145, fol. 155.
42. G. C. Moore Smith (ed.), *The Letters of Dorothy Osborne to William Temple* (1928), 46.
43. Bodleian Library, Oxford, Rawlinson Letters 53, fol. 30.
44. BL, Additional MSS 15,858, fol. 15.
45. W. A. Copinger, *The Manors of Suffolk* (1905–11), vii, 41. W. Bray (ed.), *Diary and Correspondence of John Evelyn, F.R.S.* (undated), 695, 699. M. Hadfield, *A History of British Gardening* (1979), 144.
46. See below, pp. 99–100.
47. D. Parsons (ed.), *The Diary of Sir Henry Slingsby of Scriven, Bart.* (1836), 64.
48. West Yorkshire Archive Service, Leeds, MSS of the Earl of Mexborough, MX/R1/93 and R42/52.
49. J. G. Taylor, *Our Lady of Battersea* (1925), 315. Flower of the sun was another name for the sunflower.
50. Essex Record Office, Hatfield Broad Oak MSS, D/DBa/E3, fol. 16.
51. PROB 4/9002.
52. PRO, Chancery Masters' Exhibits, C.111/120, part 1, an account of all the timber standing and growing upon the manor of Oxnead, 15 August 1692.
53. *Camden Society*, lxviii (1857), 105–6.
54. F. Bamford (ed.), *A Royalist's Notebook* (1936), 84, 95.
55. Robert Plot, *The Natural History of Stafford-shire* (1686), 227.
56. John Aubrey, *The Natural History and Antiquities of the County of Surrey* (1718, 1719), ii, 159–60. E. S. de Beer (ed.), *The Diary of John Evelyn* (1955), iii, 221. C.33/275/fol. 282.
57. C.8/505/52. *The Diary of John Evelyn*, iv, 121. C.38/265/3 July 1699. W. A. Copinger, *The Manors of Suffolk* (1905–11), vii, 41.
58. Thomas Fuller, *The Worthies of England* (ed. J. Freeman) (1952), 542. Aubrey, *op.cit.*, 97.
59. *The Diary of John Evelyn*, iii, 157. PROB 11/353/41.
60. Frances P. Verney and Margaret M. Verney, *Memoirs of the Verney Family During the Seventeenth Century* (1907), i, 6.
61. See above, p. 43.
62. *Surtees Society*, liii (1869), 270.
63. Sir Henry Wotton, *Reliquiae Wottonianae* (1672), 64–5.
64. N. E. McClure (ed.), *The Letters of John Chamberlain* (1939), i, 235. W. D. Christie (ed.), *Memoirs, Letters and Speeches of Anthony Ashley Cooper, First Earl of Shaftesbury* (1859), 26–7.
65. M. Hadfield, *A History of British Gardening* (1979), 65.
66. BL, Additional MSS 15,520, fol. 154. Thomas Fuller, *The Worthies of England* (ed. J. Freeman) (1952), 523.
67. C.5/548/28.
68. Sir Henry Chauncy, *The Historical Antiquities of Hertfordshire* (1826), i, 373.
69. PRO, SPDom, Charles II, S.P.29/lxvi/35.
70. H. Avray Tipping (ed.), *English Houses of the Early Renaissance* (1912), 181.
71. Sir William Dugdale, *The Antiquities of Warwickshire* (1730), ii, 989.
72. C.33/291/fol. 399. Stebbing Shaw, *The History and Antiquities of Staffordshire* (1798, 1801), ii, 285. Robert Plot, *The Natural History of Stafford-shire* (1686), 338–9, 359.
73. C. Morris (ed.), *The Journeys of Celia Fiennes* (1949), 228–30.
74. Somerset Record Office, Phelips MSS, DD/PH22, fol. 9. PROB 5/4751. PROB 5/2746. PROB 5/2091. PROB 4/5021. PROB 4/7594. J. P. Earwaker, *East Cheshire Past and Present* (1877, 1880), i, 314.
75. BL, Additional MSS 53,726, fol. 86.
76. PROB 5/4751.
77. *Cambridge Antiquarian Society*, liii (1935), 101.
78. John Nichols, *The History and Antiquities of the County of Leicester* (1795–1811), iv, 354.

NOTES TO CHAPTER FOUR

1. PROB 11/412/220.
2. Hertfordshire Archives and Local Studies, Lytton MSS 22,049, 22,050 and 23,452.
3. BL, Additional MSS 33,145, fols 22, 73.
4. *Bristol Record Society*, xxxv (1982), 152. B. D. Henning (ed.), *The History of Parliament: The House of Commons 1660–1690* (1983), iii, 564.
5. C.33/319/fols 233–4. BL, Additional MSS 28,250, fol. 39 and 33,148, fol. 98. C.10/133/4. C.33/279/fols 415–16. C.33/327/fol. 296. C.33/276/fol. 393 and 288/fol. 280. C.8/452/13. PRO, SPDom, Charles II, S.P.29/cdxxi/216.
6. HMC, *Twelfth Report*, Appendix, part vii, 386, 405.
7. Dr Williams's Library, London, Baxter Letters, v, fol. 3. HMC, *Ninth Report*, Appendix, part ii, 394.
8. *Surtees Society*, cxci (1976, 1977), 66–8.
9. *Surtees Society*, cxc (1975), 12–14, 185, 202, 205–6, 209–10. C.38/215/ 28 June 1683 and 218/ 7 May 1684.
10. John Locke, *The Correspondence of John Locke* (ed. E. S. de Beer) (1976–89), iii, 105.
11. Staffordshire Record Office, Paget MSS, D603/k/2/4/4, 7.
12. BL, Additional MSS 70,115, unbound letter of Lady Harley dated 22 December 1670, and 70,128, unbound letters of Sir Edward Harley dated 2 July 1664 and 10 January 1670/1.
13. BL, Additional MSS 70,012, fol. 305 and 70,128, unbound letter dated 6 July 1678.
14. See below, pp. 91–2.
15. *CSPDom, 1684–5*, 270, 271. *CSPDom, 1685*, 433, 435, 442.
16. *CSPDom, 1683–4*, 195.
17. William Gouge, *Of Domesticall Duties* (1622), 315, 317, 367. See A. J. Fletcher, *Gender, Sex and Subordination in England 1500–1800* (1995), 173–4, 177–9.
18. *Camden Society*, Third Series, xxviii (1917), 111, 137. A 'makebate' was a mischief maker.
19. William Drogo Montagu, Duke of Manchester, *Court and Society from Elizabeth to Anne* (1864), i, 344.
20. BL, Additional MSS 34,163, fol. 80.
21. E. S. de Beer (ed.), *The Diary of John Evelyn* (1955), ii, 3. C.6/268/57.
22. G. Ormerod, *The History of the County Palatine and City of Chester* (1875–82), ii, 231, 252.
23. John Wilford, *Memorials and Characters* (1741), 326. Samuel Clark, *The Lives of Sundry Eminent Persons* (1683), part ii, 204.
24. R. Challoner, *Memoirs of Missionary Priests* (1924), 354.
25. Wilford, *op.cit.*, 625.
26. Sir Henry Chauncy, *The Historical Antiquities of Hertfordshire* (1826), ii, 167. Other examples are given in Fletcher, *op.cit.*, 233–5.
27. N. F. McClure (ed.), *The Letters of John Chamberlain* (1939), ii, 90–1.
28. E. R. O. Bridgeman and C. G. O. Bridgeman, *History of the Manor and Parish of Weston-under-Lizard, in the County of Stafford*, William Salt Archaeological Society, *Collections for a History of Staffordshire*, New Series, ii (1899), 142.
29. *Surtees Society*, cxci (1976, 1977), 62–3.
30. C.8/418/130.
31. PROB 11/161/37. Suggoth or Sugworth was a hamlet in the parish of Radley.
32. PRO, Chancery Masters' Exhibits, C.108/67, letter of Lady Margaret dated 5 September 1663 and copy of a letter of the steward, Thomas Harvey, dated 13 July 1664.
33. BL, Additional MSS 37,343, fol. 138.
34. Hull University Archives, Maxwell-Constable MSS, DDEV/55/58.
35. *CSPDom, 1634–5*, 60, 90–1.
36. John Collinges, *Par Nobile* (1669), 10.
37. C.6/332/80. C.33/234/fol. 323.
38. C.33/245/fols 209, 537.
39. Thomas Hervey (ed.), *Some Unpublished Papers Relating to the Family of Sir Francis Drake* (1887), 59–60.
40. *Miscellanea Genealogica et Heraldica*, ii (1876), 297 (will dated 13 November 1613).
41. PROB 11/154/70 (will dated 26 October 1626).
42. PROB 11/332/30 (will dated 15 October 1669).
43. *Letter-Books of John Hervey, First Earl of Bristol* (1894), i, 35, 36. For a general discussion of marital relationships see A. J. Fletcher, *Gender, Sex and Subordination in England 1500–1800* (1995), 173–8.
44. *Archaeologia Cantiana*, iv (1861), 199, 201. BL, Additional MSS 34,168, fol. 62.
45. Samuel Willes, *A Sermon Preach'd At the Funeral of the Right Honourable The Lady Mary, Daughter to Ferdinando late Earl of Huntingdon, and Wife to William Jolife of Caverswell-Castle in the County of Stafford, Esq* (1679), 26, 33–4.
46. For the role and proceedings of the ecclesiastical courts see Lawrence Stone, *Road to Divorce. England 1530–1987* (1992), 27–44, 183–230. During the period 1660 to 1699 the Court of Arches dealt with 524 matrimonial cases (*ibid.*, 424).
47. Borthwick Institute of Historical Research, High Commission Act Book, 1612–25, R VII/AB9, fols 174, 343, 352.
48. Warwickshire County Record Office, Throckmorton MSS, CR 1998, Box 65, Folder 1/1/10 and 1/18/11. For the private separation agreement see Stone, *op.cit.*, 149–82.
49. G. C. Moore-Smith (ed.), *The Letters of Dorothy Osborne to William Temple* (1928), 101.
50. Norah King, *The Grimstons of Gorhambury* (1983), 42–3.
51. PRO, SPDom, James I, S.P.14/xlix/32.
52. Frances P. Verney and Margaret M. Verney, *Memoirs of the Verney Family During the Seventeenth Century* (1907), i, 420, 422–4, 521, 533 and ii, 135–6, 224–5, 227, 295. Miriam Slater, *Family Life in the Seventeenth Century. The Verneys of Claydon House* (1984), 71, 74–6, 89, 97–100.
53. *CSPDom, 1628–9*, 468, 483. *CSPDom, 1629–31*, 93, 102. *Acts of the Privy Council, 1628–9*, 263, 334. *Acts of the Privy Council, 1629–30*, 184, 185. PRO, Chancery Depositions, C.22/638/39.
54. J. R. Scott, *Scott of Scot's Hall in the County of Kent* (1876), 230–2 and Appendix, xxxiv, xxxvi–xxxviii. HMC, *Sixth Report*, Appendix, 122. HMC, *Seventh Report*, Appendix, 53, 59, 60. J. T. Rudd (ed.), *Diary of Thomas Burton* (1828), i, 204–6, 265, 297–8, 334–7, 352. Lambeth Palace Library, Court of Arches, Libels, Articles, Allegations and Interrogatories, E1/329-32. PROB 11/312/135. E. S. de Beer (ed.), *The Diary of John Evelyn* (1955), iii, 358.
55. C.7/156/74.
56. C.5/190/18. *CSPDom, 1685*, 436.
57. C.8/452/13.
58. C.8/351/120.

NOTES TO CHAPTER FIVE

1. BL, Additional MSS 24,467, fol. 250.
2. Warwickshire County Record Office, Newdegate of Arbury MSS, CR 1841/6, no pagination.
3. See Appendix A.
4. J. Hunter, *South Yorkshire: The History and Topography of the Deanery of Doncaster* (1828), ii, 84. C. V. Wedgwood, *Strafford* (1949), 28.
5. John Prince, *The Worthies of Devon* (1701), 125.
6. John Smith, *The Names and Surnames of All the Able and Sufficient Men in Body fit for His Majesty's Service in the Wars, within the County of Gloucester* (1902), 136, 296. For an

analysis of this survey see A. J. and R. H. Tawney, 'An Occupational Census of the Seventeenth Century', *Economic History Review*, v (1934–5), 25–64.

7. BL, Additional MSS 27,447, fol. 150.

8. PRO, Chancery Masters' Exhibits, C.104/54, part 1 and C.104/55, part 1, unbound notes on servants' wages.

9. PROB 11/147/130.

10. Lady Elizabeth Cust, *Records of the Cust Family, Series II. The Brownlows of Belton, 1550–1779* (1909), 62, 74, 148. PRO, Exchequer Depositions, E.134/26 Charles II/Easter 25 and E.134/29 Charles II/Easter 21.

11. PRO, Exchequer Depositions, E.134/9 and 10 William III/Hilary 15.

12. E. F. Rimbault (ed.), *The Miscellaneous Works in Prose and Verse of Sir Thomas Overbury, Knt.* (1890), 69–70.

13. Sir Hugh Cholmley, *The Memoirs of Sir Hugh Cholmley* (1787), 21–2.

14. See Joan Parkes, *Travel in England in the Seventeenth Century* (1925), chapter 6.

15. STAC 8/223/9.

16. West Sussex Record Office, Parham MSS, book of accounts 1690–1, 35.

17. See Appendix A.

18. Robert Cleaver, *A Godlie Forme of Householde Government* (1612), 383.

19. The account books of Richard Bradshaw, steward to Sir Cecil Bishop of Parham in Sussex, record monthly payments to the housekeeper, Mrs Ann Avelin, for household expenses (West Sussex Record Office, Parham MSS, account books 1690–1, 1692–3 and 1693).

20. PROB 11/336/79.

21. A. Browning, Mary K. Geiter and W. A. Speck (eds), *Memoirs of Sir John Reresby* (1991), 108.

22. PROB 11/405/121.

23. D. Parsons (ed.), *The Diary of Sir Henry Slingsby of Scriven, Bart.* (1836), 71.

24. Warwickshire County Record Office, Throckmorton MSS, CR 1998, Files of Correspondence (Tribune), Folder 47/42.

25. *Bristol Record Society*, xxxv (1982), 70, 176–7.

26. East Devon Record Office, Drake of Buckland Abbey MSS, F 693.

27. E. F. Rimbault (ed.), *The Miscellaneous Works in Prose and Verse of Sir Thomas Overbury, Knt.* (1890), 144.

28. West Yorkshire Archive Service, Leeds, MSS of the Earl of Mexborough, MX/R6/11, MX/R43/53.

29. Statute 3 James I, cap.iv.

30. *The Memorandum Book of Richard Cholmeley of Brandsby 1602–1623* (North Yorkshire County Record Office Publications No.44) (1988), 41, 44, 189, 215–17, 237, 240–3. Borthwick Institute of Historical Research, High Commission Act Book, 1607–12, RVII/AB12, fol. 77.

31. *Catholic Record Society*, liii (1961), 291–303. *Calendar of the Proceedings of the Committee for Compounding*, 1447.

32. William Perkins, *The Workes* (1608, 1609), iii, 696. Robert Cleaver, *A Godlie Forme of Householde Government* (1612), 372. BL, Egerton MSS 2645, fols 142–3.

33. John Dod and Robert Cleaver, *Three Godlie and Fruitful Sermons* (1610), 49–50.

34. William Gouge, *Of Domesticall Duties* (1622), 610.

35. Samuel Clark, *The Lives of Sundry Eminent Persons* (1683), part ii, 111.

36. BL, Additional MSS 70,130, Sir Edward Harley's notes on the character and sayings of his father. J. T. Cliffe, *The Puritan Gentry* (1984), 33. BL, Additional MSS 70,012, fol. 89 and 70,124, unbound letter dated 9 March 1673/4.

37. BL, Additional MSS 34,163, fol. 27.

38. Warwickshire County Record Office, Throckmorton MSS, CR 1998, Large Carved Box, 47, no pagination.

39. Antony House, Carew Pole MSS, Buller records, BC/26/29/4.

40. Sir Henry Chauncy, *The Historical Antiquities of Hertfordshire* (1826), ii, 360.

41. BL, Additional MSS 34,164, fol. 4.

42. William Gouge, *op.cit.*, 607, 663, 664.

43. Warwickshire County Record Office, Throckmorton MSS, CR 1998, Box 60, Folder 3/24 and Box 63, Folder 1/18.

44. PRO, Chancery Masters' Exhibits, C.108/188, part 1, unbound letter dated 17 January 1637/8.

45. *CSP Dom, 1619–23*, 462, 470, 484, 540, 554. John Rushworth, *Historical Collections* (1680), part 2, 288–93.

46. BL, Cotton MSS, Appendix XLIV, fol. 42 and Cotton Charter II 25(7), fols 1, 8.

47. PRO, Chancery Masters' Exhibits, C.108/188, part 1, unbound letter dated 4 December 1664.

48. C.6/176/3. PROB 11/364/136. PROB 11/383/59. PROB 11/332/30.

49. HMC, *Lothian MSS*, 87–8. PROB 11/374/103. C.8/426/33.

50. C.38/180/5 July 1672; 194/24 June 1676; and 200/28 July 1678.

51. PROB 11/151/26.

52. East Sussex Record Office, Firle Place MSS, SAS/G, Box 7/6.

53. PROB 11/205/135.

NOTES TO CHAPTER SIX

1. Fynes Moryson, *Itinerary* (1617), part iii, 149.

2. *Shropshire Archaeological and Natural History Society Transactions*, Series 3, i (1901), 193.

3. Sir Miles Sandys, *Prima Pars Parvi Opusculi* (1634), 162–3.

4. William Higford, *Institutions or Advice to his Grandson* (1658), 30–2, 82.

5. Cleaver's book was first published in 1598. The quotations here are drawn from the third edition (1612) which contains amendments and additions by Cleaver and his friend John Dod. Gouge's work originally appeared in 1622 and this is the edition from which the quotations are taken. A third edition was published in 1634.

6. Cleaver, *op.cit.*, 61, 365, 366, 376, 378.

7. Gouge, *op.cit.*, 601–2, 613, 616, 621, 631, 653.

8. J. E. Jackson (ed.), *Wiltshire, The Topographical Collections of John Aubrey, FRS, AD 1659–70* (1862), 15.

9. Humphrey Sydenham, *Sermons* (1630), 36.

10. Robert Harris, *Abner's Funerall* (1641), 25.

11. Sir Henry Chauncy, *The Historical Antiquities of Hertfordshire* (1826), ii, 82.

12. D. Parsons (ed.), *The Diary of Sir Henry Slingsby of Scriven, Bart.* (1836), 23–4.

13. Richard Easton, *A Sermon Preached at the Funeralls of that Worthie and Worshipfull Gentleman, Master Thomas Dutton of Dutton, Esquire* (1616), 23. West Sussex Record Office, Parham MSS, account books, 1690–1 and 1692–3, no regular pagination.

14. Warwickshire County Record Office, Finch-Knightley of Packington MSS, TD 79/21, no pagination.

15. *Thoresby Society*, xvii (1908), 152, 182–5. *Surtees Society*, xl (1861), 242–5.

16. STAC 8/293/18.

17. Statute 5 Elizabeth I, cap.iv, as amplified in Statute 1 James I, cap.vi.

18. Somerset Record Office, Popham MSS, DD/POt 121.

19. C.10/168/30.

20. West Sussex Record Office, Parham MSS, account book, 1690–1, 19–21 and unnumbered pages.

21. *Surtees Society*, clxxx (1965), 2, 8, 11–13.

22. Robert Cleaver, *A Godlie Forme of Householde Government*

(1612), 366. William Gouge, *Of Domesticall Duties* (1622), 685–6.

23. East Sussex Record Office, Glynde Place MSS, 2932 and 2933, no pagination. PRO, Chancery Masters' Exhibits, C.104/54, part 1 and C.104/55, part 1, notes on servants' wages.

24. PRO, Chancery Masters' Exhibits, C.104/110, part 3, undated note written by Margaret Danby, the widow of Thomas Danby.

25. BL, Additional MSS 28,242, fols 15, 22. Essex Record Office, Hatfield Broad Oak MSS, D/DBa/A2, fols 13–14. *Bristol Record Society*, xxxv (1982), 198–9. BL, Additional MSS 33,145, fols 141, 145. BL, Additional MSS 6688, fols 82–3. Sheffield Record Office, Wentworth Woodhouse Collection, Bright MSS 87. BL, Additional MSS 33,147, fols 272, 277. East Sussex Record Office, Firle Place MSS, SAS/G, Box 11/28. Warwickshire County Record Office, Throckmorton MSS, CR 1998, Box 65, Folder 1/2/11. C.38/232/13 July 1688.

26. *The Ancestor*, iii (1902), 159. *Herald and Genealogist*, iv (1867), 67. Sir Hugh Cholmley, *The Memoirs of Sir Hugh Cholmley* (1787), 22. C.8/505/52.

27. BL, Additional MSS 33,148, fol. 104.

28. East Sussex Record Office, Firle Place MSS, SAS/G, Box 11/28.

29. Essex Record Office, Hatfield Broad Oak MSS, D/DBa/A2, fol. 14.

30. PROB 11/371/155 and 419/70.

31. C. Morris (ed.), *The Journeys of Celia Fiennes* (1949), 25.

32. PROB 4/3988.

33. PROB 4/2865. PROB 11/311/71.

34. PRO, Chancery Masters' Exhibits, C.108/187, part 1, inventory of the personal estate of Sir Edward Zouch, 19 September 1634.

35. PRO, Chancery Masters' Exhibits, C.108/188, part 1, letter dated 4 February 1663/4. For reasons which are unclear the letter was never despatched.

36. G. Tyack, *Warwickshire Country Houses* (1994), 20.

37. PROB 4/6863. C. Morris (ed.), *The Journeys of Celia Fiennes* (1949), 15, 55, 56. Hampshire Record Office, Chute (Vyne) MSS, 31M57/629. PROB 4/9002. PROB 5/4751. *Buckinghamshire Record Society*, xxiv (1988), 268. PROB 5/3442. PROB 4/4192. PROB 5/4297. PROB 4/3425. PROB 4/7825. Lady Elizabeth Cust, *Records of the Cust Family, Series II. The Brownlows of Belton 1550–1779* (1909), 163.

38. PROB 4/9002. PROB 4/4192.

39. PROB 4/17,255. *Buckinghamshire Record Society*, xxiv (1988), 270.

40. PROB 4/15,000.

41. PROB 4/12,318.

42. BL, Additional MSS 33,148, fol. 91. Sir John Monson was seated at Burton Hall and Sir George Savile at Rufford Abbey.

43. BL, Additional MSS 70,137, no regular pagination.

44. C.33/312/fol. 39. PROB 11/351/63.

45. PROB 11/397/148. C.33/296/fol. 80.

46. PROB 11/123/20 and 183/72.

47. PROB 11/149/70. Humphrey Sydenham, *Nature's Overthrow and Death's Triumph* (1636), 184–5.

48. PROB 11/215/6.

49. PROB 11/390/43.

50. PROB 11/387/59. The will was not proved until 6 May 1697.

51. PROB 11/453/200.

52. PROB 11/321/115, 119 (16 November 1665). PROB 11/350/26 (23 December 1673). PROB 11/379/5 (23 May 1684). PROB 11/401/165 (27 February 1689/90).

53. *A Christian New-Year's Gift* (1644), 52–3. Sir Henry

54. Anthony Wood, *Athenae Oxonienses* (ed. P. Bliss) (1813–20), iii, col.1240.

Chauncy, *The Historical Antiquities of Hertfordshire* (1826), ii, 318.

NOTES TO CHAPTER SEVEN

1. Appendix B lists 192 families which had estate stewards at one time or another. The total number, however, must have been well in excess of this figure.

2. See D. R. Hainsworth, *Stewards, Lords and People* (1992), 4, 9, 13, 54–6.

3. C.10/498/27. West Yorkshire Archive Service, Leeds, MSS of the Earl of Mexborough, MX/ R17/35.

4. PRO, Chancery Masters' Exhibits, C.111/134, original Chancery decree dated 19 June 1668.

5. C.7/545/105. C.10/267/13.

6. PRO, Chancery Masters' Exhibits, C.107/16, part 1, account books, Lady Day 1686 to Lady Day 1687 and Lady Day 1687 to Lady Day 1688. C.38/240/27 November 1691.

7. East Sussex Record Office, Firle Place MSS, SAS/G, Box 7/6.

8. London Metropolitan Archives, Northwick Collection, Acc.76/776, 2006, 2183, 2184.

9. A. F. Upton, *Sir Arthur Ingram c. 1565–1642*, 184–6. For the building work at Coughton Court see above, p. 16.

10. C.33/313/fol. 326.

11. See Appendix B.

12. PROB 11/363/106. *Harleian Society*, lxii (1911), 122, 132.

13. Cheshire Record Office, Arderne Collection, Box C/91/13 and Box D/15/12.

14. C.7/564/85. *Al.Cant.*, i, 26.

15. C.38/211/30 March 1682; 214/14 July 1683; 217/1 February 1684/5; and 223/17 July 1686. *Al.Oxon.*, 477.

16. C.33/323/fol. 294. Hampshire Record Office, Kingsmill MSS, 1743–62. PROB 11/431/62.

17. PROB 11/412/220 and 497/263. C.10/267/13.

18. C.6/80/27. PROB 11/342/69.

19. Essex Record Office, Hatfield Broad Oak MSS, D/DBa/A4, fols 4, 13, 25, 27, 29; A66/36; A70/13; A76/29; and A77/4 and 8. C.38/344/166. BL, Egerton MSS 2648, fol. 364 and 2650, fols 112, 115.

20. PRO, Exchequer Depositions, E.134/26 Charles II/Easter 25. C.8/426/33.

21. BL, Additional MSS 28,250, fol. 153.

22. Hull University Archives, Maxwell-Constable MSS, DDEV/51/102; 53/50; 54/8; 55/58; 56/412; and 57/16 and 36. *Catholic Record Society*, vi (1906), 256 and xxvii (1927), 261. Borthwick Institute of Historical Research, York Registry, will of George Constable, 18 May 1672.

23. *CSPDom, 1678*, 616. *CSPDom, 1680–1*, 275.

24. Most of the information contained in this table has been derived from the post-Restoration period. In the few cases where a salary was adjusted the higher figure has been taken. For individual cases see Appendix B.

25. PROB 11/395/90 and 405/121.

26. BL, Additional MSS 33,143, fols 4–6, 29, 33, 58, 75, 82, 90, 97, 107.

27. D. R. Hainsworth (ed.), *The Correspondence of Sir John Lowther of Whitehaven 1693–1698* (*The British Academy. Records of Social and Economic History*, New Series, vii, 1983), 5.

28. PROB 11/290/236. PRO, Chancery Masters' Exhibits, C.104/42, accounts of John Cary and associated papers.

29. PROB 11/312/135.

30. PROB 11/362/19. C.38/221/8 June 1685.

31. Philip Morant, *The History and Antiquities of the County of*

Essex (1768), ii, 574. J. J. Howard (ed.), *A Visitation of the County of Essex . . . by Sir Edward Bysshe* (1888), 56.

32. C.8/344/166. PROB 11/383/59.

33. W. Knowler (ed.), *The Earl of Strafforde's Letters and Despatches* (1739), i, 169, 170. *Yorkshire Archaeological Journal*, xxv (1920), 25.

34. D. Parsons (ed.), *The Diary of Sir Henry Slingsby of Scriven, Bart.* (1836), 51, 350. Yorkshire Archaeological Society Library, Slingsby MSS, DD56/J2/1.

35. See D. R. Hainsworth, *Stewards, Lords and People* (1992), 4, 254, 256.

36. PRO, Chancery Masters' Exhibits, C.104/55, part 2, letter dated 8 March 1686/7.

37. West Yorkshire Archive Service, Leeds, MSS of the Earl of Mexborough, MX/R16/20; R19/2 and 11; R32/6; and R42/52.

38. BL, Sloane MSS 813, fols 17, 44. There were famous stone quarries at Hamdon Hill.

39. BL, Additional MSS 69,881, fol. 56.

40. Essex Record Office, Hatfield Broad Oak MSS, D/DBa/A1/fols 14, 45, 63, 75, 87 and rev. fol. 4; A2/fol. 8 and rev. fols 2, 3; and L35. BL, Egerton MSS 2646, fols 44–7.

41. BL, Additional MSS 41,502.

42. C.38/55/28 April 1627.

43. PROB 11/308/61. C.38/159/18 February 1667/8 and 174/1 June 1671.

44. PROB 11/312/104. C.6/176/3. PRO, Chancery Depositions, C.22/13/35.

45. C.7/573/74.

46. STAC 8/120/2. *Thoresby Society*, xxxvii (1936–42), 5–7, 14. The plaintiff himself was no paragon as may be seen from a letter which Sir Thomas Wentworth sent him on 29 July 1617 (*Camden Fourth Series*, xii (1973), 94–6). In this letter Wentworth chided him for wrongly accusing his wife of adultery and added that 'the world taxeth your selfe' with frequent acts of infidelity.

47. C.6/159/91. C.38/148/20 May 1663.

48. C.8/181/82.

49. C.33/259/fol. 648. Sir Thomas described Curwen as his father's bailiff but it is clear that he performed the functions of a steward.

50. STAC 8/56/18.

51. STAC 8/263/1.

52. STAC 8/24/21. Scremerston is today in Northumberland. In the seventeenth century, however, it was situated in Norhamshire, one of three enclaves which were collectively known as North Durham and which were subject to the jurisdiction of the Bishop of Durham as lord of the Palatine of Durham.

53. STAC 8/111/4.

54. Yorkshire Archaeological Society Library, Parrington Deposit of Slingsby Letters, DD 149/117.

55. John Aubrey, *The Natural History and Antiquities of the County of Surrey* (1718, 1719), i, 149 and ii, 161–2. J. G. Taylor, *Our Lady of Battersea* (1925), 83, 86, 190, 192, 316.

56. F. Blomefield *An Essay Towards a Topographical History of the County of Norfolk* (1805–10), vii, 443.

NOTES TO CHAPTER EIGHT

1. J. E. Jackson (ed.), *Wiltshire, The Topographical Collections of John Aubrey, FRS, AD 1659–70* (1862), 9.

2. HMC, *Thirteenth Report*, Appendix, part ii, 308.

3. PROB 11/462/151. PROB 11/199/48. PROB 11/412/220. PROB 4/3241. PROB 4/16,461. PRO, Chancery Masters' Exhibits, C.104/54, part 2, accounts of John Tawton, 1675, no pagination.

4. *CSPDom, 1670*, 42.

5. PROB 11/355/113. Bedfordshire and Luton Archives and Records Service, Burgoyne MSS, DDX 143/1, account book of Lady Burgoyne, no pagination.

6. BL, Additional MSS 70,115, no pagination (undated letter written in the early part of Charles II's reign).

7. Joan Parkes, *Travel in England in the Seventeenth Century* (1925), 65, 70–1.

8. Essex Record Office, Hatfield Broad Oak MSS, D/DBa/A76/14.

9. PROB 4/13,226. B. D. Henning (ed.), *The History of Parliament: The House of Commons 1660–1690* (1983), iii, 276.

10. PROB 5/4751.

11. PROB 4/257.

12. Statutes 3 William and Mary, cap.vi; 5/6 William and Mary, cap.xiv; and 9 William III, cap.xxxviii.

13. BL, Harleian MSS 7660, fols 30, 34.

14. PRO, Chancery Masters' Exhibits, C.108/188, part 1, letter dated 3 August 1665.

15. Essex Record Office, Hatfield Broad Oak MSS, D/DBa/Z2/2, no regular pagination.

16. C.38/164/20 February 1668/9. C.6/116/183. BL, Additional MSS 41,308, fol. 29(d). C.38/249/15 May 1694 and 252/9 December 1695. C.38/232/13 July 1688.

17. C.5/572/21.

18. C.38/249/3 August 1694.

19. BL, Additional MSS 70,010, fol. 223.

20. C.10/165/30.

21. Essex Record Office, Hatfield Broad Oak MSS, D/DBa/A2, fol. 56.

22. BL, Additional MSS, 33,148, fol. 60.

23. Lady Evelyn Newton, *Lyme Letters 1660–1760* (1925), 176.

24. C.38/194/24 June 1676.

25. Surrey Record Office, Guildford Muniment Room, Loseley MSS, 1105.

26. L. Tolson, *History of the Church of St John the Baptist, Kirkheaton, Yorkshire and Annals of the Parish* (1929), 136.

27. Essex Record Office, Hatfield Broad Oak MSS, D/DBa/E3, fol. 15.

28. PROB 4/4121. PROB 4/3441. PRO, Chancery Masters' Exhibits, C.107/161, inventory dated 3 May 1689. PROB 4/18,861. BL, Egerton MSS 2983, fol. 178. *Surtees Society*, cxci (1976, 1977), 173.

29. Joan Parkes, *Travel in England in the Seventeenth Century* (1925), 66, 78–9, 82–96. Thomas Birch (ed.), *The Court and Times of James I* (1848–9), ii, 347.

30. Parkes, *op.cit.*, 66, 82–4.

31. J. R. Scott, *Scott of Scot's Hall in the County of Kent* (1876), Appendix, xxxiii.

32. BL, Additional MSS 70,009, fol. 172 and 70,115, no pagination (undated letter of Dame Abigail Harley).

33. PRO, Chancery Masters' Exhibits, C.107/154, will of Sir John Fortescue, 21 March 1668/9, and associated papers.

34. BL, Additional MSS 70,017, fol. 128.

35. BL, Additional MSS 33,582, fol. 110.

36. Parkes, *op.cit.*, 79. West Sussex Record Office, Parham MSS, account books 1690–1, 19, 20; 1692–3, 12, 17 and unnumbered pages; and 1697–8 and 1699, no pagination.

37. BL, Additional MSS 28,242, fols 16, 17, 24, 30.

38. BL, Additional MSS 39,218, fol. 67.

39. PRO, Chancery Masters' Exhibits, C.104/54, part 1, 'The Coachman's Note of things in his Chamber and his receipt in full', 15 October 1700.

40. A. Browning, Mary K. Geitter and W. A. Speck (eds), *Memoirs of Sir John Reresby* (1991), 249–55. Katherine A. Esdaile, *English Church Monuments 1510 to 1840* (1946), 118.

41. HMC, *Twelfth Report*, Appendix, part vii, 203–4.

42. See J. T. Cliffe, *The Puritan Gentry* (1984), 53, 59–61.
43. E. S. de Beer (ed.), *The Diary of John Evelyn* (1955), iii, 112–13, 525.
44. BL, Additional MSS 29,564, fol. 290.
45. Sir James Harrington, *Horae Consecratae* (1682), 354.
46. Recollections of Sir William Waller in *The Poetry of Anna Matilda* (1788), 114.
47. Thomas Birch (ed.), *The Court and Times of Charles the First* (1848), i, 197–8. *Acts of the Privy Council, January to August 1627*, 53, 54.
48. Essex Record Office, Hatfield Broad Oak MSS, D/DBa/Z2/2, page 14.
49. *DNB*, Esdaile, *op.cit.*, 118.
50. College of Arms, Le Neve's Book of Baronets, i, 13b.

NOTES TO CHAPTER NINE

1. Statutes 21 Henry VIII, cap.xiii; 25 Henry VIII, cap.xvi; and 33 Henry VIII, cap. xxviii.
2. William Laud, *The Works* (1847–60), v, 308, 313. Lambeth Palace Library, Register Laud, i, fol. 217.
3. Lambeth Palace Library, Register Laud, i, fol. 255 and MS 943, fols 247, 293, 295. PRO, SPDom, Charles I, S.P. 16/cccxlv/85.
4. Lambeth Palace Library, MS 943, fol. 293.
5. *Harleian Miscellany*, x (1913), 51.
6. Sir William Waller, *Divine Meditations upon Several Occasions, with a Dayly Directory* (1680), 91.
7. BL, Egerton MSS 2539, fol. 210.
8. See, for example, J. T. Cliffe, *The Puritan Gentry Besieged, 1650–1700* (1993), Chapter 10 and Appendix.
9. Northamptonshire Record Office, Isham Correspondence, IC/242/184.
10. Sir Hughe Knatchbull-Hugesson, *Kentish Family* (1960), 5, 18–19, 26, 35.
11. BL, Egerton MSS 2650, fol. 333.
12. PROB 11/176/25.
13. HMC, *Buccleuch MSS*, i, 327. *CSPDom, 1668–9*, 133.
14. BL, Additional MSS 37,911, fols 5, 6.
15. *Life and Death of Mr Henry Jessey* (1671), 4–7. R. A. Marchant, *The Puritans and the Church Courts in the Diocese of York 1560–1642* (1960), 123. J. T. Cliffe, *The Yorkshire Gentry* (1969), 306–8.
16. BL, Additional MSS 64,921, fols 58, 67, 77, 110. HMC, *Coke MSS*, ii, 245, 259.
17. Anthony Wood, *Athenae Oxonienses* (ed. P. Bliss) (1813–20), iii, col.336. Christopher Elderfield, *Of Regeneration and Baptism* (1653), epistle dedicatory. *Catholic Record Society*, xxii (1921), 305.
18. *The Life of Adam Martindale* (ed. R. Parkinson), *Chetham Society*, iv (1845), 203.
19. BL, Egerton MSS 2643, fol. 1.
20. East Sussex Record Office, Glynde Place MSS 2932, no pagination.
21. *The Works of Symon Patrick, D. D.* (ed. A. Taylor) (1858), ix, 426–7.
22. *The Autobiography of Henry Newcome, MA* (ed. R. Parkinson), *Chetham Society*, xxvii (1852), 202–3.
23. Samuel Clark, *The Lives of Thirty-Two English Divines* (1677), 148.
24. Canon 71.
25. Dr Williams's Library, London, Baxter Letters, iii, fols 98, 102.
26. Samuel Clark, *op.cit.*, 158. HMC, *Fourteenth Report*, Appendix, part ix, 476.
27. Thomas Cawton the younger, *The Life and Death of that Holy and Reverend Man of God Mr Thomas Cawton* (1662), 14–16.
28. *The Works of Symon Patrick, D. D.* (ed. A. Taylor) (1858), ix, 426. J. G. Taylor, *Our Lady of Battersea* (1925), 84, 86, 405.
29. BL, Additional MSS 53,726, fols 62, 69, 80. Bulstrode Whitelocke, *The Diary of Bulstrode Whitelocke, 1605–1675* (ed. Ruth Spalding) (1990), 71, 112, 203, 633, 636, 777, 780, 781.
30. Statute 27 Elizabeth I, cap.ii; also 23 Elizabeth I, cap.i.
31. J. Morris (ed.), *The Troubles of Our Catholic Forefathers* (1872–7), Series iii, 467.
32. *Ibid.*, Series i, 247.
33. The sources include G. Anstruther, *The Seminary Priests: I Elizabethan 1558–1603* (1968), *II Early Stuarts 1603–1659* (1975), *III 1660–1715* (1976) and *Catholic Record Society*, lxx (1984).
34. *Catholic Record Society*, ix (1911), 107, 108, 110–12.
35. Warwickshire County Record Office, Throckmorton MSS, CR 1998, Box 65, Folder 1/2/11.
36. *Archaeologia Aeliana*, New Series, ii (1858), 160.
37. BL, Additional Charter, 19018A.
38. For a comprehensive account of priest-holes see M. Hodgetts, *Secret Hiding-Places* (1989).
39. W. M. Brady, *Annals of the Catholic Hierarchy in England and Scotland, 1585–1876* (1877), 84.
40. Rosamund Meredith, 'A Derbyshire Family in the Seventeenth Century: the Eyres of Hassop and their forfeited estates', *Recusant History*, viii, no.1 (1965), 16, 55–6, 62, 64 and 'The Eyres of Hassop, and some of their connections, from the Test Act to Emancipation', *Recusant History*, ix, no.1 (1967), 9, 11–12.
41. *The Herald and Genealogist*, iv (1867), 65–7.
42. STAC 8/19/10. For a more general account of the Yorke family see C. H. D. Howard, *Sir John Yorke of Nidderdale 1565–1634* (1939).
43. STAC 8/151/8.
44. H. Aveling, *Northern Catholics. The Catholic Recusants of the North Riding of Yorkshire 1558–1790* (1966), 247. PRO, Signet Office Docquet Book, Index 6803, December 1609 and February 1609/10 (no pagination). *The Memorandum Book of Richard Cholmeley of Brandsby 1602–1623* (*North Yorkshire County Record Office Publications No.44*), (1988), 47–9.
45. *Catholic Record Society*, vi (1909), 16.
46. J. Morris (ed.), *The Troubles of Our Catholic Forefathers* (1872–7), Series i, 237, 247. C.2/B31/38 and S22/39.
47. G. Anstruther, *The Seminary Priests: II Early Stuarts 1603–1659* (1975), 55 and *III 1660–1715* (1976), 41,170. R. Challoner, *Memoirs of Missionary Priests* (1924), 541–2. *CSPDom, 1678*, 554, 616. *CSPDom, 1679–80*, 340.
48. Hull University Archives, Maxwell-Constable MSS, DDEV/66/8.
49. *Durham Research Review*, ii, no.9 (1958), 204.
50. J. Peile (ed.), *Biographical Register of Christ's College, 1505–1905* (1910), i, 449.
51. J. Venn (ed.), *Biographical History of Gonville and Caius College, 1349–1897* (1897–1901), i, 393, 398. *Al.Cant.*, ii, 206.
52. A. G. Matthews, *Calamy Revised* (1934), 99. Catalogue of the Belsay MSS, B1/X/2 and 3.
53. PROB 11/143/45.
54. C.38/216/21 November 1683. *Al.Cant.*, ii, 464.
55. D. Parsons (ed.), *The Diary of Sir Henry Slingsby of Scriven, Bart.* (1836), 53–4. *Al.Cant.*, i, 329.
56. PROB 11/132/117. PRO, Chancery Masters' Exhibits, C.107/16, part 1, book of accounts of the acting guardian of the children of Jonathan Cope, 1698–1703, no pagination.
57. *Bristol Record Society*, xxxv (1982), introduction xx, 173–5, 199.
58. HMC, *Twelfth Report*, Appendix, part vii, 378, 381, 384,

385, 392, 394, 395, 398, 399, 404. A manichord was a multi-stringed instrument.

59. PRO, Chancery Masters' Exhibits, C.107/16, part 1, account book, 25 March 1695 to Lady Day 1696, 54, 56, 58–9. For the education of daughters see Felicity Heal and Clive Holmes, *The Gentry in England and Wales, 1500–1700* (1994), 251–4 and A. J. Fletcher, *Gender, Sex and Subordination in England 1500–1800*, chapter 18.

NOTES TO CHAPTER TEN

1. H. H. E. Craster and others, *A History of Northumberland* (1893–1940), ix,158.
2. J. Throsby, *Thoroton's History of Nottinghamshire* (1790), i, 108.
3. E. S. de Beer (ed.), *The Diary of John Evelyn* (1955), ii, 2 and v, 358.
4. Bartholomew Parsons, *A Romane Centurion Becomming a Good Souldier of Jesus Christ* (1635), epistle dedicatory. John Aubrey, *Brief Lives* (ed. R. Barber) (1975), 256. *CSPDom, 1637–8*, 169, 176. C.3/358/17 and 398/103. C.10/47/122.
5. William Shippen, *The Christian's Triumph over Death* (1688), 37, 45. B. D. Henning (ed.), *The History of Parliament: the House of Commons 1660–1690* (1983), ii, 728–9.
6. Somerset Record Office, Phelips MSS, DD/PH229, fol. 9.
7. West Yorkshire Archive Service, Leeds, MSS of Lord Mexborough, MX 359. C.8/138/74.
8. BL, Additional MSS 37,343, fol. 142.
9. PRO, Exchequer Depositions, E.134/1 and 2 William and Mary/Hilary 9.
10. BL, Additional MSS 15,858, fol. 101. Jane M. Ewbank (ed.), *Antiquary on Horseback, Cumberland and Westmorland Archaeological and Antiquarian Society*, Extra Series, xix (1963), 103. The traveller was the Rev. Thomas Machell.
11. PROB 4/17,589.
12. PROB 4/8417.
13. *Camden Society*, Third Series, xxviii (1917), 106.
14. E. S. de Beer (ed.), *The Diary of John Evelyn* (1955), ii, 4.
15. Sir William Waller, *Divine Meditations Upon Several Occasions* (1680), 43–4.
16. *CSPDom, 1637*, 478. *CSPDom, 1637–8*, 25, 352, 444, 528. *CSPDom, 1638–9*, 157. *CSPDom, 1639–40*, 356, 467. *CSPDom, 1640*, 470. *CSPDom, 1640–1*, 261, 323, 406, 518, 586. *CSPDom, 1641–3*, 61.
17. PRO, Chancery Masters' Exhibits, C.104/42, note relating to the personal estate of Sir Henry Lee, 6 July 1659.
18. Warwickshire County Record Office, Newdegate of Arbury MSS, CR 136/A25, fol. 102.
19. PRO, Chancery Masters' Exhibits, C.107/161, bill of Richard Salter.
20. *Camden Fourth Series*, xii (1973), 14. *The Record Society of Lancashire and Cheshire*, cxxxiv (1996), 32.
21. BL, Additional MSS 27,447, fol. 226.
22. PROB 11/148/38. C.33/231/fol. 853.
23. D. Parsons (ed.), *The Diary of Sir Henry Slingsby of Scriven, Bart.* (1836), 26–7. Yorkshire Archaeological Society Library, Slingsby MSS, DD 56/D5, accounts.
24. PRO, SPDom, Charles I, S. P. 16/cdxxxii/34. *Bristol Record Society*, xxxv (1982), 198–9.
25. *The Diary of Bulstrode Whitelocke, 1605–1675* (ed. Ruth Spalding) (1990), 678. C.8/444/23.
26. *The Memoirs of Sir Hugh Cholmley* (1787), 56.
27. Thomas Mannyngham, *A Sermon at the Funeral of Sir John Norton* (1687), 17.
28. *CSPDom, 1637–8*, 506. Fynes Moryson, *Itinerary* (1617), part iii, 150.
29. BL, Additional MSS 28,242, fols. 26–7, 32–3; Additional MSS 28,250, fols 9, 10; and Additional Charter 18,965, fols

4, 5, 7, 10, 16, 17, 19, 20, 25, 35, 36, 65.
30. Sir John Monson, *An Antidote Against the Errour in Opinion of Many in These Daies Concerning Some of the Highest and Chiefe Duties of Religion* (1647), 45–6, 50.
31. *The Record Society of Lancashire and Cheshire*, cxxxiv (1996), 32.
32. *The Memoirs of Sir Hugh Cholmley* (1787), 56.
33. PROB 11/353/27. C.33/248/fol. 396.
34. PROB 5/2091.
35. Bartholomew Parsons, *A Sermon Preached at the Funerall of Sir Francis Pile Baronet* (1636), 32–3.
36. Thomas Comber, *Memoirs of the Life and Death of the Right Honourable the Lord Deputy Wandesforde* (1778), 31. Samuel Clark, *The Lives of Thirty-Two English Divines* (1677), 158.
37. *Harleian Miscellany*, x (1813), 32.
38. Samuel Willes, *A Sermon Preach'd At the Funeral of the Right Honourable The Lady Mary, Daughter to Ferdinando late Earl of Huntingdon, and Wife to William Jolife of Caverswell-Castle in the County of Staffordshire, Esq* (1679), 28–31.
39. William Bagshaw, *De Spiritualibus Pecci* (1702), 58. J. T. Cliffe, *The Puritan Gentry* (1984), 31–2, 34.
40. J. Morris (ed.), *The Troubles of Our Catholic Forefathers* (1872–7), Series iii, 468.
41. John Dod and Robert Cleaver, *Three Godlie and Fruitful Sermons* (1610), 48, 51.
42. Robert Cleaver, *A Godlie Forme of Householde Government* (1612), 20, 34, 45–7, 373. William Gouge, *Of Domesticall Duties* (1622), 667.
43. J. T. Cliffe, *The Puritan Gentry Besieged, 1650–1700* (1993), 140.
44. Nathaniel Parkhurst, *The Faithful and Diligent Christian Described and Exemplified* (1684), 51, 53–4.
45. Samuel Ainsworth, *A Sermon Preached at the Funerall of that Religious Gentle-woman Mrs Dorothy Hanbury* (1645), 29.
46. BL, Additional MSS 70,019, fol. 322.
47. Bartholomew Parsons, *A Romane Centurion Becomming A Good Souldier of Jesus Christ* (1635), epistle dedicatory.
48. Robert Cleaver, *A Godlie Forme of Householde Government* (1612), 30–1, 34–5.
49. Thomas Burroughs, *A Soveraign Remedy for All Kinds of Grief* (1675), 80.
50. BL, Harleian MSS 3364, fol. 9.
51. William Higford, *Institutions or Advice to his Grandson* (1658), 90.
52. *Camden Society*, Third Series, xxviii (1917), 110.
53. HMC, *Twelfth Report*, Appendix, part vii, 114. See R. Carr, *English Fox Hunting: A History* (1976).
54. PROB 11/178/130.
55. C.6/79/40.
56. J. Hunter, *South Yorkshire: the History and Topography of the Deanery of Doncaster* (1828), ii, 137.
57. Statute 22/23 Charles II, cap.xxv. See P. B. Munsche, *Gentlemen and Poachers: the English Game Laws, 1671–1831* (1981), chapter 1.
58. PROB 4/3441.
59. PROB 4/6582.
60. *Catholic Record Society*, lvi (1964), 35, 36.
61. Somerset Record Office, Phelips MSS, DD/PH 226, fol. 9. PROB 5/4447. BL, Additional MSS 33,147, fols 6, 16, 37, 78. PROB 4/7580. C. Morris (ed.), *The Journeys of Celia Fiennes* (1949), 45, 90. J. Throsby, *Thoroton's History of Nottinghamshire* (1790), i, 108. See Felicity Heal and Clive Holmes, *The Gentry in England and Wales, 1500–1700* (1994), 293–4.
62. Essex Record Office, Hatfield Broad Oak MSS, D/DBa/A4, fols 2, 8, 12 and E3, fol. 16.
63. W. D. Christie (ed.), *Memoirs, Letters and Speeches of Anthony Ashley Cooper, First Earl of Shaftesbury* (1859), 21–2. J. T. Cliffe, *The Puritan Gentry* (1984), 140–1. HMC, *Thirteenth*

Report, Appendix, part ii, 297.

64. Cliffe, *op.cit.*, 141–2.

65. H. H. E. Craster and others, *A History of Northumberland* (1893–1940), ix, 158. William Trevethick, *A Sermon at the Funeral of the Honourable Colonel Robert Rolle of Heanton Sachville in the County of Devon Esq* (1661), epistle dedicatory.

66. G. C. Moore Smith (ed.), *The Letters of Dorothy Osborne to William Temple* (1928), 174–5.

67. PROB 4/1350. PROB 5/3404.

68. PROB 4/17,589.

69. *Anthony & Cleopatra*, Act 2, Scene 5.

70. East Sussex Record Office, Glynde Place MSS 2932, no pagination. PROB 5/2091 (Shuckburgh). PROB 4/3425 (Halford). C.38/235/15 June 1689 (Clifton). PROB 11/362/54 (Assheton). PROB 5/5003 (Harris). PROB 4/257 (Hesilrige). A 'press' was a cupboard.

71. William Higford, *Institutions or Advice to his Grandson* (1658), 77–8.

72. PRO, Chancery Masters' Exhibits, C.107/154. will of Sir John Fortescue, 21 March 1668/9 and associated papers.

73. C.6/30/98. C.38/237/24 July 1690.

74. Hull University Archives, Maxwell-Constable MSS, DDEV/69/1. PROB 4/9996. PROB 5/2991.

75. Norfolk Record Office, Kimberley MSS, KIM 9/2. PROB 11/278/354. BL, Additional MSS 15,857, fol. 18. R. W. Ketton-Cremer, *Norfolk in the Civil War* (1969), 28, 41.

76. *Chetham Society*, Third Series, v (1953), introduction xx and 152. The cittern and the gittern were guitar-like instruments.

77. *Chetham Society*, xxxv (1856), 185, 187, 191, 202, 210, 225 and xli (1856), 302, 305, 306.

78. HMC, *Twelfth Report*, Appendix, part vii, 371, 372, 389, 395, 406. Indoor entertainment, including music and drama, is discussed in Felicity Heal and Clive Holmes, *The Gentry in England and Wales, 1500–1700* (1994), 294–7.

NOTES TO CHAPTER ELEVEN

1. *Yorkshire Archaeological Journal*, xxxiv (1929), 190, 193.

2. PRO, Chancery Masters' Exhibits, C.108/187, part 1, inventory dated 19 September 1634.

3. PROB 4/15,259 (Springett). PROB 4/8654 (Hoby). PROB 4/17,269 (Yelverton). BL, Additional MSS 38,175, fol. 48 (Digby). PROB 4/3988 (L'Estrange). Cf. M. Girouard, *Life in the English Country House* (1980), 165–6, 169–70.

4. Anthony Wood (ed. A. Clark), *The Life and Times of Anthony Wood* (1891–1900), ii, 321, 475 and iii, 102–3.

5. D. J. McKitterick, *The Library of Sir Thomas Knyvett of Ashwellthorpe c. 1539–1618* (1978). *Chetham Society*, Third Series, v (1953), introduction xix and 108–50. PROB 4/11,402. PROB 4/2355. PROB 4/10,177. PROB 5/5275. PROB 5/3442. See also S. Jayne, *Library Catalogues of the English Renaissance* (1956).

6. PROB 4/11,402. PROB 4/2355.

7. BL, Additional MSS 70,001, between fols 230 and 231. Mary Elizabeth Bohannon, 'A London Bookseller's Bill: 1635–1639', *The Library*, Fourth Series, xviii (1938), 417–46. A. G. Watson, *The Library of Sir Simonds D'Ewes* (1966). BL, Harleian MSS 646, fol. 174.

8. *Camden Society*, lviii (1854), 230.

9. BL, Additional MSS 70,060, unbound catalogue dated 9 October 1662.

10. *Chetham Society*, Third Series, v (1953), 108–50.

11. PROB 4/3536.

12. Warwickshire County Record Office, Lucy of Charlecote MSS, L6/1095 (Z22). Alice Fairfax-Lucy, *Charlecote and the Lucys* (1958), 127, 137–40, 165. Robert Harris, *Abner's Farewell* (1641), 27.

13. PROB 5/4751.

14. Warwickshire County Record Office, Newdegate of Arbury MSS, CR 1841/9, 39–80.

15. PRO, Chancery Masters' Exhibits, C.107/161, receipts and bill of Gabriel Rogers.

16. Cf. S. Jayne, *Library Catalogues of the English Renaissance* (1956), 46.

17. BL, Egerton MSS 2983, fol. 78.

18. PRO, Chancery Masters' Exhibits, C.104/82, library catalogue dated 25 October 1680.

19. Sir William Waller, *Divine Meditations Upon Several Occasions* (1680), 29.

20. W. H. Long (ed.), *The Oglander Memoirs* (1888), 148–9.

21. BL, Harleian MSS 384, fol. 63.

22. John Bridges, *The History and Antiquities of Northamptonshire* (1791), ii, 163. PROB 4/17,269. BL, Hargrave MSS 107. Anthony Wood, *Athenae Oxonienses* (ed. P. Bliss) (1813–20), iii, cols 906–7.

23. John Prince, *The Worthies of Devon* (1701), 475.

24. Anthony Wood, *op.cit.*, iv, cols 172–4.

25. P. Styles, *Sir Simon Archer 1581–1662* (*Dugdale Society Occasional Papers*) (No.6, 1946), 9–10, 15–44, 48, 51.

26. *Chetham Society*, Third Series, v (1953), introduction xiii, xiv, xviii–xxiii and 112, 114, 118, 127, 140, 143.

27. *Harleian Society*, viii (1873), 284. Cheshire Record Office, Arderne Collection, DAR/A/59.

28. BL, Additional MSS 28,564, fol. 206. Sir John Ramskill Twisden, *The Family of Twysden and Twisden* (1939), 176, 186–251. *Archaeologia Cantiana*, iv (1861), 168, 198–9. *DNB* (Dering and Twysden).

29. *DNB*. Sir William Pole, *Collections Towards a Description of the County of Devon* (1791).

30. Sir Henry Chauncy, *The Historical Antiquities of Hertfordshire* (1826), i, 444 and ii, 207.

31. BL, Harleian MSS 646, in particular fols 2–5, 20.

32. R. Clutterbuck, *The History and Antiquities of the County of Hertford* (1815–27), i, 407–10.

33. BL, Additional MSS 34,239, fols 14–15.

34. Sir Hugh Cholmley, *The Memoirs of Sir Hugh Cholmley* (1787). BL, Additional MSS 29,442 and 29,443. *Camden Society*, Third Series, xxviii (1917).

35. *Catholic Record Society*, vii (1909), 36.

36. William Prynne, *Canterburies Doome* (1644), 524–6. *DNB*.

37. Harbottle Grimston, *A Christian New-Year's Gift* (1644), 105. Sir Roger Twysden, *An Historicall Vindication of the Church of England* (1657). Sir Edward Harley, *A Scriptural and Rational Account of the Christian Religion* (1695). J. T. Cliffe, *The Puritan Gentry* (1984), 31, 51, 94, 103, 120, 145 and *The Puritan Gentry Besieged, 1650–1700* (1993), 203–4.

38. Dame Damaris Masham, *A Discourse Concerning the Love of God* (1696). J. T. Cliffe, *The Puritan Gentry Besieged, 1650–1700* (1993), 202.

39. These men all have their place in *DNB*.

40. Warwickshire County Record Office, Newdegate of Arbury MSS, CR 1841/9, 45. *DNB*.

41. J. Hunter, *South Yorkshire: the History and Topography of the Deanery of Doncaster* (1828), ii, 137. BL, Additional MSS 29,443, fol. 8. Sir Francis Wortley, *Characters and Elegies* (1646). *DNB* (Wortley). F. Madan, *The Greslies of Drakelowe, William Salt Archaeological Society, Collections for a History of Staffordshire*, New Series, i (1898), 83. John Nichols, *The History and Antiquities of the County of Leicester* (1795–1811), iii, 886.

42. J. T. Cliffe, *The Puritan Gentry* (1984), 46–7, 51, 105, 106, 123.

43. Nichols, *op.cit.*, iii, 656, 658–9 and iv, 559–63.

44. Anthony Wood, *Athenae Oxonienses* (ed. P. Bliss) (1813–20), iv, cols 128–30. *DNB*.

45. *Catholic Record Society*, lv (1963), 479. *DNB*.
46. William Sampson, *Virtus Post Funera Vivit* (1636), 62.
47. BL, Additional MSS 5832, fols 203–4.
48. BL, Additional MSS 39,218, fol. 65. Joseph Hall, *The Works* (1625), 296. L. P. Smith, *The Life and Letters of Sir Henry Wotton* (1907), ii, 396–7, 405, 460.
49. PROB 4/257.
50. Anthony Wood, *op.cit.*, iv, Fasti Oxonienses, ii, col. 246. *DNB*. PRO, Chancery Masters' Exhibits, C.107/161, bookseller's bill of 1702. Warwickshire County Record Office, Newdegate of Arbury MSS, CR 1841/9, 40.
51. BL, Harleian MSS 646, fols 78, 142.

NOTES TO CHAPTER TWELVE

1. STAC 8/249/4.
2. *CSPDom, 1635–6*, 475, 500, 501.
3. *CSPDom, 1635–6*, 420, 536–7. PROB 11/387/83.
4. Oliver Heywood, *His Autobiography, Diaries, Anecdote and Event Books* (ed. J. Horsfall Turner) (1882–5), iii, 97. PROB 11/327/104.
5. John Aubrey, *The Natural History and Antiquities of the County of Surrey* (1718, 1719), iii, 88–9. Helen Evelyn, *The History of the Evelyn Family* (1915), 208–10, 212–15. HMC, *Seventh Report*, Appendix, 489.
6. Sir Peter Leycester, *Historical Antiquities* (1674), 207.
7. Anthony Wood, *The Life and Times of Anthony Wood* (ed. A. Clark) (1891–1900), ii, 311. *CSPDom, 1668–9*, 108–9, 184.
8. Anthony Wood, *op.cit.*, ii, 519, 523 and *Athenae Oxonienses* (ed. P. Bliss) (1813–20), iv, Fasti Oxonienses, col. 43. C.7/374/57. C.33/268/fol. 475. Lambeth Palace Library, Court of Arches, Act Book, 1672–4, A10, fol. 87. PROB 11/378/156. PROB 5/5275.
9. Lambeth Palace Library, Court of Arches, Act Book, 1660–3, A2, fols 164, 183, 190, 230, 244, 249, 266, 311, 317; Libels, Articles, Allegations and Interrogatories, E1/268; Personal Answers, Ee1, fols 517–18; and Depositions, Eee1, fols 88–93, 113–14, 122–9, 147–52, 167–86, 482–3. B. D. Henning (ed.), *The History of Parliament: The House of Commons 1660–1690* (1983), ii, 21 (where Isabella Jones is called Isabella Falkingham). For a general discussion of clandestine marriages see Lawrence Stone, *Road to Divorce. England 1530–1987* (1992), Part I, Chapter IV.
10. Robert Cleaver, *A Godlie Forme of Householde Government* (1612), 378.
11. STAC 8/55/26.
12. STAC 8/118/19. *Collectanea Topographica et Genealogica*, v (1838), 126, 128. PROB 11/143/28.
13. C.8/94/20.
14. C.9/6/146.
15. STAC 8/197/23.
16. STAC 8/183/1.
17. STAC 8/200/1.
18. STAC 8/131/17 and 263/11.
19. STAC 8/111/19. John Nichols, *The History and Antiquities of the County of Leicester* (1795–1811), iv, 989–90.
20. Philip Morant, *The History and Antiquities of the County of Essex* (1768), ii, 621. Browne Willis, *The History and Antiquities of the Town, Hundred and Deanery of Buckingham* (1755), 140, 143.
21. BL, Additional Charters 71,704 and 71,751. *Camden Society*, New Series, xv (1875), 166.
22. C.10/7/68.
23. BL, Additional MSS 70,002, fols 181, 240, 259, 271–3, and 70, 129, unbound papers in the handwriting of Dame Martha Button and letter of Sir Richard Strode dated 4 March 1649/50. West Devon Record Office, Strode MSS, 72/147.
24. BL, Additional MSS 70,124, unbound letter of Richard Stephens dated 24 April. C.5/132/30. C.6/87/1.
25. Bulstrode Whitelocke, *The Diary of Bulstrode Whitelocke, 1605–1675* (ed. Ruth Spalding) (1990), 793, 805, 806, 808, 812, 813, 819, 827, 833, 835.
26. Somerset Record Office, Phelips MSS, DD/PH/164, unbound letter of Christopher Dodington dated 7 July 1638, and 229, fol. 16. Bristol Record Office, Ashton Court MSS, AC/C56/1, 2, 4, 5.
27. C.33/255/fols 458–9. PRO, Chancery Depositions, C.22/222/5.
28. PRO, SPDom, Charles I, S.P. 16/cdiii/22–3.
29. Lambeth Palace Library, Court of Arches, Act Book, 1666, A4A, fols 26, 32, 42, 46, 58, and Depositions, Eee 2, fols 103–18, 138–40, 152–3, 172–3. This may be compared with the case involving Sir Oliver Boteler of Teston in Kent (Lawrence Stone, *Broken Lives. Separation and Divorce in England 1660–1857* (1993), 33–7).
30. C.10/171/143.
31. C.33/248/fol. 532. C.38/195/3 March 1676/7. Lambeth Palace Library, Court of Arches, Act Book, 1674–6, A11, fols 165, 175. Sir Henry Chauncy, *The Historical Antiquities of Hertfordshire* (1826), i, 382–3.
32. Bulstrode Whitelocke, *The Diary of Bulstrode Whitelocke, 1605–1675* (ed. Ruth Spalding) (1990), 702, 714. Lambeth Palace Library, Court of Arches, Depositions, Eee2, fols 459, 468–511, 557–66, 569–73. A. G. Matthews, *Calamy Revised* (1934), 462. HMC, *Eighth Report*, Appendix, part i, 136 and *Ninth Report*, Appendix, part ii, 3.
33. STAC 8/38/9. Northamptonshire Record Office, ROP 374, John Cotta, *The Poysoning of Sir Euseby Andrew* (1881), 15–24. PRO, Court of Wards, Miscellaneous Books, Wards 9/217/fol. 30.
34. BL, Harleian MSS 797, fol. 15.
35. Thomas Birch (ed.), *The Court and Times of Charles the First* (1848), ii, 46, 70. F. Bamford, *A Royalist's Notebook* (1936), 96–7.
36. BL, Additional MSS 34, 164, fol. 77. *Harleian Miscellany*, x (1813), 23–67. A. M. Everitt, *The Community of Kent and the Great Rebellion 1640–60* (1966), 50–2.
37. R. H Gretton, *The Burford Records* (1920), 282–3. PROB 5/4751. C.38/243/31 January 1692/3. Anthony Wood (ed. A. Clark), *The Life and Times of Anthony Wood* (1891–1900), iii, 195. Narcissus Luttrell, *A Brief Historical Relation of State Affairs from September 1678 to April 1714* (1857), iv, 251, 253, 255. *Oxford Historical Society*, lxv (1914), 221. HMC, *Twelfth Report*, Appendix, part vii, 349.

NOTES TO THE EPILOGUE

1. BL, Lansdowne MSS 238, fol. 148.
2. BL, Egerton MSS 2716, fol. 56.
3. Buckinghamshire County Records and Local Studies Service, Claydon House MSS (Letters), letter dated 14 February 1675/6.
4. BL, Harleian MSS 382, fol. 89.
5. Thomas Fuller, *The Worthies of England* (ed. J. Freeman) (1952), 87. C. Morris (ed.), *The Journeys of Celia Fiennes* (1949), 254.
6. *Somerset Record Society*, xv (1900), 61.
7. John Prince, *The Worthies of Devon* (1701), 114.
8. Jane M. Ewbank (ed.), *Antiquary on Horseback, Cumberland and Westmorland Archaeological and Antiquarian Society*, Extra Series, xix (1963), 133–5.
9. STAC 8/209/23.
10. C.33/273/fols 322–3; 283/fol. 180; and 313/fol. 324. C.38/251/29 May 1695. C.5/146/15.
11. C.8/204/48.

12. C.38/232/28 February 1688/9 and 235/15 June 1689.
13. J. T. Cliffe, *The Yorkshire Gentry* (1969), 157–8.
14. Anthony Wood, *The Life and Times of Anthony Wood* (ed. A. Clark) (1891–1900), ii, 136–7. C.33/277/fols 78–9.
15. Jane M. Ewbank, *op.cit.*, 69. C.33/275/fols 947–9.
16. College of Arms, Le Neve's Book of Baronets, iii, 90.
17. *Bristol Record Society*, xxxv (1982), 184.
18. O. Ogle, W. H. Bliss and others (eds), *Calendar of the Clarendon State Papers in the Bodleian Library* (1892–1970), iv, 92.
19. HMC, *Seventh Report*, Appendix, 464. BL, Additional MSS 36,916, fol. 228. W. A. Copinger, *The Manors of Suffolk* (1905–11), iv, 178.
20. Anthony Wood, *op.cit.*, iii, 441. C.8/543/87. PROB 11/425/52.
21. John Collinson, *The History and Antiquities of the County of Somerset* (1791), iii, 603, 605, 607. BL, Additional MSS 34,239, fol. 16. *Abstracts of Somersetshire Wills*, Sixth Series (1890), 67–9. C.33/217/fol. 188.
22. PROB 11/382/45. C.5/307/42.
23. C.10/505/89. C.33/263/fol. 776 and 265/fol. 201.
24. PROB 11/233/71. PRO, Chancery Depositions, C.22/35/31. C.33/235/fols 112, 187, 722. PROB 4/17,589.
25. BL, Additional MSS 33,142, fol. 274, and 33,148, fols 56, 62.
26. *Fragmenta Genealogica*, xiii (1909), 135–8.
27. BL, Additional MSS 34,168, fol. 61.
28. E. A. B. Barnard, *A Seventeenth Century Country Gentleman* (1944), 80, 83.
29. Anthony Wood, *The Life and Times of Anthony Wood* (ed. A. Clark) (1891–1900), iii, 97–8.
30. HMC, *Thirteenth Report*, Appendix, part ii, 271.
31. Lady Evelyn Newton, *The House of Lyme* (1917), 350.

NOTES TO APPENDIX A

The following additional abbreviations have been used in these notes:

E.179 PRO, Exchequer, Lay Subsidy Rolls (poll tax returns, 1641 and 1660)
S.P.28 PRO, State Papers Domestic Series, Commonwealth Exchequer Papers (returns of persons contributing to the relief of Irish Protestants, 1642)

1. PROB 11/321/115, 119.
2. Lady Elizabeth Cust, *Records of the Cust Family. Series II. The Brownlows of Belton, 1550–1779* (1909), 62.
3. PROB 11/132/117.
4. C.38/232/13 July 1688.
5. PROB 11/165/45.
6. PROB 11/160/116.
7. PROB 11/454/22.
8. Hertfordshire Archives and Local Studies, Verulam (Gorhambury) MSS, IX.A.57.
9. C.8/566/49.
10. C.38/219/30 June 1684.
11. BL, Additional MSS 12,518, fol. 27.
12. HMC, *Lothian MSS*, 87–8.
13. PROB 5/4751.
14. Warwickshire County Record Office, Lucy of Charlecote MSS, L6/1009, no pagination.
15. BL, Additional MSS 33,143, fols 58–9.
16. BL, Additional MSS 33,152, fols 8, 43, 48, 53, 58, 168.
17. Somerset Record Office, Popham MSS, DD/POt 121.
18. PROB 11/401/165.
19. *Archaeologia Aeliana*, New Series, i (1857), 104–5.
20. E.179/384/17.
21. PROB 11/323/29.
22. E.179/244/30, no pagination.
23. J. Hunter, *South Yorkshire: the History and Topography of the Deanery of Doncaster* (1828), ii, 84.
24. BL, Additional MSS 6688, fols 82–3.
25. PROB 11/143/28.
26. PROB 11/132/70.
27. E.179/272/44.
28. H. Foley (ed.), *Records of the English Province of the Society of Jesus* (1877–83), iii, 199.
29. S.P.28/191, unbound documents.
30. *Camden Society*, xlix (1850), 217–19.
31. PROB 11/148/40.
32. Essex Record Office, Hatfield Broad Oak MSS, D/DBa/A2, fol. 14.
33. North Yorkshire County Record Office, Newburgh Priory MSS, Box 3, Bundle 15, account book of Sir Henry Bellasis, no pagination.
34. E.179/244/30.
35. West Sussex Record Office, Parham MSS, account book 1697–8, no pagination.
36. PRO, SPDom, Charles I, S.P.16/cxciii/1.
37. PROB 11/121/43.
38. PRO, Chancery Masters' Exhibits, C.104/55, part 1, unbound accounts.
39. PRO, Chancery Masters' Exhibits, C.104/54, part 1 and C.104/55, part 1, unbound documents.
40. S.P.28/194, part 4, unbound documents.
41. Sir Hugh Cholmley, *The Memoirs of Sir Hugh Cholmley* (1787), 56.
42. E.179/245/14(3), fol. 3.
43. *Catholic Record Society*, xxvii (1927), 265–6.
44. Borthwick Institute of Historical Research, Wills in the York Registry, will of George Constable, 18 May 1672. Hull University Archives, Maxwell-Constable MSS, DDEV/56/412.
45. E.179/255/21.
46. North Yorkshire County Record Office, Cunliffe-Lister (Swinton) MSS, Bundle 11, account book of Sir Thomas Danby, no pagination.
47. C.10/165/30.
48. C.8/309/73. PROB 11/371/117.
49. PROB 11/181/146.
50. C.38/221/8 June 1685. PROB 11/362/19.
51. Warwickshire County Record Office, Finch-Knightley of Packington MSS, TD79/21, no pagination.
52. E.179/248/18.
53. BL, Additional MSS 27,399, fols 219, 220, 227.
54. E.179/244/39, fol. 66.
55. E.179/191/390.
56. HMC, *Sixth Report*, Appendix, 330.
57. *Surtees Society*, clxxx (1965), 2, 4, 8, 11–14, 26.
58. BL, Additional MSS 33,581, fols 76–7.
59. BL, Additional MSS 33,582, fols 110, 111, 167.
60. Sheffield Record Office, Wentworth Woodhouse Collection, Bright MSS 87.
61. Dorothy M. Meads (ed.), *The Diary of Lady Margaret Hoby 1599–1605* (1930), introduction, 40.
62. Northamptonshire Record Office, Isham MSS, IL 3613.
63. BL, Additional MSS 24,467, fol. 250.
64. C.38/266/12 June 1699.
65. C.8/186/43.
66. PRO, Chancery Masters' Exhibits, C.104/42, unbound account.
67. *Surtees Society*, cxci (1976, 1977), 33.
68. PRO, SPDom, Charles I, S.P.16/cxciii/1.
69. East Sussex Record Office, Glynde Place MSS 2932 and 2933, no pagination.
70. E.179/250/4.

71. E.179/102/481.
72. E.179/244/39, fol. 46.
73. E.179/168/220.
74. S.P.28/191, unbound documents.
75. Borthwick Institute of Historical Research, Wills in the York Registry, will of Sir Henry Savile, 13 June 1632.
76. E.179/256/26.
77. E.179/250/4.
78. PROB 5/2091.
79. *Chetham Society*, xxxv (1856), 187. E.179/250/4.
80. D.Parsons (ed.), *The Diary of Sir Henry Slingsby of Scriven, Bart.* (1836), 279.
81. *Ibid.*, 26–7.
82. *Bristol Record Society*, xxxv (1982), 198–9.
83. C.38/250/22 February 1694/5.
84. Warwickshire County Record Office, Throckmorton MSS, CR 1998, Box 63, Folder 1/18.
85. Throckmorton MSS, CR 1998, Large Carved Box, 26, irregular pagination.
86. Throckmorton MSS, CR 1998, Large Carved Box, 47, no pagination, and Box 65, Folder 1/2/11.
87. E.179/250/4.
88. E.179/255/21.
89. C.38/169/3 March 1669/70. PROB 11/330/78.
90. PROB 11/364/136.
91. PROB 11/350/26.
92. BL, Additional MSS 53,726, fol. 69.
93. E.179/256/26.
94. STAC 8/19/10.
95. *The Memorandum Book of Richard Cholmeley of Brandsby 1602–1623* (*North Yorkshire County Record Office Publications No.44*), (1988), 138, 148–52, 155, 158, 160.
96. E.179/248/18.
97. E.179/255/21.
98. E.179/274/10.
99. PRO, SPDom, Charles I, S.P.16/cxciii/1.
100. E.179/256/26.
101. E.179/244/39, fol. 77.
102. S.P.28/192, no pagination.
103. PRO, Court of Wards, Miscellaneous Books, Wards 9/xcix/fol. 487.
104. C.6/219/23.
105. S.P.28/193, no pagination.
106. E.179/255/21.
107. E.179/256/26.
108. E.179/244/30, no pagination.
109. PRO, Chancery Masters' Exhibits, C.107/161, unbound accounts.
110. *Chetham Society*, Third Series, v (1953), 156, 157.
111. C.38/252/4 June 1695.
112. E.179/250/4.
113. C.7/385/69.
114. E.179/256/26.
115. C.38/270/6 June 1700.
116. E.179/255/21.
117. E.179/244/30, no pagination.
118. Yorkshire Archaeological Society Library, MS 311, no pagination.
119. E.179/102/481.
120. Eleanor C. Lodge (ed.), *The Account Book of a Kentish Estate 1616–1704*, *British Academy, Records of Social and Economic History*, vi (1927), 223, 225–7.
121. Hertfordshire Archives and Local Studies, Lawes-Wittewronge of Rothamsted MSS, D/ELw/F18.
122. E.179/244/39, fol. 30.
123. E.179/250/4.
124. E.179/250/4.
125. E.179/244/39, fol. 54.
126. E.179/256/26.

127. E.179/274/10.
128. E.179/244/39, fol. 43.
129. E.179/244/30, no pagination.
130. E.179/244/30, no pagination.
131. E.179/205/487.
132. E.179/260/3X.
133. E.179/244/39, fol. 43.
134. E.179/244/30, no pagination.
135. E.179/244/39, fol. 30.
136. E.179/256/26.
137. E.179/244/30, no pagination.
138. E.179/205/488.
139. E.179/205/487.
140. E.179/250/4.
141. E.179/172/416.

NOTES TO APPENDIX B

1. C.38/275/20 August 1702.
2. C.7/564/85. *Al.Cant.*, i, 26.
3. BL, Additional MSS 28,564, fols 212, 213 and Additional Charters 17,777–9, 17,782, 17,784, 17,786–8, 17,794, 17,797, 17,802.
4. C.33/259/fol. 648.
5. PROB 11/338/47. C.7/534/64.
6. C.38/267/18 February 1700/1.
7. *Camden Society*, xlix (1850), 218. PROB 11/382/13. PRO, Exchequer Depositions, E.134/4 William and Mary/Easter 22 and Trinity 6. C.38/231/26 June 1688. H. A. C. Sturgess (ed.), *Register of Admissions to the Honourable Society of the Middle Temple* (1949), i, 219.
8. C.38/275/23 January 1702/3 and 279/12 July 1703.
9. Robert Plot, *The Natural History of Stafford-shire* (1686), 211.
10. C.38/271/17 May 1701.
11. J. Hutchins, *The History and Antiquities of the County of Dorset* (1861–73), iii, 236.
12. C.38/267/4 December 1700.
13. *Camden Fourth Series*, xxviii (1983), 4, 12, 20. PROB 11/154/70 and 383/59. Essex Record Office, Hatfield Broad Oak MSS, D/DBa/A1, fols 14, 45, 63; A3; fols 6, 16, 29, 42, 51, 60, 68; A4; A21, fol. 2; A66/36; A70/13; A72/4; A76/29; A77/8; A84/1. C.38/237/10 February 1690/1.
14. PROB 11/321/115, 119.
15. C.38/55/28 April 1627. C.6/18/26 and 28. PROB 11/272/19 and 361/137. C.38/247/15 November 1693 and 270/5 March 1700/1.
16. C.38/154/11 May 1665; 156/15 June 1666; and 190/24 November 1675.
17. PROB 11/371/127. C.38/239/16 December 1691. C.5/186/183.
18. C.33/249/fol. 687.
19. West Sussex Record Office, Parham MSS, account books, 1690–1, 1692–3, 1693, 1696, 1698 and 1699.
20. PRO, Exchequer Depositions, E.134/36 and 37 Charles II/Hilary 18.
21. PROB 11/312/104. C.6/176/3.
22. C.8/505/52.
23. PRO, Chancery Depositions, C.22/769/2, and Chancery Masters' Exhibits, C.108/67, various unbound papers. C.38/190/30 April 1675. PROB 11/462/151.
24. Bedfordshire and Luton Archives and Records Service, Trevor-Wingfield MSS, TW 800.
25. C.38/214/14 June 1683.
26. C.38/265/3 July 1699. PROB 4/4480.
27. PROB 11/331/157 and 376/69.
28. C.38/65/22 June 1630.
29. STAC 8/56/18.

30. Lady Elizabeth Cust, *Records of the Cust Family. Series II. The Brownlows of Belton, 1550–1779* (1909), 62, 77, 104, 156–7.
31. PROB 11/308/61. C.38/159/18 February 1667/8 and 174/1 June 1671.
32. C.10/267/13. C.33/307/fols 298–9. PROB 11/412/220 and 497/263.
33. John Aubrey *The Natural History and Antiquities of the County of Surrey* (1718, 1719), ii, 161–2.
34. Felicity Heal and Clive Holmes, *The Gentry in England and Wales, 1500–1700* (1994), 113. PROB 11/132/117 and 371/155. C.33/259/fols 676–7. C.38/214/9 September 1683; 245/27 December 1693; and 248/16 March 1694/5.
35. PRO, Chancery Masters' Exhibits, C.104/54, part 2 and 55, parts 1 and 2, various unbound papers.
36. *Catholic Record Society*, liv (1962), 163. BL, Additional MSS 28, 242, fols 15, 31, 34 and 28,250, fol. 153.
37. C.5/260/19. PRO, Chancery Depositions, C.22/536/32.
38. PROB 11/300/206.
39. C.6/134/107. C.38/202/12 June 1679; 228/7 July 1687; 232/13 July 1688; and 235/15 June 1689. C.8/426/19.
40. PROB 11/337/128.
41. BL, Additional MSS 69,881, fols 86, 88. HMC, *Coke MSS*, ii, 309.
42. *Catholic Record Society*, liii (1961), 432–5. Hull University, Archives, Maxwell-Constable MSS, DDEV/50/140; 51/102; 53/50; 54/8; 55/58; 56/15, 16, 25, 412; and 57/16, 36. Borthwick Institute of Historical Research, Wills in the York Registry, will of George Constable, 18 May 1672.
43. C.7/477/27. C.8/160/45. C.8/162/19.
44. PROB 4/4121. PROB 11/323/18.
45. Cheshire Record Office, Arderne Collection, DAR/C/91/13; D/15/12; D/68/39; D/75/15; E/123; and F/3, 9. C.105/9, part 2, Crewe papers.
46. C.38/197/22 June 1677. PRO, Chancery Depositions, C.22/35/31.
47. STAC 8/120/2 and 8. *Thoresby Society*, xxxvii (1936–42), 5, 6, 7, 14. North Yorkshire County Record Office, Cunliffe-Lister (Swinton) MSS, Bundle 11, account book of Miles Danby.
48. BL, Harleian MSS 587, fols 49–50, 52–4, 56–7, 59–64, 66–75 and Additional MSS 41,502.
49. BL, Additional MSS 38,175, fols 50, 61. Buckinghamshire County Records and Local Studies Service, Gayhurst Estate Deeds, 1/31.
50. PROB 11/330/104. C.10/165/30. G. Eland (ed.), *Shardeloes Papers* (1947), 55–7. C.33/306/fol. 131.
51. C.38/254/27 February 1696/7.
52. PROB 11/324/61. *Al.Oxon.*, 425.
53. PROB 11/346/143.
54. J. Forster, *Sir John Eliot* (1864), ii, 634–5.
55. C.38/246/22 July 1693 and 252/21 June 1695.
56. PROB 11/362/19. C.38/221/8 June 1685. C.7/573/74.
57. G. W. Johnson (ed.), *The Fairfax Correspondence. Memoirs of the Reign of Charles the First* (1848), i, introduction, xxv.
58. PROB 11/363/106. *Harleian Society*, lxii (1911), 122, 132.
59. Warwickshire County Record Office, Finch-Knightley of Packington MSS, estate account books, vols 1 to 4 (on microfilm) and vol. 5 (TD79/21). PROB 11/373/83.
60. J. P. Earwaker, *East Cheshire: Past and Present* (1877, 1880), ii, 561–3, 617. *Al.Oxon.*, 733.
61. C.38/264/9 June 1699.
62. *Yorkshire Archaeological Society Record Series*, xl (1909), 84 and liv (1915), 287.
63. HMC, *House of Lords, New Series, 1693–95*, 47.
64. C.5/260/19. PRO, Chancery Depositions, C.22/536/32.
65. C.33/334/fol. 75.
66. East Sussex Record Office, Frewen MSS 7321 and 7322.
67. HMC, *House of Lords, New Series, 1693–95*, 504.
68. East Sussex Record Office, Firle Place MSS, SAS/G, Box 11/27 and 28.
69. Hertfordshire Archives and Local Studies, Garrard of Lamer Park MSS, E/13, 15, 16.
70. C.5/577/24.
71. PRO, Chancery Depositions, C.22/81/23.
72. Derbyshire Record Office, Chandos-Pole-Gell MSS, Box 7/10c, Box 47/15c. HMC, *Ninth Report*, Appendix, part ii, 398.
73. C.38/241/7 December 1691; 247/22 July 1693; and 256/12 July 1696.
74. *Thoroton Society Record Series*, ix (1942), 20.
75. R. Barber (ed.), *The Worlds of John Aubrey* (1988), 112.
76. Hertfordshire Archives and Local Studies, Verulam (Gorhambury) MSS, IX.A.75.
77. C.6/195/40.
78. C.33/303/fols 523–4. BL, Additional Charter 18,990.
79. C.38/191/28 July 1675.
80. Edward Hasted, *The History and Topographical Survey of the County of Kent* (1797–1801), vi, 95 and vii, 234. PROB 11/237/221.
81. C.5/186/163.
82. Francis Blomefield, *An Essay Towards a Topographical History of the County of Norfolk* (1805–10), vii, 443.
83. BL, Additional MSS 70,006, fols 177–8; 70,062, no pagination; and 70,123, no pagination.
84. PRO, Chancery Masters' Exhibits, C.107/16, part 2, account book of Sir John Harpur's guardians, fols 51, 55, 57.
85. PROB 11/370/57. PROB 4/10,096.
86. BL, Sloane MSS 813, fols 11, 15–17, 37, 41, 42, 44, 49, 58, 60, 64, 72. C.38/219/30 June 1684.
87. C.33/237/fol. 602.
88. Lancashire County Record Office, Hesketh MSS, DDHe/55/10–15, 18, 19.
89. HMC, *Lothian MSS*, 87. C.8/426/33.
90. PROB 11/330/86 and 335/28.
91. C.5/613/34.
92. C.8/181/82.
93. C.10/498/27.
94. C.38/194/30 June 1676 and 203/22 April 1679. PROB 11/315/131.
95. *Surtees Society*, xvii (1843), 206–8, 234, 248.
96. PRO, State Papers Supplementary, S.P.46/lxxxviii/fols 129, 132, 149, 158, 167B.
97. G. Lipscomb, *The History and Antiquities of the County of Buckingham* (1847–51), ii, 593.
98. A. F. Upton, *Sir Arthur Ingram c. 1565–1642* (1961), 183–91. West Yorkshire Archive Service, Leeds, Temple Newsam MSS, TN/EA/13/7–33; 15/5 and 8; and 18/4/1. *Yorkshire Archaeological Society Record Series*, ix (1890), 160.
99. PRO, Chancery Depositions, C.22/388/39. C.38/152/20 January 1664/5; 176/13 December 1671; 188/7 July 1674; 191/28 June 1675; 197/24 July 1677; and 200/25 July 1678. C.33/323/fol. 294. Hampshire Record Office, Kingsmill MSS, 1434, 1435, 1667, 1743–62.
100. PROB 11/381/110.
101. BL, Egerton MSS 2716, fols 361–2, 366–8, 370, 372–3, 379, 390.
102. C.38/228/7 July 1687; 231/5 July 1688; 234/22 June 1689; and 237/24 July 1690.
103. C.6/159/89 and 91.
104. STAC 8/24/21.
105. PROB 11/290/236. PRO, Chancery Masters' Exhibits, C.104/42, unbound accounts and other papers.
106. Lady Evelyn Newton, *The House of Lyme* (1917), 72–3, 127, 137, 189, 219.
107. PROB 5/4751. C.38/243/31 January 1692/3.
108. Staffordshire Record Office, Leveson-Gower MSS,

D593/P/8/2/2.

109. C.6/42/13.
110. *Surtees Society*, cxci (1976, 1977), 21, 22, 24, 29, 34, 70, 77, 81, 89–145, 148, 193.
111. C.33/313/fol. 326.
112. D. R. Hainsworth, *Stewards, Lords and People* (1992), 11, 12, 26, 27, 31, 39.
113. F. G. Emmison (ed.), *Wills at Chelmsford (Essex and East Hertfordshire)*, ii (1961), 255.
114. C.7/142/25. PROB 11/323/47. C.38/214/14 July 1683; 217/1 February 1684/5; and 223/17 July 1686. *Al.Oxon.*, 477.
115. Warwickshire County Record Office, Lucy of Charlecote MSS, L6/1009, no pagination.
116. PROB 11/346/129 and 383/47. C.33/225/2 December 1686.
117. C.33/200/fol. 610.
118. West Yorkshire Archive Service, Leeds, Vyner MSS, 5378.
119. PROB 11/405/121.
120. C.5/164/34.
121. C.38/193/29 June 1676.
122. East Sussex Record Office, Glynde Place MSS 2932, no pagination.
123. C.10/83/70.
124. Warwickshire County Record Office, Newdegate of Arbury MSS, CR 136/B571. PROB 11/358/143. J. Foster (ed.), *The Register of Admissions to Gray's Inn, 1521–1889* (1889), part 1, 279.
125. C.38/247/29 June 1693.
126. STAC 8/212/13.
127. C.5/260/19.
128. PROB 11/311/71. *Al.Cant.*, iii, 392.
129. PROB 11/311/53. PROB 4/12,216.
130. C.38/271/2 July 1701.
131. BL, Additional MSS 33,143, 33,145, 33,147 and 33,148.
132. Somerset Record Office, Phelips MSS, DD/PH 224, fol. 109; 225, fol. 25; and 229, fols 8, 9.
133. C.7/261/16.
134. PROB 11/352/156.
135. C.8/139/88.
136. *CSPDom, 1676–7*, 339–40. Somerset Record Office, Popham MSS, DD/PO C/62 2a and DD/POt 121.
137. PRO, Chancery Depositions, C.22/810/36. PRO, SPDom, Charles II, S.P.29/cdxxiv/143. PROB 11/401/165.
138. PROB 11/342/69. C.6/80/27.
139. *Archaeologia Aeliana*, New Series, i (1857), 104.
140. Lambeth Palace Library, Court of Arches, Depositions, 1665–8, Eee 2, fols 5–8.
141. West Yorkshire Archive Service, Leeds, MSS of the Earl of Mexborough, MX/R15/45, 46, 98; R16/2, 20, 23; R17/1; R19/2, 11; R22/7; R32/6; R36/10, 35, 38; R42/4, 52, 65, 69–71; and R44/7, 20, 27, 29.
142. *CSPDom, 1685*, 60. C.38/250/19 December 1694. C.38/262/16 March 1698/9.
143. London Metropolitan Archives, Northwick Collection, Acc.76/2009, 2010.
144. J. G. Taylor, *Our Lady of Battersea* (1925), 79, 80, 82, 83, 86, 190, 313–16. John Aubrey, *The Natural History and Antiquities of the County of Surrey* (1718, 1719), i, 149.
145. PRO, Chancery Masters' Exhibits, C.111/134, Chancery decree dated 19 June 1668. C.38/165/18 June and 17 December 1668.
146. Borthwick Institute of Historical Research, Wills in the York Registry, will of Sir Henry Savile, 13 June 1632.
147. STAC 8/263/1. W. Knowler (ed.), *The Earl of Strafforde's Letters and Despatches* (1739), i, 169, 170. *Yorkshire Archaeological Journal*, xxv (1920), 25, 26.
148. PROB 11/312/135. J. R. Scott, *Scott of Scot's-Hall in the County of Kent* (1876), Appendix, xli.
149. BL, Additional MSS 36,583, fols 5, 13. *CSPDom, 1645–7*, 240–1.

150. *CSPDom, 1680–1*, 275.
151. Hull University Archives, Maxwell-Constable MSS, DDEV/54/9; 56/449; and 69/48, 49, 58, 64.
152. C.7/545/105. C.38/165/19 February 1668/9.
153. *Chetham Society*, xxxv (1856), 168.
154. Yorkshire Archaeological Society Library, Slingsby MSS, DD56/J1/7; J2/1; and J3/3 and 4, and Parrington Deposit of Slingsby Letters, DD149/102, 103, 105, 112–18. D. Parsons (ed.), *The Diary of Sir Henry Slingsby of Scriven, Bart.* (1836), 50–1, 350.
155. Anthony Wood, *Athenae Oxoniensis* (ed. P. Bliss) (1813–20), iii, col. 1048. R. Barber (ed.), *The Worlds of John Aubrey* (1988), 141.
156. *Bristol Record Society*, xxxv (1982), 99, 157, 169, 173.
157. C.33/314/fol. 210.
158. G. D. Stawell, *A Quantock Family* (1910), 99, 374, 379, 400, 404, 407.
159. H. Hornyold, *Genealogical Memoirs of the Family of Strickland of Sizergh* (1928), 130, 135, 160.
160. PRO, Exchequer Depositions, E.134/11 William III/Easter 24 and Michaelmas 9.
161. C.10/133/4. PROB 11/353/41.
162. BL, Additional MSS 40,670, fol. 11.
163. C.10/253/48.
164. D. R. Hainsworth, *Stewards, Lords and People* (1992), 77.
165. Warwickshire County Record Office, Throckmorton MSS, CR 1998, Files of Correspondence (Tribune), Folder 48/27 and 33; Large Carved Box, 26; and Box 65, Folders 1/1/10, 1/2/11 and 1/18/1. E. A. B. Barnard, *A Seventeenth Century Country Gentleman* (1944), 4.
166. Lambeth Palace Library, Court of Arches, Depositions, Eee 2, fols 107, 111.
167. MSS of Lord Tollemache, Helmingham Hall (East Suffolk Record Office catalogue), B1/10/1; 13/10, 11; and 14/2.
168. PROB 11/344/3.
169. *Dorset Natural History and Archaeological Society Proceedings*, cxv (1994), 15.
170. Frances P. Verney and Margaret M. Verney, *Memoirs of the Verney Family During the Seventeenth Century* (1907), i, 513–16, 519, 520 and ii, 110–11, 385, 397, 451, 484, 495, 498.
171. C.7/500/124.
172. *Chetham Society*, New Series, lxxx (1921), 13–14.
173. H. B. McCall, *Story of the Family of Wandesforde of Kirklington and Castlecomer* (1904), 262. Yorkshire Archaeological Society Library, Duke of Leeds Collection, Box 38, accounts. C.38/145/12 February 1662/3.
174. *Dorset Natural History and Archaeological Society Proceedings*, cxv (1994), 17.
175. PROB 11/350/26 and 404/90.
176. W. Knowler (ed.), *The Earl of Strafforde's Letters and Despatches* (1739), ii, 433.
177. C.38/247/2 December 1693.
178. C.38/235/9 July and 12 December 1689; 250/22 May 1694; 259/10 May 1697; and 270/6 May 1700.
179. C.33/308/fols 246–7.
180. Norfolk Record Office, Ketton-Cremer MSS, WKC5/150, 154, 157. PROB 11/395/90. R. W. Ketton-Cremer, *Felbrigg* (1962), 60.
181. PRO, State Papers Supplementary, S.P.46/c/fols 61–3, 68, 128.
182. C.8/444/23.
183. C.38/242/7 November 1692.
184. C.38/194/30 June 1676; 195/16 February 1676/7; 204/15 July 1679; 210/2 July 1681; 219/26 June 1684; 229/9 December 1687; and 235/2 July 1689.
185. PROB 11/327/104.
186. PRO, Chancery Masters' Exhibits, C.107/112, accounts of John Moon. PROB 11/438/132.

187. C.38/204/17 December 1679; 219/8 November 1684; and 235/11 December 1689.
188. PROB 4/6863. C.38/274/20 July 1700.
189. PROB 11/364/136. *Recusant History*, xxii, no. 2 (1994), 172.

190. C.5/575/29. PROB 11/362/39.
191. STAC 8/19/10.
192. PRO, Chancery Masters' Exhibits, C.108/187, parts 1 and 2, and 188, part 1, Zouch papers.

INDEX

PHOTOGRAPHIC ACKNOWLEDGEMENTS

1, 7, 20, 35, 54, 66, 72, 98, 99 Harland Walshaw; 2, 18, 51 National Trust Photographic Library/Rupert Truman; 3, 45 National Trust Photographic Library/Mike Williams; 4, 16, 50 National Trust Photographic Library/John Hammond; 5, 13, 46, 49, 63, 69, 75, 82, 87, 88, 89, 90, 91 by permission of the British Library; 6, 10, 21, 22, 28, 30, 67, 86, 101 A. F. Kersting; 11, 17, 23, 33, 34, 36, 77, 97 Crown Copyright, RCHME; 12 Canon M. H. Ridgway/The Conway Library, Courtauld Institute of Art; 14 National Trust Photographic Library/Angelo Hornak; 15 British Architectural Library, RIBA London; 19 National Trust Photographic Library/Roy Fox; 25, 29 National Trust Photographic Library/Andreas von Einsiedel; 27 National Trust Photographic Library/Charlie Waite; 32, 80, 83 Country Life Picture Library; 41, 48 National Trust Photographic Library/Derrick E. Witty; 42 © Manchester City Art Galleries; 43 Yale Center for British Art; 52 Birmingham City Archives; 53 Peter Burton; 56 Weston Park Foundation/Courtauld Institute of Art; 57, 100 The Conway Library, Courtauld Institute of Art; 58, 64, 65, 79 by courtesy of the National Portrait Gallery, London; 59, 60 Coughton Court (The National Trust)/Courtauld Institute of Art; 68 Leeds Museums and Galleries (Lotherton Hall)/Courtauld Institute of Art; 76 © Dean and Chapter of Westminster; 84 John Nicoll; 85 Crown Copyright, Public Record Office, reproduced by permission of the Controller of Her Majesty's Stationery Office; 94 The Witt Library, Courtauld Institute of Art; 96 Grosvenor Museum, Chester.